Vegetarian Times

Cooks

Mediterranean

Vegetarian Times

Cooks

Mediterranean

From the Editors of *Vegetarian Times*

Introduction by Melissa Clark
Photographs by Mary Ellen Bartley

William Morrow and Company, Inc., New York

Library of Congress Cataloging-in-Publication Data

Vegetarian times cooks Mediterranean / from the editors of Vegetarian times.—1st ed.
   p.   cm.
  ISBN 0-688-16209-6
  1. Vegetarian cookery. 2. Cookery, Mediterranean. I. Vegetarian times.
TX837.V4267   2000
641.5'636'091822—dc21   99–38251
                                                      CIP

Printed in the United States of America

First Edition

1 2 3 4 5 6 7 8 9 10

BOOK DESIGN BY BONNI LEON-BERMAN

www.williammorrow.com

Contents

Foreword

The Mediterranean Diet became famous a few years ago when research showed it to be incredibly healthful. Food cognoscenti have embraced the cuisines of Italy, the Provençal region of France, Spain, Morocco, and Greece. Dishes from other, less well-known regions of the Mediterranean also are being served up in restaurants and at home. They are popular because they taste great, not because they are healthful. Calling the luscious tastes, colors, and variety of foods available through the Mediterranean a "diet" doesn't do justice. I have had the pleasure and privilege of visiting the region half a dozen times. I am drawn to it by its incredible richness—its beautiful palette, rich history, varied cultures and religions, its warm people and, of course, its spectacular food. Yes, I believe in the long-lasting health benefits of consuming a plant-based diet rich in fresh vegetables, grains that aren't overprocessed, plenty of olive oil, and a bit of wine here and there. However, I prepare the recipes in this book not because they are good for me but because they please my palate. I've been lucky. I learned to make fresh pasta alongside plump, smiling women in the Apulian region of Italy without understanding a word they were saying; I learned how to gather wild greens by the roadways of a Greek isle from men and women who were taught it by their ancestors; and I have tasted enough wines and olive oils to distinguish types grown in different regions, even just a few miles apart. But I didn't need to do all of this to appreciate the area's special cuisine. After all these trips and all the hands-on education, the most important lessons I learned are these:

- Look in your pantry for what you have on hand. Build a dish around that.
- Keep it simple: simple ingredients, simple preparation.
- Respect the purity and flavor of the food.
- Don't overcook.
- Use spices very sparingly. When in doubt, leave it out.
- Use more olive oil than you think you should.

One other thing I love about the Mediterranean region: A plant-based diet holds tremendous respect. Say you're a vegetarian in parts of the Western Hemisphere and you may get a sneer or, at best, a quizzical look. In every country I've visited in this region, my decision to eat vegetables and grains is met with understanding and respect. These foods make up the bulk of the everyday diet and are part of the area's culture and history. Both home cooks and chefs understand that the traditional way of preparing foods has a value far beyond its nutritional advantages. It is no coincidence that the cradle of civilization still holds secrets about life and longevity that we are just now uncovering. This book will help you discover more about a cuisine that is truly for the gods. Enjoy!

—Toni Apgar
Publishing Director
Vegetarian Times

Acknowledgments

The editors of *Vegetarian Times* would like to thank author Melissa Clark for all the effort she put into writing this book. Her knowledge and additional research of the Mediterranean region allow us to bring you a comprehensive view of the countries and people who, over hundreds of years, developed this healthy and delicious cuisine. In addition, Melissa's diligence in assuring the authenticity of our recipes, as well as the creation of new ones, is greatly appreciated.

Terry Christofferson, *Vegetarian Times*'s copyeditor, is to be generously thanked for selecting the recipes included in the book and for making suggestions for additional recipes, which Melissa carefully created. Terry also lent her copyediting skills to the manuscript, as did our good friend Janet Cappiello Blake, whom we must also thank for her meticulous work.

Finally, we must not let the opportunity slip by to thank all our dedicated readers and recipe developers who have contributed to the magazine over the years, making it possible for us to bring this book to you.

—Kristen Riggs Thudium
Special Projects Manager

The Mediterranean

A Region Rich and Diverse

The Mediterranean region is made up of the many different countries whose shores abut the turquoise waters of the Mediterranean Sea. From the northern African countries of Morocco, Tunisia, Algeria, and Libya, to the Levantine lands of Egypt, Syria, Lebanon, Israel, and Turkey, to the European nations of Greece, Italy, France, and Spain, the area is rich in history, culture, religion, and glorious food. There is no one cuisine of the Mediterranean, but many shared characteristics unite the cuisines of these disparate nations. Centuries of maritime trade have circulated ingredients, ideas, cooking techniques, and traditional methods among the major port cities. The resulting cuisines are lush and enticing, and feature an abundance of sun-ripened fruits and vegetables brightened with zesty fresh herbs, aromatic spices, and plenty of garlic—all glossed with fragrant, deep-green olive oil. The temperate climate of the Mediterranean means that the fields, orchards, and vineyards receive many hours of hot sun and many inches of rain, making them some of the most productive in the world. Even in the era of mega-agricultural complexes, the region remains dotted with small family farms, centuries-old olive groves, and rambling vineyards. These produce many of the raw ingredients that creative cooks tailor to the tastes and customs of their individual cultures. It is in this process that Mediterranean food is at is best: in the transformation of ripe, fresh, high-quality ingredients into dishes that reflect both the traditions of the cook's homeland and the overarching cuisine of the entire region.

Indeed, the beauty of Mediterranean cooking lies not only in its unity but also in its diversity. Each country's cuisine is marked by its own use of herbs and spices, its special combinations of vegetables, and the character of its olive oil and wine. Together the nations weave a wonderfully varied culinary mosaic, whose flavors and aromas harmonize in the best possible way.

But even beyond the food is the spirit of the Mediterranean, which is as warm and as welcoming as the brilliant sun. Generous hospitality and a tradition of healthful home cooking comes naturally to the people of these shores. It's a Mediterranean tradition to sit with family and friends around the dinner table, sipping wine, until well into the night. Perhaps it is because of their hospitable natures that those who reside in Mediterranean countries are blessed with fair weather, clear blue skies, and a warm sun that shines down on fertile soils. Or, perhaps it is just good luck. Whatever the cause, the inhabitants of these lands know how to take advantage of their blessing and imbue their cuisine with it.

A PLANT-BASED CUISINE

The traditional Mediterranean diet is firmly rooted in the earth. The warm, sunny climate, long growing season, mild winter, and fertile soil of this region have long provided its inhabitants with delicious fresh fruits, vegetables, grains, legumes, and nuts. It is, and has always been, a plant-based cuisine, one that never depended upon animal products to any large extent. The reason for this is more happenstance than by design. For the most part, the people of the Mediterranean region were poor; they typically made their livings as farmers, shepherds, and fishermen. As peasants they could not afford expensive foods like meat and poultry, and instead turned to what was literally in their own backyards. In doing so, they created a legacy of flavorful, hearty, and healthy meals using legumes, pastas, breads, rice and other grains, and plenty of fresh vegetables, herbs, and spices. This legacy has become known as the Mediterranean diet, and it is reflected in the recipes in this book.

Many of the recipes and ingredients that make up Mediterranean cooking are, in fact, ancient. Olives and olive oil, the cornerstones of Mediterranean cuisine, have had a particularly long and fascinating history. Olive oil was considered sacred by the ancient Etruscans and Romans, who used it as food, as well as an ingredient in healing balms, fuel for lamps, a magical restorer of youth, and a massage oil for athletes. Both olives and olive oil appear at almost every meal, and contribute both to the vibrant flavor of Mediterranean dishes and to the good health of its people. By using olive oil as a cooking medium, salad dressing, and overall flavor enhancer, the inhabitants of the region have reduced their reliance on other kinds of fats, including animal fat.

Over the centuries, trade has influenced and enriched the cultures and cuisines of countries around the world. This is especially true in the Mediterranean, where every country had at least one port where merchants could introduce foods and flavors from all parts of the globe. In the years following the Crusades and the "discovery" of what the Europeans dubbed the New World, trade among Mediterranean countries, Asia, India, and the Americas grew at a galloping rate, and the cultivation of new fruits and vegetables began in earnest.

Carrots were shipped in from Afghanistan and spinach arrived from Persia. Peppers, beans, squash, corn, and tomatoes all came from the Americas during the sixteenth century. Many varieties of tomato were bred in Italy, including the now ubiquitous plum tomato. Most legumes (besides lentils and chickpeas, which are native to the Mediterranean) arrived from Mexico and Central America. Broccoli and cauliflower were cultivated in Italy centuries ago and derive from the cabbage. The artichoke probably developed wild in Sicily, then spread to the mainland and to France. Artichokes are now found growing wild in fields and olive groves in most Mediterranean countries.

In the early seventh century, the Arabs became a dominant force and would occupy part of Spain for the next seven hundred years. They established vast trading networks and introduced sugarcane, apricots, pomegranates, dates, bananas, and eggplants, first to Spain, then eventually to all of Europe. Rice also came to Spain via the Arabs, though the grain had been eaten in India and China since the beginning of recorded history. The Arab influence is still felt in non-Arab Mediterranean countries today. Certainly the widespread use of nuts and flower waters, and the popularization of saffron, can be attributed to the Arabs. As each new wave of vegetables and grains was introduced into the Mediterranean region, the variety of plant-based dishes grew, further lessening the region's need for meat.

One could even say the dairy products of the Mediterranean are based on plants. Goat, sheep, and cow herds were nourished on grassy pastures, and their milk was turned into cultured products like yogurt and *smen,* as well as into delicious cheeses, which were traditionally made with an artichoke-derived rennet. But cheese and yogurt, and even milk and cream, are used more as condiments and flavorings than as a main source of nourishment in this region. That distinction belongs to plants.

The history of Mediterranean cuisine revolves around a trinity of wheat, wine, and olive oil. Wheat was first cultivated in the fertile crescent—the land between the Tigris and Euphrates Rivers, which is now the country of Iraq. The first flat breads were made there and throughout the surrounding lands. For many thousands of years the people of the Mediterranean and most of Europe have depended greatly on wheat, a versatile grain that is high enough in protein to allow people to survive without meat or fish.

Both the cultivation of wheat and the making of bread have been documented in ancient texts. The Hebrews are said to have created the first leavened bread by accident. As the tale goes, a mixture of flour and water was set aside and forgotten about. It started to ferment and eventually rise in the heat and humidity. After this breakthrough, leavened bread became the norm, while unleavened bread was considered ritual fare. The Jews who were forced to flee Pharaoh's Egypt during Passover had no time to bake leavened bread, so they made flat cakes, called matzos, instead. Now matzos are the ritual bread eaten during the eight days of Passover, to the exclusion of leavened bread. And then there are communion wafers, also unleavened.

The Bible also touts the Egyptians as great bread makers, and ancient Egyptian paintings depict wheat being grown, harvested, and made into loaves. In Greece in about 1000 B.C., mills and ovens were refined, and herbs, oils, and fruits were added to enhance bread dough. But bread had been the cornerstone of Western consumption since well before the time of the ancient Greeks. It was not until the twentieth century that meat would become a basic food in most societies.

Wine is extensively documented in the Bible and is used in many Jewish and Christian rituals. All sorts of fruits, including blackberries, raspberries, wild strawberries, and pears, have been used to make wine throughout the years. The oldest known alcoholic beverage was the Greek *hydromel,* which was made from fermented honey. Grapes were soon found to produce the best wines, and, as viticulture and the drinking of wine spread outward from Greece, the Mediterranean became a region dependent on its vineyards. Today, except on Muslim tables, a glass or two of wine accompanies the main meal. Ironically, in ancient Greece wine was drunk only at special gatherings and rarely taken with meals.

The Berbers, northern Africa's indigenous people, were the first to begin cultivating the olive tree. They also developed the practice of grafting to improve production. Their diet consisted mainly of native foods such as fava beans, lentils, wheat, and honey, and relied heavily on olives and their greenish-golden oil. It is also believed that the Berbers were the inventors of couscous. Olive oil was considered sacred by the ancient Greeks and Romans, and was used by early Jews as a ritual offering and to light the lamps in temples. Today, the Italians still honor this flavorful oil and, when it's mixed with spicy whole hot red peppers, give it the name *olio santo,* or "sacred oil." Olive trees are indeed wondrous, and can live a productive life for hundreds, sometimes thousands of years. Desirable dark green oil comes from the ripest, most sun-kissed olives, and every family-owned olive grove is sure to contain a number of unique and regional varieties.

THE INCREASING INFLUENCE OF TRADE

As regional networks were expanded, northern Africa was increasingly influenced by the Phoenicians, masters of trade, and the Carthaginians, masters of agriculture. During the Roman Empire, the Maghreb supplied much of the Romans' food supply, mostly wheat and olive oil. But by the beginning of the fifth century, the Roman Empire was in decline and northern European tribes were able to expand southward. Spain, Morocco, and Italy were swept into a frenzy of trade. Islam was introduced to the north Africans by Arabs at the beginning of the seventh century. The northern African culinary tradition was thus exposed to Middle Eastern influences, including an array of fragrant spices and Turkish bulgur. Reciprocally, the Maghreb introduced couscous to the Middle East. These Arabs—the Moors—then crossed the Strait of Gibraltar to conquer Spain and remained there until 1492, the beginning of the Spanish Inquisition. At this time, Spain's Catholic monarchs forced Muslims and Jews either to convert to Christianity or flee the country.

Many exiled Spanish Moors settled in the Maghreb region of northern Africa. The Spanish and Middle Eastern heritage of these people carried over into their new homeland. They brought with them flaky phyllo-type pastry; fruits and vegetables including apricots, Valencia oranges, eggplant, and carrots; and tomatoes, potatoes, and chiles, which had been brought to Spain from the Americas by the conquistadors.

At the close of the sixteenth century, the Ottomans invaded Tunisia and Algeria, and introduced Turkish and Persian cuisines to those lands. The final influence was from the French colonizers, who ousted the Ottomans in the early nineteenth century, although the French were probably more influenced by the exotic cuisine of northern Africa, which they brought back to Europe, than vice versa.

The food of the ancient Hebrews has had great influence on modern Jews, as well as on many non-Jewish Middle Eastern countries. In addition to the ritually significant bread, salt, honey, and wine mentioned in the Bible, nomadic flat bread, wild herbs, and other wild fruits and vegetables have persisted as part of the region's diet. The biblical diet also includes grains and legumes, both wild and cultivated, and figs, dates, grapes, nuts, and wines, as well as wild melons, cucumbers, leeks, onions, and garlic.

RELIGIOUS INFLUENCES AND DIETARY LAWS

Muslim dietary laws are outlined in the Koran, a sacred Muslim text said to have been received by the Prophet Muhammad from God. Food is mentioned many times throughout the Koran as a gift from God that must be eaten in accordance with God's rules. The foods that are forbidden include pork, blood, animals that die before they can be slaughtered, animals slaughtered as an offering to a pagan deity, and alcohol. Strict adherence to these rules is a personal choice; for example, most Turkish Muslims drink alcohol or at least use it in cooking.

Jewish dietary laws were said to be revealed by God to Moses, and have been interpreted and expanded by scholars of the Torah. Permitted are animals with cloven hooves and that chew their cud, as well as domesticated fowl and fish with fins and scales. Animals that do not meet these criteria are not considered kosher. All fruits and vegetables are considered kosher; in fact, vegetarianism is regarded as the ultimate kosher diet. As with Muslim laws, blood is forbidden and animals to be consumed must be ritually slaughtered. In addition, meat and dairy must be kept completely separate and may not be served at the same meal. Furthermore, silverware and dishes that are used to serve and eat meat-based meals are kept separate from those used for dairy meals.

The Regions of the

Mediterranean

The Mediterranean comprises three culturally distinct regions: the Maghreb, the Levant, and southern Europe. While together the cuisines of these regions form the hybrid known as Mediterranean cuisine, when looked at individually, each cuisine unfolds to reveal the wonderfully unique flavors of its own culture. Here is a closer exploration of the countries that make up this remarkable whole.

THE MAGHREB AND NORTHERN AFRICA

The Maghreb includes the westernmost countries of northern Africa: Morocco, Tunisia, and Algeria. Meaning "the land where the sun sets," the name Maghreb was bestowed on this region by medieval Arabic scholars, and it has remained to this day. It is a well-chosen name, for the region's setting sun is indeed remarkable as it dispenses golden shadows across the salmon-colored sand dunes. Libya and Egypt, two other northern African countries that border the Mediterranean, are not recognized as part of the Maghreb. Since these nations are not poised on the western edge of the continent, they could not share in the vivid designation. Yet, out of the two, we have included Libya here because the spirit and soul of its cooking is much the same as that of its western neighbors.

The vibrant colors and aromas of northern African cooking are evident in the crowded, bustling open-air markets located in village and city centers all over the region. These bazaars are very much the center of economic and social life, a place where people congregate to meet friends and purchase ripe, locally grown produce, dried legumes and couscous, and whatever else they need to prepare the day's meals. Most people visit the market every day, since freshness is key to the integrity of the cuisine.

It is an exciting, varied diet bursting with the ruddy colors and spicy flavors that mirror the sun-drenched land. The cuisines of the region are all based on an oral tradition: recipes and cooking techniques are passed down from mother to daughter, thus keeping alive age-old cooking secrets.

The richness of the cuisine is based in part on the wide variety of produce cultivated throughout these countries. There are quinces, Valencia oranges, cherries, apricots, turnips, carrots, eggplant, potatoes, tomatoes, and chiles, all of which came from Spain, or from the Americas via Spain. Artichokes are a popular native vegetable that is both cultivated and found growing wild in the countryside. Commonly used spices include deep yellow saffron, spicy red paprika (both sweet and hot), sweet cinnamon, and sharp powdered ginger. Fresh ginger is never used in traditional Mediterranean dishes. Ground cumin seed, coriander, and cloves have all been imported to this region from Portugal. The people of the Maghreb rely heavily on legumes such as fava beans, *ful mudammas* (brown fava beans), chickpeas, and navy beans for use in protein-rich soups, stews, and main dishes. Nuts such as almonds, pistachios, walnuts, and pine nuts are commonly used in desserts and some main courses, while sesame seeds find their way into many breads, pastries, and savory dishes.

The cuisine of Morocco is probably the best known (in the United States) among all northern African countries. In fact, couscous, a Moroccan staple, has become as common in American supermarkets as brown rice. Couscous is also a favorite in the other northern African countries. While Italians have their pasta and the Spanish have their rice, the northern African starch of choice is, without a doubt, couscous. The term *couscous* refers to both the little pellets made from cracked durum wheat or semolina and the savory dish they become once steamed over broth and covered with a rich stew. Couscous usually makes an appearance at both lunch and dinner. Sometimes, it is sweetened and cooked with milk to be eaten at breakfast or for dessert.

Couscous dishes are traditionally prepared with seven vegetables. They are always made with an intense bouillon over which the couscous steams until it is both plump and firm. Ripe, seasonal vegetables are seasoned with saffron, ginger, cumin, and hot and sweet paprika, and then spooned over the couscous, which is usually mounded in the center of a ceramic platter. Chickpeas, raisins, and honeyed onions serve as toothsome garnishes. Sweet couscous is dusted with powdered sugar and cinnamon, and is often decorated with geometrical patterns of dates, raisins, or prunes and served hot with cold buttermilk, almond milk, goat's milk, or plain cow's milk. Belboula, a hull-less cracked barley, is coarser and nuttier than its couscous cousin, but is prepared similarly.

Another Moroccan favorite is *harira*, a bean soup tinged with powdered cinnamon and ginger that is traditionally eaten by Muslims to break the daily fast during the month of Ramadan. It is a hearty soup that is also vastly popular throughout the region. The stewlike *tagine* is also a widely popular dish. The word *tagine* refers both to the stew and to the special earthenware pot in which the stew is slowly simmered.

The Moroccans love their pastries made from paper-thin leaves of dough called *warhka*. *B'stilla* is a lusty dish made from layer upon buttery layer of *warhka*, which is even thinner and more delicate than Greek phyllo dough. Algerian *dioul* and Tunisian *malsouka* are similar pastry doughs. Northern African sweets rely heavily upon almonds and other nuts, sugar syrups, and sweet spices such as cinnamon, cloves, allspice, ginger, nutmeg, mace, and even ground dried rosebuds. Prepared spice blends using these and sometimes a vast number of other spices are sold in markets, or mixed at home by northern African cooks. In Morocco, these spice blends are called *ras el hanout*, while in Tunisia they are called *bharat*. Perfumed essences, such as orange blossom water and rose water, are sprinkled onto pastries, puddings, beverages, and other sweets, and in Tunisia, a fragrant water infused with rose geraniums is also beloved.

Northern Africans, and especially Tunisians, prefer their dishes to be hot and spicy, and will dab peppery sauces on almost anything. *Harissa* is fiery sauce made from chiles, garlic, and *tabil,* which is a ground blend of coriander seed, caraway seed, red pepper flakes, and dehydrated garlic. The word *tabil* actually means "caraway seed," which is the dominant flavor of the mix. *Hrouss,* another hot and spicy paste, comes from Gabes, a city in southern Tunisia, and is made from sun-dried onions, chiles, and other spices.

Given the range of fruits and vegetables grown in the region, it is not surprising to find that northern Africa has a rich agricultural tradition. There are more than 100 million fruit trees in

Morocco alone, including oranges, lemons (many Moroccans preserve lemons in salt), almonds, apricots, figs, pomegranates, dates, and, of course, olives, which are mixed into almost every savory dish, in addition to being eaten on their own.

Olive oil in northern Africa is generally golden, clear, and fragrant. In Islam, the olive tree is associated with light, the symbol of the Prophet Muhammed, and with virility. In certain tribes of northern Africa, men drink olive oil to increase their sexual power and stamina. Argan oil is a lesser-used oil made from the nuts of the argan tree. The light-footed goats of the region actually climb the small trees to nibble on the intensely flavored nuts. The oil itself is pungent and acidic, and is often mixed with thick almond paste and honey to make a rich spread called *amalou.*

Northern Africans are overflowing with true Mediterranean hospitality. A guest in Morocco or Algeria will usually begin a feast by being offered *kemia*, a northern African version of Spanish *tapas* or Greek *mezze. Kemia* can include Moroccan spinach *briouats* (phyllo pastries), savory Algerian cheese puffs, and sweet grilled sun-dried red peppers. Green tea infused with fresh sprigs of mint is the ritual drink of Moroccan hospitality and is served, well sweetened, at the end of every meal. It is traditional for guests to drink three cups of this tea. Tunisians also enjoy mint-flavored teas and use other mints (often powdered) to flavor stews, egg dishes, and soups.

Friendly community spirit is apparent when dining in Morocco. Everyone sits on sofas and hassocks around low round tables, which are often situated in the tiled, flowered courtyards of traditional Moroccan homes. Diners use their thumbs and first two fingers plus a piece of bread to scoop up morsels of the highly seasoned food from a central communal platter.

Northern African cuisine, like all the cuisines of the Mediterranean, has been greatly affected by outside influences. Couscous, *tagines* and *harira* were developed by the ancient nomadic Berbers. Breads, another key component in the northern African diet, also originated with the Berbers. In fact, it is supposed that all breads in the world today originated from nomadic flat breads made of wheat or barley flour and baked on a griddle over a fire or buried in the hot sand by a fire. In Morocco, it is still traditional to make bread dough at home and then take it to a professional bakery for baking.

Smen (cooked and aged butter), dates, milk, and grain came from the Bedouin Arabs, who also brought back nutmeg, cloves, cinnamon, ginger, turmeric, and saffron from their expeditions to the Spice Islands. Relatively recent influences have come from Spain and France, the two European countries that ruled Morocco from 1913 to 1956. Many Moroccans speak French, and imported French cheeses and wines are common.

THE LEVANT

The term *Levant* describes the coastal Mediterranean region that covers the countries of Turkey, Lebanon, Israel, Syria, and Egypt. (Do not, by the way, confuse this term with *Levante*, a region within Mediterranean Spain.) The earliest wheats and the first breads are said to have originated within this region, cultivated in that famed fertile crescent that lies between the Tigris and Euphrates rivers. The countries of this area are all blessed with rich soils and a temperate climate, which makes them well suited to growing a cornucopia of delicious fruits, vegetables, and grains most of the year.

The location of the Levantine countries has also benefited them in terms of trade, since their ports sit right on one of the world's major trade routes. This path means that Maghrebi and European influences can often be spotted in Levantine cuisine, and vice versa.

Some of the influences in Levantine cuisine are so long held that they are not considered anything but native. But there can be no doubt that among the hot sauces popular in Israel, Tunisian *harissa* is the most common, and that thick, hearty stews filled with potatoes, vegetables, and grains came from Eastern Europe. Originally from India, eggplant, known as "poor man's meat," is one of the region's most essential vegetables, and it is prepared in myriad ways, from roasting to stuffing to pureeing into spicy dips.

Garlic has been part of this region's cuisine since time immemorial, and was supposedly fed to the Egyptian slaves to promote their strength when they were building the pyramids. It is used as the base for many of the region's savory dishes, and its flavor is traditionally brought out by lightly salting it, then grinding it into a paste with an old-fashioned mortar and pestle. Yogurt, another integral, age-old ingredient, is the dairy product of choice here. Usually made from whole milk, it is a rich, thick cream that is often transformed into delicious minted sauces and spicy dips, spooned into soups, and eaten with honey and fruit.

Turkey

The ancient Turkish diet was rather a limited one, by today's standards. Yogurt, unleavened bread, horse meat, milk, and game were probably the main food sources for the predecessors of today's Turks—the Oguz Turks from the Turan Basin in Central Asia. But by the Middle Ages, Turkish food had developed into a close cousin of the varied and multilayered cuisine it is today. While the origins of today's Turkish food have been widely debated, Turkey's influence on other countries has not. As the Ottoman Empire spread across the Mediterranean, so did its exuberant cuisine. And since then, the ingredients and techniques used in Turkish cooking have developed even further owing to booming reciprocal trade with other Mediterranean countries.

Glossy, taut-skinned eggplant is a key vegetable in even the fanciest of Turkish cooking. Eggplant may be dried, reconstituted, and stuffed; grilled; fried; or made into jam. It is also mixed with other vegetables such as tomatoes and green peppers and made into subtly spiced vegetable stews. As in most Mediterranean countries, tomatoes, zucchini, peppers, onions, grape leaves, and olive products are essential to a cook's larder. Turkish olive oil tends to be slightly cloudy but intensely flavored, and it is used both in salads and for cooking. Tangy cheeses, made from either cow's or sheep's milk, are eaten plain with bread, in colorful salads, fried with eggs, and used to stuff flaky *borek* pastries.

In Turkey, and indeed throughout the eastern Mediterranean, pungent garlic is believed to contain special healing powers that increase blood circulation. It is used constantly, both fresh and dried. Fresh garlic is crushed with salt in a mortar and pestle and is then used in sauces, salads, soups, and stews. Dried garlic is sprinkled on savory dishes for a more subtle flavoring. Unlike in the traditionally spicy cuisine of northern Africa, Turkish cooks use hot peppers sparingly. But not so with fresh herbs, which grow in fragrant profusion all over the Turkish countryside, including basil, sage, rosemary, tarragon, thyme, marjoram, and bay leaf. Turkish sage is unusually aromatic and the leaves are often dried and made into a soothing and cleansing tea.

Since food preservation is a pressing issue in hot countries, many foods are pickled, including fish, lemons, eggplant, and even fruit such as apricots. Walking down a busy street in a Turkish town, you will pass many a vendor or shopkeeper whose stall or window has row upon row of colorful jars of homemade pickles. Pickled vegetables are commonly served plain as appetizers or used to give a kick to main dishes. And pickled fried fish is actually eaten all over the Mediterranean (think of Spanish *escabeche*).

As in many Mediterranean countries, most meals in Turkey begin with a diverse and generous selection of appetizers known as *mezze*. In its most elegant form, *mezze*, which translates as "a pleasant taste," is served twice at one meal: first comes a huge platter of cold *mezze*, followed by another assortment of hot *mezze*. Salads, both creamy and crisp, stuffed grape leaves, eggplant dips, yogurt sauces, and baked savory pastries are all part of a grand Turkish *mezze*.

Mezze may be accompanied by *raki*, the national alcoholic drink, traditionally consumed only by men. It is made from dried raisins, dried figs, or fresh grapes, and is scented with plenty of sweet anise. *Raki* is also sometimes called *aslan sutu*, which means "lion's milk," because it turns cloudy when water is added to it before drinking. *Raki* can also be drunk with the main meal to open up and refresh the palate.

The Turks love to eat sweet, ripe fruit, and do so on a daily basis. Peaches, apricots, oranges, tangerines, mulberries, figs, cherries, bananas, grapes, lemons, and pomegranates are all cultivated in the neat, lush orchards that dot the fertile regions of the Turkish countryside. Fruits are also used to make jams and compotes. Sour cherries are a particular favorite, and, in season, are cooked in rice dishes or puddings, or made into tarts and refreshing fruit drinks. Pomegranate juice is also a popular drink. A tradition in many parts of the eastern Mediterranean is to squeeze grapes for their juice, concentrate the juice into a sticky syrup, and then mix it with tahini to spread on slices of fresh bread.

As in northern Africa, rose water is added to pastries and milk puddings to provide a delicate flowery flavor and perfume. It is also used in an elegant rose petal sorbet—a suave, scented ice topped with crystallized rose petals. Nuts are used in both sweet and savory dishes such as vegetable dishes, pilafs, and *lokum*, the classic sweet and gooey "Turkish delight." Favorite nuts include almonds, chestnuts, hazelnuts, pine nuts, pistachios, and walnuts. Almond-flavored *keskul* is a popular milk pudding that is presented chilled and garnished with flaked coconut and ground pistachios. It is served, as are most sweets, with bracing cups of thick, rich Turkish coffee.

Lebanon, Egypt, Syria

The cuisine of Lebanon is more varied than some of its Middle Eastern neighbors because of influences from the ancient Egyptians and Greeks, the Persians, the Ottomans, and, more recently, the French. Another difference is that since Lebanon has no blistering, sandy desert, there is no culinary tradition of nomadic peoples. Although they are larger countries, the cuisines of Syria and Egypt are considerably less known than that of their tiny neighbor Lebanon. However, the cuisines of all three countries are similar in many respects, and so it is not unfitting to talk about them all at once.

The cooks of this region, extending from the eastern edge of northern Africa to the Middle East, do not hold back when it comes to adding fragrant spices, and they use almost as many, in myriad combinations, as is possible. Some favorites include cinnamon sticks and powder, ground allspice, finely ground black and white pepper, cloves, nutmeg, and coriander. Anise, whole or ground, is used to make infusions or to flavor puddings. *Mahlab* is the aromatic dried kernel of a black cherry. It has a haunting flavor, and is often ground and mixed into biscuits, breads, and puddings. *Zatar* is a bright-green herb mixture made from dried thyme, sumac, and toasted or raw sesame seeds. It is sprinkled over flat bread and used as a general seasoning for all kinds of savory dishes. *Dukkah* is a spice mixture containing sesame, coriander seeds, and hazelnuts. It is an Egyptian specialty served as a dip for olive oil–soaked bread.

There are two unusual staples in the Lebanese kitchen. One of them is the dried inner bark and surface roots of the South American tree *Quillaja saponaria*, or soap bark. It is used for its foaming qualities and bittersweet flavor to make *natef*, a frothy, lightly sweet dessert mousse. Surprisingly, the same powder is also used as carpet soap. Another unfamiliar staple is *sahlab*, a fine white powder extracted from dried orchid leaves, which is used as a thickening agent in milk puddings or ice creams. Cornstarch is the American substitute for *sahlab*.

While the Lebanese, Syrians, and Egyptians also eat couscous, it is quite different from northern African couscous. The "grains" are made from flour and salted water, and they are finer than those of northern Africa. Couscous is always cooked with chicken and/or lamb, and baby onions are the only vegetable garnish. The popular grain *freekeh* is roasted green wheat that is cooked like bulgur or rice and has a distinctive, smoky taste.

Dried figs and other dried fruits and vegetables are eaten out of hand or reconstituted and cooked in soups, stews, and pastries. Most people of the region dry their own produce, and even in cities it's not uncommon to see the flat roofs covered with white sheets on which drying fruits and vegetables shrivel in the hot sun. As in Turkey, all sorts of vegetables are pickled in brine and spices, to be eaten as part of a *mezze* or added to prepared dishes. Lupine seeds (also called *lupini* beans in Italy and southern France) are an ancient legume; they are salted or pickled and served as a snack or part of a *mezze*. The thick, parchment-colored skins must be removed before eating the flat, round, yellow seeds. Olives, of course, are native to the region and make up a substantial part of the cuisine. They're eaten at breakfast and at the end of lunch or dinner, and are as much a staple as bread. Olive oil is also an integral ingredient in the region, as it is everywhere in the Mediterranean. Lebanese olive oil is of particularly good quality, and is reminiscent of the intensely flavored oils of southern Italy.

Pine nuts (also called *pignoli*), harvested from the pine forests in Lebanon, are eaten in all kinds of ways. The green pine cone is sometimes sliced into wedges, dipped in salt, and eaten as a snack. The mature nuts are sautéed until golden in salted butter and used as a garnish for salads and sweets. Sesame seeds play an important role in Lebanese, Egyptian, and Syrian cooking. Raw or roasted sesame seeds are used to flavor breads, biscuits, falafel, or sweet candies. Tahini, or sesame paste, is mixed into salads or made into a savory, rich dressing. Sweet, candy-like halvah is also made from pounded sesame seeds.

The cheeses of the region are made from either ewe's or goat's milk. Fresh cheeses include feta and curd cheeses that are made with yogurt (often homemade) and lemon juice. A traditional Lebanese and Syrian cheese called *shankleesh* is made with fermented curd and seasoned with cayenne pepper and salt, and then coated with thyme. In Egypt, fried slabs of cheese are eaten with bread and a squirt of lemon juice. *Samneh*, similar to northern African *smen*, is salted and aged clarified butter that is used as a sandwich spread.

Like most of the Levantine people, the Lebanese, Syrians, and Egyptians adore sweet, sticky desserts and cool milk puddings. Some typical treats include carob molasses, which can be served with pita bread as a syrupy dip, eaten alone, or mixed with tahini. Children also chew on carob pods for a sweet snack. As in Turkey, molasses is made from cooked grape juice, and the resulting tangy paste is eaten with pita bread. Other fruits are cooked down into syrups and pastes as well, and provide a concentrated, fruity sweetness that can be eaten alone, with bread, or used as a flavoring. For example, *amar el-deen*, or "moon of the religion," is a sticky sheet of Syrian candy made from dried apricot puree. It is chewed as a sugary treat and is also used to flavor ice cream.

In Lebanon, orange flower water is distilled from the blossoms of the Seville orange. It is extremely aromatic, if slightly bitter, and is used sparingly to flavor puddings and cakes. It is also used as a beverage; a teaspoonful of orange flower water stirred into a cup of boiling water makes a coffee substitute called white coffee. Rose petals are made into jam as well as rose water. The blush-colored preserve is riddled with candied strips of deep-pink rose petals, which are used to garnish creamy sweets.

Thick, black coffee is widely consumed, as are delicate herbal teas. *Arak* is a clear alcoholic drink made from distilled white grape juice and flavored with anise. Recently, Lebanese vineyards have been producing notable wines, some of which have been referred to by the French as *vins d'or*, or "wines of gold." Naturally, they go well with the robust, flavorful cuisine of this region.

Israel and the Sephardic Jews

Israeli cuisine has experienced somewhat of a renaissance during the past decade. We have begun to shift our preconceived notion of Israeli food from what might be considered typical "Jewish" food derived from the Ashkenazi Jews of Eastern Europe, such as borscht, strudels, and *cholents* (stews), toward more of an all-encompassing Mediterranean fusion. The influences of the Sephardic Jews who, during the Spanish Inquisition, were forced to leave Spain and ended up scattered throughout Italy, France, Algeria, Greece, Morocco, and the remains of the Ottoman Empire, are being appreciated more and more. Taking a holistic look at Israel, one realizes that all of the ethnic and cultural influences on the country—including Maghrebi, Yemenite, Arab, Russian, and Polish—play an equally important role in defining Israel's cuisine. Since Israel's establishment in 1948, Jews from Arab regions, northern Africa, Turkey, Syria, Lebanon, and Jordan have moved there in vast numbers, taking their cultures' recipes with them. There, they traded their culinary knowledge with European Jews who were Holocaust survivors from France, Italy, Germany, Poland, and Russia. So, while most food eaten in Israel may not be necessarily indigenous to the eastern Mediterranean, it is a genuine and distinctly Israeli cuisine that has grown from many great cultures' culinary traditions.

Other influences have come from dietary laws that promote dishes slowly braised and stewed; the separation of meat and dairy; the exclusion of pork and shellfish; and the use of wine and spirits in cooking and as ritual. Muslims also exclude pork but not shellfish. They mix dairy with meat, but completely forbid the use of alcohol. Jews adapted many recipes so that they would conform to the dietary rules, *kashrut* or kosher. Vegetarianism is considered to be the ideal lifestyle, according to Jewish tradition, but it is not a requirement of Jewish law. Since all plant foods are inherently kosher, vegetarians who do not eat any animal products are abiding by the laws of *kashrut*.

EUROPE

The Mediterranean countries of Europe—namely Spain, France, Italy, and Greece—are lands characterized by patchwork fields of grains, vegetables, and sunflowers, terraced vineyards, and silvery, shimmering olive groves. This sunny region is also a beacon to vacationers from all over the world, who flock to Barcelona, the French Riviera, Sardinia, and Athens. There is no lack of Mediterranean hospitality in these countries, and no lack of delicious and tempting gastronomical treats, either.

The cuisines of these countries have all been influenced by the Arabs, who moved through the Middle East into northern Africa and Europe, bringing with them many new ingredients and recipes. The circle of trade is apparent when we notice that Grecian desserts are often flavored with Arabic-derived flower waters, and that the French love of couscous has been inspired by its former colonial possessions in northern Africa. An enormous variety of cheeses, fine wines, fresh herbs, and pasta and rice dishes also characterize the cuisine of this region.

Spain

Catalonia, Levante, and Andalusia are the three regions of Spain that border the Mediterranean Sea. Catalonia is unique in that it has its own language and culture, and its cuisine is distinct from that of the rest of Spain. Barcelona, its capital, is the largest city in Spain. About 6 million people live in Catalonia, a region that extends south from the Pyrenees to the Cape of Tortosa, and includes the French province of Roussillon, Andorra, the Balearic Islands (Ibiza, Majorca, and Minorca) and the city of Alghero on Italy's Sardinia.

Catalan cuisine is representational of Mediterranean Spain. There are two main styles of Catalan cooking: one, built around the tradition of fishing, that includes such delicacies as seafood stews, black rice with squid, grilled fish and *suquet* (fish and potato stew); and the other, from the mountains, that features dishes such as rabbit and other game stews in red wine.

Catalan cuisine has adopted French and Italian ingredients such as tomatoes, olive oil, garlic, onions, nuts, dried fruits, and fresh herbs and put them together in the region's unique ways. Lemon, honey, and cinnamon are borrowed from the Arabs and Jews, and are also used in profusion. Brandy (Catalan brandy is less sweet than Spanish brandy), olive oil (which tends to be fruity and aromatic), olives, orange liqueur, short-grain Valencia rice, saffron, sea salt, red wine, sherry and sherry vinegars, garlic, almonds, hazelnuts, and pine nuts are used to flavor the food in myriad ways.

Tapas (like Greek and Turkish *mezze*) are small plates of appetizers served with wine or dry sherry. They are served before dinner in all of Spain in bars and restaurants—never at home. However, in Catalonia, tapas are more of a culinary footnote and not as elaborate as non-Mediterranean Spanish tapas, which sometimes can suffice as a meal in themselves. Catalan cooking is characterized by its varied fish and seafood dishes, which are typically combined with local fruits—a combination unique to Catalonia.

Levante (or Valencia) is the heart of rice country, an area of tidal flatlands. Rice is eaten daily and mixed with a wide and intriguing variety of vegetables, fish, and meats. Paella, which is made with short, stubby Valencia rice, comes in many different varieties, but is usually flavored with saffron.

Andalusia is an arid region best suited to grapevines and olive trees. The food here is simple, rustic, and delicious, filled with fresh vegetables and lusty stews and soups. Gazpacho, that spicy cold soup made with fresh tomatoes, peppers, cucumbers, and, of course, plenty of garlic and olive oil, is native to the region of southern Andalusia, where it provides a cool balm on a blistering summer afternoon.

Because of its mostly mountainous terrain, Spain is generally not well suited for cattle grazing, but it is ideal for growing olives and grapes and raising small animals like sheep and goats. Those livestock provide milk for the wonderful and varied cheeses enjoyed throughout the region. *Queso machego* is a ubiquitous, mild, sheep's milk cheese, while *queso de Mahon* is a unique, strong, semisoft cow's milk cheese made on the Baleric island of Minorca.

Spanish desserts have been influenced greatly by the Moors and commonly include almonds, egg yolks, and honey. Custards such as flan and *crema Catalena*, sugary puff pastries, and fried dough crisps are perennial favorites. Anise, cinnamon, and almond are the most common flavorings, and they find their way into breads, rolls, puddings, tarts, candies, cakes, and pastries.

Spanish Mediterranean wines of note are mainly red, and have markedly increased in quality over the last ten years. They are full and fleshy wines that sometimes age for years to reach their fruity potential.

France

The Mediterranean regions of France include Provence (which contains the city of Nice and the famous resort town St. Tropez), the Côte d'Azur, and the rocky island of Corsica in the Mediterranean Sea.

Provence was one of the earliest regions outside of Italy to be settled by the ancient Romans. Today, the region is home to flourishing vineyards, olive groves, wild mushrooms (including chanterelles, truffles, and morels), and artichokes. Provençal recipes always include plenty of garlic and tomatoes, and tend to be imbued with the flavors of fresh herbs: basil, rosemary, thyme, and savory. In winter, Provençal cooks sprinkle their creations with a dried combination of those same herbs, called *herbes de Provence*, which also includes bay leaves, marjoram, and lavender flowers. Wild lemony sorrel also grows in Provençal gardens and is used fresh in salads, soups, and some sauces.

As in most other regions of the Mediterranean, the towns and cities of southern France are centered on the market square, which bursts to life at least several times a week, if not every day. Mounds of vibrant, perfectly ripe fruits and vegetables are displayed in stalls and purchased a few at a time (just enough for the day's meal) by discerning cooks. They are taken home and made into ratatouille (a rich stew of well-cooked eggplant, tomatoes, zucchini, red peppers, garlic, onions, olive oil, and herbs); *pistou*, a thick vegetable soup flavored with an herbal paste made from garlic, basil, and olive oil; and *bourride*, a thick seafood stew seasoned and bound with *aïoli*—a thick and heady garlic mayonnaise.

Other than the produce, French Mediterranean markets offer staple ingredients of the region. There is always at least one vendor displaying buckets brimming with olives in every one of their earthy hues—from bright green to khaki to deep purple and wrinkled shiny black. Since Provençal soil is generally richer than that of Greece or Italy, the olives produced in this region tend to be more robust and less bitter. At the same stand are other salty preserves, like *lupini* beans, *cornichons* (tiny, very tart cucumber pickles), capers, and anchovies. Sometimes, that stall will also carry the nuts used in the region's cooking—the pale almonds, hazelnuts, walnuts, and pine nuts that are baked into pastries and cakes, used for garnish, or, occasionally, eaten out of hand.

Down the row but only a few feet away is the dry goods stand, where vendors hawk couscous, bulgur, polenta, dried white beans in varying sizes, the tiny green lentils preferred all over France (called *lentilles du Puy*), and chickpeas and their beige-colored flour. Chickpea flour, with its earthy taste, is a favorite ingredient and a good source of protein. It is made into *panisse*, a thick porridge that is molded, fried, and served sprinkled with sugar. Another chickpea flour snack is *socca*, which is a thin, soft, salty wafer served warm in paper cones in the Cours Saleya market of Nice.

Another beloved regional snack is the overstuffed sandwich known as *pan bagnat*. It is a classic Niçoise street food made from whole round loaves of bread that are halved, drizzled with fruity olive oil, and stuffed with tuna, olives, anchovies, tomatoes, and capers. These sandwiches are prepared in the morning and set under a weight. By lunchtime they have flattened and condensed, and the olive oil has moistened and flavored the bread. They are often packed for an afternoon picnic on the beach.

Cheeses in Mediterranean France are varied and distinct. Chèvres, which are goat's milk cheeses, are very popular, and are sold in various stages of the aging process. Soft, mild fresh goat cheeses are eaten on salads, spread on crusty loaves of bread, or drizzled with olive oil and herbs. Slightly older, with a firm consistency and a slightly chalky flavor, goat cheeses are eaten on dense loaves of bread with fruit after a meal. The hardest and most pungent chèvres are eaten in tiny quantities, usually by themselves or as part of a cheese course. Using a fork and knife is the proper way to eat these intense little morsels. Other common cheeses include creamy, sharp Roquefort and nutty Gruyère, which is used in gratins and other baked dishes.

For dessert, the people of Cavaillon and the surrounding area can indulge in their famous fragrant melons, eaten plain or filled with port, candied, or pureed and made into sorbets. As in most of the Mediterranean, fig trees are located in many a backyard, and the luscious, ruby-fleshed fruits are eaten with fresh white cheese or with almonds. The southern French also adore ice creams and intensely flavored sorbets, which are sold in cafés or licked from small cones while strolling along the avenues. Parisian-style pastries and cakes are also favored, with their rich, silky buttercreams, soft spongy cakes, and crisp meringues.

The wines of southern France are some of the best in the whole Mediterranean. Wine making has been practiced for thousands of years, and the result is a variety of styles, from the light, pink, rosé wines of Bandol and the hearty, robust, red wines of the Rhône to citrusy, floral white wines of Cassis (not to be confused with the liqueur, which hails from Burgundy).

The island of Corsica was sold to France by Genoa in 1768 and has remained under the country's sovereignty since. It lies more than a hundred miles off France's coast and is generally not visible from the mainland. It is an arid island, relatively isolated and uncrowded, with a largely undeveloped interior.

Corsican cuisine is a meld of French, Italian, and Arabic influences. It combines Arabic couscous with hearty French stews and roasted meats, and Italian-style hard cheeses and sausages with the island's own version of pasta. Chestnuts grow abundantly on the island and chestnut flour is used in breads, cakes, and desserts, which are often flavored with almond or anise. Unlike the subtle spices preferred by the Provençal, fiery peppers tend to inflame the already strongly spiced Corsican dishes.

Wine is made on the little island, but it is somewhat harsh. Still, it's drinkable, and, best of all, flows abundantly from earthenware pitchers in homes and cafés. The favorite apéritif, as it is all over France, is strong licorice-flavored *pastis*. Here, as in the northern regions, *pastis* is diluted with cool water, turning straw colored and cloudy in the process.

Italy

Mediterranean Italian food is overwhelmingly popular in the United States, and rightly so. It is rich with ripe vegetables, sprightly fresh herbs, pliable homemade pastas, crusty breads, and handmade cheeses. Just as there is no one Mediterranean cuisine, so there is no one Mediterranean Italian cuisine. From the southern islands of Sardinia and Sicily, up the boot to Naples and Rome, and along the coast to Genoa, Italian cuisine is as varied as it is united.

One unifying facet of Italian cooking is pasta. However, Italy is also home to many kinds of rice (including the short-grained Arborio rice that is stirred into risotto), semolina or potato gnocchi, and polenta. They are all combined with sauces, which can range from a simple drizzle of garlic-scented olive oil to a rich ragoût of vegetables, herbs, spices, and cheese.

Pasta is usually made from either finely ground, soft wheat flour or semolina flour, which is a more coarsely ground, hard wheat flour. Eggs are only sometimes added to the dough, and never to semolina pastas. Pastas come in dozens of shapes, many with whimsical names such as *orecchetti* (little ears) and *capellini* (angel's hair). Italians always cook their pasta al dente, until the pasta is cooked but still firm.

Polenta is a relative newcomer in terms of its use in Italian cuisine. Cornmeal was brought to Italy in the sixteenth century, after European exploration of the Americas. Polenta can be made from both white and yellow cornmeal and may be cooked in milk, broth, wine, or water. Soft polenta is scooped into bowls and served as is or with a thick sauce. Leftover soft polenta is usually poured into pans and allowed to get cold and firm. It is then sliced and fried or baked.

Couscous, an Arabic influence, is more commonly eaten in Sicily than on the Italian mainland. It is often served as a first course, usually with a hearty meat and vegetable sauce. Even the soups are usually based on grains—vegetable soups have pasta added, and are often made especially hearty with the addition of beans. Soups are also served ladled over toasted croutons or thick slices of crusty country bread.

As with all Mediterranean diets, the Italian one is largely vegetarian, and seafood is eaten more often than meat. Vegetables are prepared in a dazzling variety. Italian antipasto, akin to *mezze*, is a colorful selection of carefully cooked vegetable dishes. Roasted red peppers, fried eggplant, steamed asparagus, artichokes with olive oil and lemon, garlicky sautéed broccoli rabe, marinated mushrooms, olives, grilled zucchini, and lightly dressed mixed salads (made with pleasantly bitter arugula, radicchio, and endive) are all part of the array. Other favorite vegetables include wild mushrooms, such as porcini and white truffles, which grow densely in the Italian forests. The Italians grow an impressive number of eggplant varieties, ranging from tiny, tomato-size white eggplant to the wandlike violet-hued type. They are made into antipasti and used in sauces, soups, and baked casseroles, especially in southern Italy.

Vegetables always appear in main dishes, and when served as sides, vegetables are always respectfully presented on separate plates. Italians have a passion for serving fresh, local vegetables in season. They are often cooked with fava beans, chickpeas, lentils, and cannellini, which are the Italians' favorite legumes.

Italian food, like most Mediterranean cuisine, is impregnated with the flavors of fresh herbs. Bay, a shrubby evergreen, is so common as a hedge that Italians can use fresh bay leaves year-round. Fragrant basil, which is grown in small-leafed bushes, is used fresh in season, as are oregano, parsley, and mint. Dried herbs are not as commonly used. It is far more likely for an Italian cook to use parsley, which is available year-round, than dried basil in a dish. Spices are popular, too, although not to the extent that they are in northern Africa and the Levant. Cinnamon, allspice, and anise are used in sweet dishes, and anise is also used in certain meat and fish preparations.

In addition to the subtle and delicate olive oil from central Italy and the strong, intensely flavored olive oil of southern Italy, sunflower seed oil is commonly used. It is a light oil with no marked taste, and is used for frying and, occasionally, for salads.

There are even more varieties of cheese in Italy than there are in France. Common ones include soft, stretchy mozzarella, eaten fresh in salads or by itself; robust provolone, Parmesan, and pecorino (from sheep's milk); buttery, creamy mascarpone (Italian cream cheese); and mild, milky ricotta, which is used in pastas and desserts.

Out of all the Italian breads, pizzas and focaccia are probably the two best known in the United States. But there are many other types of Italian breads, from the wheaty, thick-crusted peasant loaves baked in wood ovens to the pale, soft rolls eaten for breakfast. Bread usually accompanies meals, and is also often a central ingredient in many dishes, where it is crumbled and used as a stuffing, sliced and toasted as croutons (*crostini*), mixed into salads or soups, or layered into a casserole.

Pastries (made with fruits, nuts, and cheese), semolina cakes, and sorbets and ice creams are all eaten for dessert, but the most popular dessert by far is simply ripe, seasonal fruit. It is far more common to see an Italian peeling an orange or cracking some nuts after a meal than indulging in a fancy torte or cake. Those desserts are left for special occasions such as weddings and holidays. But sweet treats are eaten in the afternoon with espresso or in the mid-morning with a frothy *caffè latte*.

For the excellent wines of Italy, most of the grapes are grown in Tuscany and the Piedmont area, which do not border the Mediterranean sea. But these rich, heady wines are enjoyed all over the country. The greatest Italian wines are red, lush, and full bodied, and often require several years of aging. Italian white wines are crisp and pleasant, just right to sip on sultry nights and hot afternoons.

Greece

Some scholars believe that the origin of Mediterranean cooking (and all cooking for that matter) was in ancient Greece, and Greece is probably the first country that comes to mind when the topic of Mediterranean cuisine comes up.

For the most part, Greek cooking is simple and pure. Olive oil, garlic, lemon, and herbs flavor most of what the Greeks consume, from their soft, creamy dips and the plainly grilled fresh fish, to the soups, stews, and vegetable dishes popular throughout the land.

In terms of herbs, the favorite is pungent, dried oregano, followed by fresh mint, dill, flat-leaf parsley, bay leaf, and thyme. Less frequently used are rosemary, allspice, celery leaves, coriander seeds, cilantro, ground nutmeg, caraway seeds, cumin, anise, fennel seeds, and ground mace. Basil is grown for religious purposes and as a fly repellent, but hardly ever appears in cooking.

Some other key ingredients in Greek cooking include capers, giant white beans, grape leaves, honey, orange blossom water and rose water (used sparingly in desserts and beverages), sesame seeds, squash blossoms, red wine vinegar, and yogurt.

The Greeks eat a lot of cheese and serve it daily in some form or another. Most popular is the tangy feta, made from sheep's or goat's milk and then preserved in brine. Feta is crumbled over the crisp salads that are Greek mainstays. Other favorite cheeses include *kefalotiri*, which is similar to Parmesan, *kasseri*, a hard cheese made from sheep's or goat's milk, and *kefalo-graviera*, a hard cow's-milk cheese. Clarified butter is also prepared and used in Greek cooking, especially brushed between the layers of flaky *spanakopita* and other phyllo pastries.

Greeks are the masters of grilled vegetables and have been grilling all sorts of food over open fires for thousands of years. Bell peppers, eggplant, fennel, mushrooms, squash, and onions are all at their Greek best when marinated with garlic and lemon, coated in olive oil, and grilled over an outdoor fire or red-hot coals.

Olives, including the famous dark-purple Kalamata olives that are indigenous to the country, are a Greek mainstay. Olive trees flourish in the favorable climate and rocky dry soils of the countryside. Most olive farms are small family-run operations that have been passed down from generation to generation. Olive trees have a life span of hundreds—and sometimes thousands—of years, so they generally outlive several generations of farmers. Bowls of olives appear at bar counters instead of peanuts or pretzels. A favorite snack or light meal is made from simply a handful of marinated olives, a slab of bread, and a chunk of tangy feta cheese. And it was the Greeks who introduced golden olive oil to the rest of the Mediterranean. No Greek meal would be truly Greek without the liberal use of the fragrant oil, which, in this country, tends to be fruity, deep-scented, and rich.

The *mezze* in Greece is primarily the precursor to the main course, though it can be eaten at all times of the day, and usually accompanies a glass of wine or an *ouzo*, the national alcoholic beverage, made from the residues of pressed grapes and flavored with anise, mastic, lime, and coriander. A fundamental part of Greek hospitality and a longstanding cultural tradition, *mezedes* commonly served include a variety of delicious treats including roasted eggplant salad, stuffed grape leaves, phyllo-wrapped *spanakopita*, *tzatziki* (yogurt and cucumber salad), *skordalia* (a garlicky potato dip), marinated and roasted vegetables, and a big plate of marinated or oil-cured olives.

Greek soups are quintessentially vegetarian. They are never served as starters but always stand alone as the main course. Steaming bowls full of chunky vegetables, beans or lentils, and rice or pasta, these soups are inexpensive and delicious. They are often served with thick slices of homemade bread. Big round loaves of crusty country wheat breads are the standard. Not a scrap of bread is wasted; leftovers are made into bread crumbs and used in *skordalia* or in bread salads.

After the Italians, the Greeks consume the most pasta per capita in the Mediterranean region. However, the Greeks tend not to be as discerning as the Italians and call all pasta by one name, *makaronia*. They also prefer their noodles cooked until very soft and generally toss them with whatever sauce happens to be bubbling on the stovetop. Still, the creamy, cheese-laced *pastitsio* is a perennial favorite.

Two of the most famous Greek desserts are honey-sweetened baklava and creamy, cinnamon-topped rice pudding. Again, these two sweets reflect the dessert styles all over the Mediterranean, but especially Turkey and the rest of the Levant. Fruit jams, another favorite dessert, are syrupy preserves, often made from quinces or cherries, that are eaten with a spoon, accompanied by nothing more than a glass of iced water or a cup of coffee. A refreshing beverage can also be made from the fruit syrup left over from a jar of jam, mixed with water and ice.

Wine is central to Greek culture and is a traditional drink that dates back to the days of Mount Olympus and Dionysus, the god of wine. Like most Mediterranean peoples, the Greeks have few pretensions or stigmas regarding wine drinking. Regionally produced wines are made to be consumed in moderation and always accompany a meal. Greek wines are produced, not to compete with the renowned French vintages, but to be enjoyed as one of life's simple pleasures. *Retsina*, an age-old traditional Greek favorite, is tinged with pine resin and served ice cold. This strangely flavored and overwhelmingly popular wine is protected by law and may only be produced by Greece.

The Mediterranean

WHAT IS THE "MEDITERRANEAN DIET"?

During the past decade, it's been hard not to notice the excitement surrounding the much-touted Mediterranean diet. While each country in the Mediterranean is unique, with its own culture and specialized cuisine, the diets of all these countries are unified in several important aspects relating to good health. Mediterranean people consume a plant-based diet consisting mostly of grains, legumes, pasta, and bread, and plenty of fresh, ripe fruits and vegetables. Pungent garlic, fresh herbs, sea salt, and fragrant spices enhance the flavors in myriad ways. Throughout the Mediterranean, healthful monounsaturated olive oil is used as the primary source of fat, while very few meats or sweets are eaten. All kinds of cheeses, yogurt, and eggs are consumed in moderation, and small glasses of wine are sipped with meals. The healthful results of abiding by this seemingly decadent diet are astounding. In studies conducted on the Greek isle of Crete, researchers found that Cretan men who followed this traditional diet were much less likely to die of heart disease than their American counterparts. Moderate consumption of wine and reduced intake of saturated fats (mainly from animal products) have both been linked to a reduced risk of coronary disease and some forms of cancer. Additionally, the traditional Mediterranean diet is high in fiber, complex carbohydrates, vitamins, minerals, and antioxidants, which also help keep diseases at bay.

All that said, it's important to add that the Mediterranean diet is not just what you eat. It is a way of life. Researchers are finding that how you eat is as significant as what you eat. Relaxed, social meals, a strong network of family and friends, and a daily siesta are as health giving as fresh, unprocessed vegetables and large amounts of fiber. Furthermore, including vigorous physical activity as a part of a daily routine prevents obesity and increases a person's quality of life.

So, without even splurging on an airline ticket, anyone can adapt aspects of the Mediterranean diet to his or her own lifestyle and possibly lead a fuller, better, and longer life. What other "diet" offers you that?

THE CRETAN MODEL

Although today we take for granted the link between heart disease and diet, in the late 1950s and early 1960s, it was a radical departure in thinking. Ancel Keys and Henry Blackburn were two of the first scientists to make that connection, which they published in their ground-breaking tract, *The Seven Countries Study*. The investigators noted the cholesterol levels, lifestyles, and diets of more than 12,000 middle-aged men in Greece, Finland, Italy, Japan, the Netherlands, the United States, and the former Yugoslavia. What they found was that the men on the Greek island of Crete were 70 percent less likely to develop heart disease than men in the United States. And people in Crete were living longer and more active lives than their counterparts in any of the other countries studied. What were the Cretans doing that much of the rest of the world wasn't?

The answer lay in the combination of a practically meatless diet rich in vegetables, fruits, grains, and olive oil; plenty of daily exercise; and a small glass or two of wine drunk with meals on a daily basis. This is how Blackburn (as quoted in the Center for Science in the Public Interest Nutrition Action Healthletter, December 1994) rather poetically portrayed his healthy research subjects:

> He's a shepherd or small farmer, a beekeeper or fisherman, or a tender of olives or vines. He walks to work daily and labors in the soft light of his Greek Isle. His midday, main meal is of eggplant, with large mushrooms, crisp vegetables, and country bread dipped in golden olive oil. Once a week there is a bit of lamb. Once a week there is chicken. Twice a week there is fish fresh from the sea. Other meals are hot

dishes of legumes seasoned with condiments. The main dish is followed by a tangy salad, then by dates, Turkish sweets, nuts, or fresh fruit. A sharp local wine completes the meal.

This picturesque rendering of a typical Cretan lifestyle forms the basis for what we are now calling the Mediterranean diet. Although the above sketch was specific to Crete, it could also be that of any poor Mediterranean country.

Unfortunately for richer countries, Keys and Blackburn also discovered that keeping healthy and living longer was a by-product of a peasant lifestyle. Most Mediterranean peoples could not afford to eat differently and were compelled to exercise by laboring vigorously in the fields. Fruits and vegetables were a cornerstone of their diet because they were free—most households grew them in their gardens and orchards. Grains were cheap and plentiful, and cheese and yogurt could be made from the milk of one's own family goat. Olives, growing abundantly on the hillsides, were pressed into inexpensive, flavorful oil. Meat was costly, so seldom consumed.

The consensus, proved by other studies, seems to be that the more affluent a culture becomes, the more harmful and dangerous its eating habits become. Once poorer regions, Crete included, taste what amounts to a wealthier region's diet—high in animal products and saturated fat—they seldom look back. The rates of heart and other diseases rise accordingly.

MEDITERRANEAN FOOD PYRAMID VS. UNITED STATES DEPARTMENT OF AGRICULTURE'S FOOD GUIDE PYRAMID

At first glance, the Mediterranean food pyramid, which was jointly created by Oldways Preservation and Exchange Trust, the Harvard University School of Public Health and the World Health Organization, seems to echo the recommendations made by the U.S. government in the *USDA Food Guide*.

Both pyramids are built on a foundation of plants, such as grains, fruits, and vegetables. Both promote a moderate amount of dairy intake. However, the Mediterranean food pyramid encourages legumes over animal proteins, severely limits meat, and advocates greater olive and olive oil consumption, regular exercise, and a daily glass of wine with a meal. The USDA pyramid makes no distinction between types of fats, whereas the Mediterranean pyramid specifies olive oil. Also, the U.S. guideline places meat in the same category as fish, beans, nuts, and eggs, thereby permitting up to 9 ounces of meat per day!

Obviously, for vegetarians, the Mediterranean diet pyramid comes much closer to the way we already eat (if you just knock that meat-filled peak right off the top). But it also gives a clear blueprint to help us choose the right quantities of the foods we already eat. Basing a diet on grains and legumes, fresh fruits, and vegetables is the way many of us want to eat, but may not be the actuality. The pyramid is a clearly organized reminder that cheeses, dairy products, and sweets should be only the tip of our diet iceberg, and that exercise is as important as eating well.

A CLOSER LOOK AT THE MEDITERRANEAN PYRAMID

The Mediterranean diet pyramid gives us a guide for good eating, but it does not explain the logic behind its recommendations. Here's a more searching look at some of the theories behind it.

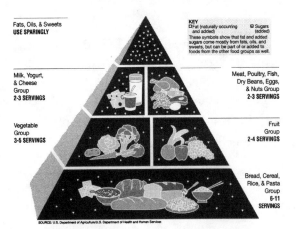

Grains: Good Sources of Protein and More

Grains, which make up the foundation of the Mediterranean diet pyramid, appear at most every Mediterranean meal, in some form or another. Whether it's flat bread or risen loaves, oven-baked or skillet-fried bread, it is usually at least part whole wheat and is eaten most every day, sometimes alongside rice, couscous, bulgur, polenta, or pasta. Grains provide the bulk of protein and many of the calories of a Mediterranean diet; they also break down into complex carbohydrates, which are the body's preferred energy source.

While not all of the grains consumed in the Mediterranean are whole, whole wheat is often made into breads, couscous, and bulgur. These foods are excellent sources of insoluble fiber, which helps keep digestive tracts clear. Studies show that insoluble fiber may also protect against rectal and colon cancer by carrying out carcinogens quickly through the large intestine.

Fruits and Vegetables

The Mediterranean region has been blessed with a particularly long growing season, thanks to the warm sun that shines brilliantly over the landscape. Fresh fruits and vegetables are diverse, abundant, and available all year long. Such bounty has left its mark on the diet of its inhabitants, who often find it more convenient to pick a ripe fig or orange off a tree near their homes than to go to a supermarket to buy a packaged, processed product. Greeks average nine servings of fruit and vegetables per day compared to the USDA food pyramid's minimum recommendation of five servings and the average American's actual intake of about two to three. And Mediterranean peoples don't necessarily eat that many servings of fruits and vegetables just because they are practically fat-free, nutrient-rich, and contain no additives or preservatives. They eat fruits and vegetables because they taste ripe and delicious, and because it is part of their culture. No matter where you travel around the Mediterranean, you'll see that people eat fruit every single day, often as snacks and desserts, and serve fresh vegetables and salads with almost every meal, sometimes even with breakfast, as in Israel.

Among the health benefits of fruits and vegetables are these: they provide plenty of fiber, vitamins, and minerals, as well as antioxidants, including beta-carotene and vitamin C. Antioxidants are important for guarding the body against many kinds of cancer and heart disease. They do so by keeping unstable molecules known as free radicals from wreaking havoc in the bloodstream. Free radicals can damage blood cells and encourage the growth of cancerous tumors. These free radicals can also oxidize "bad" LDL (low-density lipoprotein) cholesterol, which causes the cholesterol to clog arteries, leading to heart disease. Furthermore, studies have shown that a plant-rich diet may reduce the risk of developing hypertension, which in turn is a major risk for heart disease.

Olive Oil

Fruity, golden-green olive oil is ubiquitous in every Mediterranean country. It is used as the primary cooking medium, drizzled on salads and breads, and even used in baking both sweet and savory dishes. Olive oil is extremely rich in monounsaturated fat and low in saturated fat. It lowers levels of potentially harmful LDL cholesterol while raising beneficial HDL (high-density lipoprotein) cholesterol. While every country in the Mediterranean produces olive oil, Spain, Greece, and Italy are the region's largest producers and exporters.

The question that often comes up concerning olive oil is: How much is too much? According to Dr. Walter Willet, one of the creators of the Mediterranean pyramid, olive oil is a nutritionally desirable food and there is no scientific reason to restrict its use (other than in cases of obesity, in which instance all fats should be limited). Research done in 1960 on the Greek island of Crete found that in the traditional Mediterranean diet, 35 to 40 percent of calories come from fat from olive oil. The U.S. public health agencies currently recommend 30 percent or less, and some people even advocate a 20 to 25 percent limit. But the study showed that the Cretans were much less likely to die of coronary heart disease or cancer than Americans. This finding is what led the European office of the World Health Organization and the Harvard School of Public Health to endorse the Mediterranean diet as nutritionally superior to the American diet and challenge the notion that the restriction of all fats is necessary to a healthy diet.

This theory was endorsed by researchers who had begun looking at how the different kinds of fats influence the risk of disease. The American diet is typically rich in polyunsaturated fats from vegetable oils that are high in omega-6 fatty acids and low in omega-3 fatty acids. Omega-6 fatty acid has been found to cause tumors in animals and blood clotting in humans. Monounsaturated oils such as olive oil are high in omega-3 and low in omega-6. So the fat from olive oil was found to be superior not just to saturated fat, but to the fat from other, polyunsaturated vegetable oils as well.

Olive oil helps reduce the risk of heart disease by lowering "bad" cholesterol without lowering "good cholesterol." Harmful cholesterol, called LDL, is the kind that clogs arteries; HDL is the good cholesterol. LDL gets stuck in artery walls only when it has been oxidized, or chemically damaged by unstable molecules called free radicals. Eating monounsaturated fats like those in olive oil may reduce LDL's susceptibility to oxidation. Antioxidants, which help neutralize harmful free radicals, are found in many Mediterranean foods; these antioxidants include vitamin E, found in olive oil, and beta-carotene and vitamin C, which are present in many vegetables. They have also been tied to reduced rates of certain cancers, including breast and colon cancer.

Still, when cooking, keep in mind that merely substituting a monounsaturated fat such as olive oil (or canola or certain nut oils) for saturated fat such as butter or margarine does not necessarily transform the recipe into a healthful one. If a recipe is chockfull of cream and cheese or sugar, nothing short of a complete makeover will render it good for you.

Legumes

Since the Mediterranean diet does not rely on animal products as a source of protein, it is not surprising to find that legumes are consumed in great quantity. Legumes such as beans, peas, and lentils are eaten as part of a main meal almost every day. They may be stewed with other vegetables or by themselves, served as a cold salad dressed in olive oil and lemon, made into hearty and satisfying soups, or mashed into a soft dip to be scooped up with bread or vegetables.

Legumes are an excellent low-fat source of protein (about 14 grams per cooked cup). They contain an abundance of soluble fiber, which helps the heart by lowering elevated cholesterol levels. They are also a source of complex carbohydrates. In the late 1950s and early 1960s, the average Greek ate three times the amount of legumes we Americans eat today, and the Italians and Spaniards ate twice as much. The Mediterranean diet advocates eating some kind of legume preparation every day, which is not a hard task given the number of delicious ways in which legumes may be used.

Nuts are placed in the same category as legumes in the Mediterranean diet because of their high protein count. They are also high in fat, but it's good, monounsaturated fat. Nuts are traditionally included in many kinds of dishes; they can be pounded into sauces such as in Italian pesto, folded into breads and pastries, added to stews and salads, or eaten with fruit for dessert. One thing to note: nuts are seldom eaten by the bowlful with cocktails or in front of the television set as they are in the United States. So, if you are trying to follow the Mediterranean diet, eat nuts as they do in the Mediterranean—in small quantities to add flavor and texture to dishes.

Dairy Products

Some sort of dairy product—be it cheese, milk, or yogurt—is eaten on a daily basis throughout the Mediterranean. Out of all the dairy products, cheese is probably the most prevalent in Europe, while yogurt dominates in the Levant and the Maghreb regions.

When cheese is eaten, it isn't consumed in large quantities; cheese is generally used as a condiment to enhance the flavor of vegetable or grain dishes, rather than as the main ingredient. Tangy feta is crumbled on Greek salads; soft, fresh goat cheese is eaten with bread and fruit in France; and the Italians grate Parmesan on pasta. It is rare to see a cheese sandwich or an extra-cheese pizza as you do in the United States. Although cheese is high in saturated fat, it also provides protein and plenty of calcium. So, even though experts say that cheese and other saturated fats should be limited, a little bit eaten every day can be made part of any lacto-ovo vegetarian's diet.

Yogurt plays an important role in northern Africa, in the Middle East, and in Greece. It is mixed into salads with garlic and olive oil; made into a thin, cold soup; spooned onto vegetable dishes; or eaten with honey and fruit. Most of the yogurt eaten is whole milk yogurt, but there is no reason not to substitute low-fat or nonfat yogurt to cut down on unnecessary, non-olive oil–based fat.

Fish

For thousands of years, people of the countries that border the Mediterranean have depended on the fruits of the sea to supplement their plant-based diet. Although fish is not at the base of the Mediterranean food pyramid, it is certainly a part of the diet that deserves mentioning, and is placed in between cheese and eggs in the hierarchy (one should eat it less often than cheese and more often than eggs). Fish was generally considered peasant fare since it was much cheaper than red meat or poultry (which were reserved for special occasions). In fact, many coastal inhabitants made their livings as fishermen. Even the poorest family could sustain itself on homegrown fruits and vegetables, grains, and freshly caught fish. Fish are still abundant in the aqua waters of the Mediterranean, though less so than in the past. Owing to ecological abuse and neglect, the fish populations have suffered, and fish farms have increased in number and popularity. However, fresh fish and other seafood can still be found in fishermen's stalls at every city marketplace.

While fish is generally not served more than a few times a week, it is appreciated as a valuable alternative source of protein. Fish is low in cholesterol and saturated fat and supplies omega-3 polyunsaturated fatty acids, which have been shown to help prevent the type of blood clotting in arteries and plaque buildup in blood vessels that can eventually lead to heart disease and heart attacks. Other oils present in fish are thought to act against inflammatory and immune system reactions, which are symptoms of diseases such as arthritis and psoriasis. Fish also provide trace minerals such as copper, zinc, and selenium, which are hard to get from other foods. Sardines, in particular, provide calcium, which is important in developing bone mass, controlling blood pressure, and lowering the risk of colon cancer.

Eggs

The Mediterranean diet suggests that eggs be eaten only a few times per week. Indeed, this is the custom in the Mediterranean, where eggs only occasionally serve as a main course. It is far more common to find them acting as a binder for sauces or fillings; a garnish in salads, soups, and stews; or as part of a pudding or other sweet, rather than as the star of a meal. And even when eggs are the main dish, they are usually combined with plenty of fresh vegetables, as in an omelet or *frittata*, or in a casserole such as a Moroccan *tagine*.

The current wisdom espouses that people at risk of heart disease eat no more than one or two eggs a week. However, as the concern with overall cholesterol levels is refined to reflect new information about the ratio of "good" HDL cholesterol to "bad" LDL cholesterol, healthy people have been given the green light to make eggs a moderate part of their diets, especially if they don't eat much other saturated fat. Nutritionally in their favor, eggs are an excellent source of protein and are low in calories.

Sweets

Although sweets are not exactly encouraged in either the Mediterranean or U.S. pyramid, they are allowed more space in the Mediterranean diet. This is because sweets, though not eaten every day, are an integral part of Mediterranean cuisine. Fruit jellies, pastries, tarts, tortes, cakes, sweetened grains, creamy puddings, and candies are all treats that are eaten several times a week. Unlike in the United States, sweets are not usually served to cap off a meal. Instead, they are enjoyed as an afternoon snack with coffee or tea. It is a custom that results in a moderate, if consistent, consumption of sweets.

Wine

While wine does not appear in the actual pyramid graphic, it is nonetheless an essential part of Mediterranean cuisine, as indicated by the little wineglass set next to the pyramid. Wine is customarily sipped with meals, and drinking one or two glasses with lunch or dinner is a usual part of the culture (except with Muslims, who don't drink any alcohol, as it is forbidden by the Koran). This type of moderate wine consumption has been linked to lower rates of heart disease, according to researchers, probably by inhibiting blood clots (alcohol thins the blood) and by boosting levels of protective HDL cholesterol.

Although the research into why wine is associated with lower early death rates in general is still being probed, there are some known facts. So far, the majority of research has shown that both red and white wine have the same positive effects on reducing heart disease (although there is one small study that espouses red wine over white). Also, it is not the alcohol in wine that is the cause of its benefits. There are other chemicals that may prove to be antioxidants, which could explain the lower heart rates.

Another way in which wine contributes to overall health is that it helps people relax and enjoy their meals. Studies have shown that relaxation is as important to good health as exercise, although it seldom gets the same attention.

One downside to wine is that it is high in calories. A small glass of wine has 120 calories, which is more than even the most sugary soda. Another problem is that some people are not inclined to drink alcohol because of a history of alcoholism or a general dislike. So while experts are encouraging the consumption of a moderate amount of wine (some say women should be limited to one glass daily and men, two), it is not a recommendation made necessarily for everyone.

THE IMPORTANCE OF AN ACTIVE LIFESTYLE

Research has made it clear that exercise is key to a longer, healthier life. It has been linked to reductions in cancer rates, heart disease, diabetes, and stroke. Still, Americans are slow to find the time to make exercise a part of their daily routine.

Americans who view the Mediterranean diet alone, without exercise, as a miracle method of losing weight and becoming instantly healthy are misleading themselves. The 35 to 40 percent of calories from monounsaturated fat averaged by Cretan men following traditional Mediterranean diets and lifestyles would most likely lead to weight gain for the average American. It is our sedentary lifestyles that set us so far apart from those sheep-herding Cretans. Even if we exercised religiously every day for the requisite twenty to twenty-five minutes, we would still not come near to meeting the amount of physical activity expended by the Cretans. (What would be equivalent to six hours of ploughing?)

The compromise, according to some experts, is to exercise as much as we can every day and to make sure to include some weekly vigorous exercise (like running, stair climbing, speed walking, or bicycling), along with more moderate daily exercise (gardening, walking, yoga, stretching). If weight gain is still a problem when following an exercise regime, then reducing fat and calorie intake is essential for good health.

There is hardly anyone in America who does not know about the evils of obesity. Numerous studies have shown that excessive weight gain raises the risk of heart disease, cancer, diabetes, and hypertension. Many experts do believe that if a person is physically active and can maintain a normal body weight, consuming more than 30 percent of calories from fat should not be harmful if most of the fat is monounsaturated. But if weight gain is a concern, limiting overall fat intake to closer to 20 or 25 percent should help shed pounds.

TAKING TIME TO ENJOY

If there is one central, essential component missing from the American lifestyle as compared to the Mediterranean, it is taking the time to stop and enjoy life. Our hyper-paced lives leave little room for two-hour lunches and three-hour dinners. But it is precisely these long, relaxed meals, surrounded by friends and family, that can create an environment conducive to the very best health.

All too often, Americans who sit down to dinner, even if they do surround themselves with their families on a nightly basis, finish eating within thirty minutes and are off to watch television or to do even more work brought home from the office. Food is quickly swallowed, not slowly savored. The enjoyment of food and company, and in general a network of friends and family, can provide much-needed social support. Theories abound that people who have heart disease and are without adequate social support are three times more likely to die from their disease than those with high levels of social support. People in the southwest of France have a lower risk for heart disease than those living in more northern areas of the country, where social networks tend not to be as strong. Meals taken together provide a foundation for support. The dinner table can be a place where family members relate to one another and share and soothe the stresses of the day.

This kind of relaxation, and really any type, is more important to people's health than is usually given credit. It is as important for our physical health as it is for our mental health. When you are in a state of relaxation, your stress hormones (catecholamines) become regulated. If there are too many stress hormones in your system, extra fat will be released into the bloodstream and will end up in the liver, where it is converted into cholesterol and reenters the bloodstream. A lifetime of social support may buffer you against these harmful hormonal increases.

A daily siesta is also an integral part of the traditional Mediterranean lifestyle and provides health benefits by allowing the body and mind to rest and relax. Originally, the siesta was taken to avoid laboring in full sun at the hottest part of the day. Now, it is as ingrained in the culture as the sun itself. Even in our age of consumerism and fast-paced living, many Mediterranean-region stores close down every day for an hour or two at midday. Two separate studies of heart patients have shown that a daily thirty-minute nap may be related to a 20 to 30 percent decrease in coronary episodes. Although it is difficult, if not impossible, for most Americans to schedule a catnap into their day, as public awareness grows it just may get easier.

The Mediterranean

Today

■ While the picturesque images of the Greek shepherd tending his flocks on the craggy hillside or the Italian peasant wife spending her days in the kitchen turning out crusty loaves of bread and miles of homemade pasta might not be those you'll often stumble upon in today's Mediterranean countries, much of the vibrant, traditional lifestyle remains intact. But the fact is, there is no escaping technology and global modernization, and some of these advancements have taken their toll in terms of health. ■ According to Dr. Marion Nestle, head of nutrition and food studies at New York University, "the classic Mediterranean diet is becoming an endangered species." Among Cretan men—those bellwethers of Mediterranean health— caloric intake is down, but calories expended are down, too. Cholesterol levels, rates of heart disease, blood pressure, body weight, and abdominal obesity are all higher (though still lower compared to the United States). Cretans today eat less bread, potatoes, fruit, and olive oil and more meat, fish, and cheese. Fifty years ago, 61 percent of the Cretan diet came from plant foods and only 7 percent came from animals. Researchers thought this was a wonderful and healthful diet, but the Cretans wanted more meat. A study done in 1989 observed an increase in meat consumption and a decrease in legume intake. Since the 1940s, scientists have proved that whenever more meat is introduced into a plant-based diet such as that of the traditional

39

Mediterranean, the incidence of coronary heart disease and certain cancers rises, often dramatically. Since the 1950s, Greece and many other Mediterranean countries have moved from agrarian to urbanized societies. This has often been coupled with the increased availability of processed foods and a more sedentary lifestyle. Affluence has been a mixed blessing in terms of health. ■ But even in the most developed and urban Mediterranean areas, fundamental parts of the traditional lifestyle remain. Strong family and community ties are still extremely important to the diverse people of this region, who are also endowed with the precious gift of overwhelmingly warm hospitality. While the working Provençal might have to commute in a car, relaxed lunch breaks and long family dinners persist. Fast-food chains and prepackaged foods may be finding their ways into even the most remote Turkish towns, and eating habits may be tending toward diets that are higher in refined sugar and saturated fats, but the traditional Mediterranean diet has deep roots. Peoples of the Mediterranean still depend greatly on seasonal local produce, homemade meals, and healthful olive oil. It is doubtful that these eating habits will ever fully disappear.

Appetizers and Hors d'Oeuvres

The Mediterranean tradition of what we would call appetizers and hors d'oeuvres is as vast and colorful as the region itself. In every Mediterranean country, when meals commence, a striking array of small dishes appears at the table, both to stimulate the appetite and to begin to satisfy it in as varied a way as possible. ■ Sometimes these starters are so elaborate and filling that they can serve as a meal. In fact, in northern Africa and parts of Greece, the plates of savory morsels served before dinner are left out for the whole meal, allowing the diners to help themselves to whatever their appetites call for. Hot and cold appetizer salads, made with artichoke hearts, eggplant, zucchini, cooked or raw carrots, grains, and legumes; flaky pastries filled with vegetables and cheese; and stuffed vegetables and grape leaves are served first but continue to be nibbled throughout the meal. For light eaters, these mouthfuls need no follow-up. ■ In Turkey, lavish dinners usually start with cold *mezze,* which may consist of *dolmas* (stuffed grape leaves) and stuffed eggplant, followed by hot *mezze* like *borek* (phyllo pastries). *Mezze* is presented on a communal platter for everyone to help themselves to whatever they like. Lebanese *mezze* commonly includes hummus and a variety of lentil or bean dishes with vegetables. Greek *mezze* might offer *skordalia* (potato and garlic dip), olives, *dolmas,* pickled vegetables, *spanakopita* (spinach and cheese phyllo pastries), and leafy green salads. ▪ In Italy, appetizers are called antipasti and consist of myriad multihued dishes such as sautéed or cured olives, stuffed mushrooms or fried zucchini, sliced fresh cheeses, and *bruschetta* (toasted bread with garlic and olive oil, usually topped with tomato). The Spanish variant of *mezze* is tapas, which are served only at bars and restaurants (never at home) to satisfy hunger pangs during the long stretch of time between lunch and a characteristically late-night dinner. Simple tapas may include just a few dishes of olives; roasted, salted almonds; and chunks of *manchego* cheese. More hearty tapas may consist of stuffed vegetables, potato tortillas, stuffed eggs, and *pa amb tomàquet,* the Spanish version of Italian *bruschetta*. In Mediterranean France, hors d'oeuvres are usually fairly simple, such as platters of fresh fruits (melon and figs) and vegetables, served with olive oil and *tapenade* (olive paste), or cheeses. ▪ In this chapter, we have gathered a feast of tempting small dishes. Don't limit them just to supper's prelude; serve several of them together to make an unforgettable meal.

herbed white bean pâté

This herb-imbued, smooth pâté gets even better if you let it sit in the refrigerator for an hour or more before serving. Serve it as a dip with whole-grain crackers and sliced radishes or carrots, or spread it on a thick piece of crusty bread and garnish with watercress and cucumber slices.

You can make the pâté up to one day in advance and store it, well covered, in the refrigerator.

makes 3 cups

½ cup diced shallots or scallions (white part only)
2 garlic cloves, minced
2 cups cooked white beans (rinsed if canned)
3 tablespoons minced fresh parsley or chives
1 tablespoon capers, drained
1 tablespoon fresh lemon juice
1 tablespoon extra-virgin olive oil
½ teaspoon dried thyme
½ teaspoon dried dill
½ teaspoon dried tarragon
½ teaspoon ground white pepper
½ teaspoon salt, or more to taste
¼ teaspoon ground nutmeg
Dash of hot pepper sauce (optional)

Per 2 tablespoons: 28 calories • 1g protein • 1g fat • 4g carbohdrates • 0 cholesterol • 19mg sodium • 1g fiber

1. Place the shallots or scallions and garlic in a food processor or blender. Process or blend for a few seconds, until finely chopped.
2. Add the beans and remaining ingredients, except for the hot pepper sauce. Puree the mixture until very smooth. Adjust seasoning for taste—if pâté needs more zip, add a little hot sauce or more lemon juice.

bruschetta with salsa cruda

Bruschetta is the original garlic bread—thick slices of Italian bread are speared on a giant fork and grilled over an open flame, then rubbed with the cut side of a garlic clove and brushed with an intensely flavored olive oil. In this recipe, the *bruschetta* are topped with *salsa cruda,* which literally means "raw sauce" in Italian. No topping could be simpler or more robust.

You can make the *salsa cruda* mixture up to 4 hours in advance.

makes 6 servings

6 thick slices Italian bread
1 large garlic clove, cut in half
1 to 2 tablespoons extra-virgin olive oil
4 plum tomatoes, diced
½ teaspoon salt
¼ teaspoon freshly ground black pepper
¼ teaspoon dried oregano
12 fresh basil leaves, shredded

Per serving: 128 calories • 4g protein • 3g fat • 22g carbohydrates • 0 cholesterol • 360mg sodium • 2g fiber

1. Preheat the broiler or grill. Lightly toast the bread slices until they are golden brown on both sides. Rub one side of each of the slices with the cut side of the garlic. Brush the slices with olive oil and set aside.
2. In a bowl, combine the tomatoes, salt, pepper, and oregano. Mound the mixture onto the bread and top with fresh basil. Let sit for 10 minutes before serving so that the juices can partially soak into the bread.

crostini with porcini mushroom topping

Crostini are thin, delicate slices of Italian bread that are toasted and brushed with either olive oil or melted butter. Here, they are scented with garlic, brushed with fruity olive oil, then topped with flavorful wild porcini mushrooms, which are sold fresh in open air markets throughout Italy. Porcini are the most popular wild mushrooms in Italian cuisine. They are almost always used dried, which allows their unique flavor to deepen and intensify.

For an equally delicious topping, you may substitute dried shiitake mushrooms for the porcini.

makes 6 servings

For the *crostini*

6 thin slices Italian bread

1 large garlic clove, cut in half

1 to 2 tablespoons extra-virgin olive oil

For the topping

2 ounces dried porcini mushrooms, snipped into small pieces

1 cup water

1 tablespoon olive oil

3 garlic cloves, minced

¼ cup red wine (optional)

½ teaspoon dried rosemary

¼ teaspoon dried oregano

¼ teaspoon salt

¼ teaspoon freshly ground black pepper

⅓ cup chopped fresh parsley

3 tablespoons fresh lemon juice

Per serving: 98 calories • 2g protein • 5g fat • 11g carbohydrates • 0 cholesterol • 180mg sodium • 1g fiber

1. Preheat the broiler or grill. Lightly toast the bread slices until they are golden brown on both sides. Rub one side of each of the slices with the cut side of the garlic. Brush the slices with oil and set aside.

2. To prepare the topping, in a heavy skillet over medium heat, combine the dried mushrooms and water and simmer for 10 minutes. When the water is reduced in volume by half, add the olive oil, garlic, wine if desired, dried herbs, salt, and pepper. Continue simmering until most of the liquid has evaporated, about another 8 minutes.

3. Add the parsley and lemon juice, stirring to combine. Spoon the topping onto the bread and serve immediately.

skewered cheese tortellini with garlic-parmesan sauce

This recipe is fail-safe and takes a minimal amount of effort. Just purchase ready-made tortellini, cook, and thread them onto skewers. For a delicious variation, substitute fresh spinach, porcini, or pumpkin tortellini for the cheese tortellini. If you don't have skewers, spread the tortellini out on a large serving platter and spear them with toothpicks. Serve the sauce in a large bowl on the side.

A time-saver when preparing for a big party, the sauce can be made up to a week in advance. The skewers can be prepared several hours in advance.

makes 24 skewers

72 cheese tortellini, preferably fresh (about 25 ounces)
6 tablespoons minced fresh parsley
½ cup olive oil
½ cup freshly grated Parmesan cheese
⅓ cup fresh lemon juice
3 garlic cloves, minced
Salt and freshly ground black pepper to taste

Per skewer: 93 calories • 4g protein • 3g fat • 12g carbohydrates • 1mg cholesterol • 44mg sodium • 0 fiber

1. In a pot, cook the tortellini according to package directions. Drain well. Thread twenty-four 4-inch skewers with 3 tortellini each. Arrange the skewers on a platter and sprinkle with 2 tablespoons of parsley.
2. In a small mixing bowl, make the sauce by mixing the remaining 4 tablespoons parsley, the olive oil, Parmesan cheese, lemon juice, garlic, and salt and pepper. If desired, puree the sauce in a blender for 1 minute (it gives the sauce a smoother consistency).
3. With a pastry brush, dab sauce on the skewered tortellini. Reserve the remaining sauce to serve as a dip alongside the skewers.

stuffed garlicky mushroom caps

Wild mushrooms grow in abundance in the woods and fields of the European Mediterranean countries. Italians make wild mushroom tarts and beautifully molded mushroom *sformatini,* while the French stuff, marinate, and sauté the mushrooms with fragrant fresh herbs and garlic. In this recipe, mushrooms are stuffed with a heady garlic, cheese, and herb mixture. Serve them, hot, straight from the oven.

makes 24 stuffed mushrooms

24 large white mushrooms, cleaned and trimmed
2 cups loosely packed fresh basil
¼ to ⅓ cup olive oil
1 to 2 tablespoons water
⅓ to ½ cup freshly grated Parmesan cheese
½ cup dry bread crumbs
4 garlic cloves, minced
Salt and freshly ground black pepper to taste

Per mushroom: 38 calories • 1g protein • 3g fat • 2g carbohydrates • 1mg cholesterol • 28mg sodium • 1g fiber

1. Preheat the oven to 325°F. Remove all of the mushroom stems and set aside. Reserve the caps.
2. In a food processor or blender, puree together the mushroom stems, basil, olive oil, water, Parmesan, bread crumbs, garlic, and salt and pepper. Fill the mushroom caps with the mixture and place on an ungreased baking sheet. Bake for 12 to 14 minutes, until the mushrooms are tender. Serve immediately.

spinach phyllo kisses

These flaky little pastries make perfect party hors d'oeuvres—you can pop them into your mouth in one clean bite. Although they are at their best when served while still warm from the oven, they can also be served at room temperature. Or, prepare the kisses ahead, freeze them, unbaked, then bake them while still frozen, allowing about 15 minutes more baking time.

makes about 50 kisses

1 package (10 ounces) frozen spinach, thawed and squeezed dry

2 cups low-fat ricotta cheese

8 ounces feta cheese (about 1 cup)

1 small onion, minced

3 garlic cloves, minced

2 tablespoons packed fresh dill (or 2 teaspoons dried)

½ teaspoon freshly ground black pepper

¼ teaspoon ground nutmeg

Salt to taste

1 pound phyllo dough, thawed

½ cup melted butter, plus more as needed

Per kiss: 70 calories • 3g protein • 4g fat • 7g carbohydrates • 12mg cholesterol • 139mg sodium • 0 fiber

1. Preheat the oven to 325°F. In a food processor, puree the spinach, ricotta, feta, onion, garlic, dill, pepper, nutmeg, and salt. Set aside.

2. To make the kisses, unfold one sheet of phyllo onto a dry surface, keeping the rest of the phyllo under a slightly damp towel (it dries out very quickly). Using a pastry brush, brush the phyllo lightly with melted butter. Top with another sheet of phyllo and repeat until there are 4 sheets layered. With kitchen scissors, cut layers into 9 equal squares. On each square, put a dollop of the spinach-cheese filling (about 2 tablespoons). Bring up the corners of the phyllo and twist them together to form a kiss. Lightly brush the outside with melted butter. Repeat until the phyllo and filling are used up.

3. Bake the kisses on greased baking sheets for 12 to 15 minutes, or until golden brown. Serve warm or at room temperature.

herb and walnut-stuffed new potatoes

These little red potatoes topped with yogurt, walnuts, and a festive sprig of dill look perfect for the holidays. They are a welcome time-saver if you are preparing for a party, since the potatoes can be boiled and scooped out up to two days in advance. Filled potatoes can be prepared up to several hours in advance, but they are best served when freshly assembled.

makes 24 potatoes

24 baby red potatoes
¾ cup plain whole-milk yogurt
24 walnut halves, toasted (see Note, page 153)
24 sprigs fresh dill

Per potato: 51 calories • 3g protein • 3g fat • 718g carbohydrates • 1mg cholesterol • 9mg sodium • 1g fiber

1. Cook the potatoes in boiling water for 8 to 12 minutes, until just tender. Drain and cool.
2. Slice off the bottom end of each potato so it sits upright, and slice off one-third of the top. (If the potatoes are medium-small, cut them in half and use both halves.) With a melon baller, scoop out some of the potato and fill the cavity with a dollop of yogurt. Top each with a walnut half and tuck in a sprig of dill. Serve immediately.

greek garlic and potato dip

Like most of their Mediterranean neighbors, Greeks love garlic. This dip, thickened by the addition of potatoes, is called *skordalia*. It is traditionally smeared onto fresh crusty bread and eaten for lunch, or served with bean casseroles or boiled beets for supper. Using a mortar and pestle is important because it brings out the full flavor of the pureed garlic. Spread this dip on bread or crackers, or use it to accompany fresh vegetables.

makes 2 cups or 32 tablespoons

2 large potatoes
5 garlic cloves, coarsely chopped
1 cup parsley leaves
¼ cup extra-virgin olive oil, or more to taste
1½ tablespoons white wine vinegar, or more to taste
Salt and freshly ground black pepper to taste

Per 2 tablespoons: 39 calories • 0 protein • 3g fat • 2g carbohydrates • 0 cholesterol • 20mg sodium • 0 fiber

1. In a large pot of boiling water, cook the potatoes with skins on until tender, about 20 minutes.
2. Meanwhile, crush the garlic with a mortar and pestle.
3. When the potatoes are tender, peel and cut them into small pieces. Place the potatoes, garlic, parsley, olive oil, and vinegar in a blender or food processor. Blend for 3 minutes, stop, and adjust the taste by adding more oil, salt and/or pepper. Blend until smooth.

marinated olives

It would be nearly impossible to travel in the Mediterranean region and not notice the countryside dotted with small family-run orchards full of silvery-leafed, gnarled olive trees. In addition to the oil derived from the fruit, the olive itself is a Mediterranean mainstay. Only perfectly formed, unblemished olives are fit for the table; all others are pressed for their oil. There are dozens of different olive varieties as each region grows its specialty. Cured olives can be broken into two broad categories: black and green (although they come in various shapes, sizes and shades, including brown and purple). This zesty marinade makes already tangy green olives even more flavorful.

The longer you leave them in the marinade, the more intense the olives become.

makes 1½ cups

8 ounces good-quality green olives
  (about 1½ cups)
3 tablespoons fresh mixed herbs, such as thyme,
  oregano, basil, marjoram, chives, and sage
1 tablespoon coarsely chopped garlic
1 teaspoon finely chopped fresh rosemary
  (or ½ teaspoon dried)
1 teaspoon fennel seeds, crushed
½ teaspoon paprika (hot or sweet, to taste)
¼ teaspoon whole black peppercorns
¼ teaspoon salt
⅛ teaspoon crushed red pepper flakes
3 bay leaves
1-by-3-inch piece of lemon peel
Extra-virgin olive oil

Per ¼-cup serving: 98 calories • 0 protein • 10g fat • 3g carbohydrates • 0 cholesterol • 736mg sodium • 0 fiber

1. Put the olives into a medium bowl. Add the herbs, garlic, rosemary, fennel seeds, paprika, peppercorns, salt, and red pepper flakes and mix thoroughly.
2. Pack the seasoned olives into a jar, layering them with bay leaves; add the lemon peel. Pour the olive oil over the olives to cover, then tightly cover the jar. Refrigerate for at least 4 days, shaking occasionally.
3. To serve, drain the olives, remove and discard the peppercorns, bay leaves, and lemon peel. Serve at room temperature.

baked feta cheese with spicy tomato sauce

The salty white cheese known as feta (which literally translates as "slice" in Greek) appears daily on every Greek table. Traditionally made from sheep's milk, feta can also be made from goat's milk. Each region's feta varies in its pungency, saltiness, and firmness, depending on how long the cheese is left to age in barrels of brine. If the feta you buy seems too salty, you can soak it in water overnight in the refrigerator to de-salt it somewhat.

In this hearty recipe, slices of feta cheese are baked until soft and creamy inside, then topped with a lively tomato sauce. Make an extra batch or two of the tomato sauce for your vegan friends to spread on slices of oven-warmed or toasted baguette. The sauce freezes well and can be kept for up to three months.

makes 8 servings

½ tablespoon olive oil
1½ cups chopped onions
Pinch of sugar
3 garlic cloves, minced
1 small serrano chile pepper, seeded and minced
1 pound vine or plum tomatoes, peeled, seeded, and chopped (or one 15½-ounce can whole tomatoes)
½ cup fresh orange juice
2 tablespoons dry white wine (optional)
1 tablespoon minced fresh parsley
Salt and freshly ground black pepper to taste
8 ounces feta cheese

Per serving: 38 calories • 2g protein • 2g fat • 3g carbohydrates • 8mg cholesterol • 110mg sodium • 0 fiber

1. Preheat the oven to 350°F. In a large skillet, heat the olive oil over medium-high heat. Add the onions and sugar and cook, stirring often, until the onions begin to brown, about 5 minutes. Add the garlic and chile and cook, stirring often, until the vegetables are tender, 3 to 4 minutes.
2. Stir in the tomatoes, orange juice, and wine if using. Reduce the heat to low and simmer, stirring occasionally, for about 30 minutes. Add small amounts of water if the mixture becomes too dry. Remove from the heat; stir in the parsley and season with salt and pepper.
3. Put the feta in a small, shallow baking dish and surround with the tomato sauce (do not cover the cheese with sauce).
4. Bake, uncovered, until the sauce begins to bubble at the edges and the cheese is hot, about 20 minutes. Serve warm with toasted baguette rounds.

marinated goat cheese

Goat's milk cheeses are generally more popular than cow's milk cheeses in the Mediterranean. This is probably because goats fare much better than cows on the region's rocky land and during the dry, hot summers. Mild fresh white goat cheese tastes wonderful when marinated in olive oil, garlic, herbs, and spices. You can then serve it spread on fresh or toasted bread or crumble it over freshly cooked pasta.

This cheese will keep in the refrigerator for up to a month as long as it is covered by a thin layer of olive oil.

makes 8 servings

One 11-ounce log mild goat cheese

2 tablespoons olive oil, plus more as needed

3 tablespoons shredded fresh basil (or 1 teaspoon dried)

4 sprigs rosemary (or 1 teaspoon dried)

2 garlic cloves, minced

½ teaspoon freshly ground black pepper

Pinch of salt (optional)

Per serving: 135 calories • 6g protein • 11g fat • 2g carbohydrates • 34mg cholesterol • 435mg sodium • 0 fiber

1. Cut the cheese log into 1-inch pieces; pack the pieces tightly into a jar.
2. In a small bowl, combine the remaining ingredients; stir.
3. Pour the seasoned oil over the cheese. (Add more oil if needed to cover the top of the cheese.) Cap the jar and shake to distribute the seasonings. Refrigerate for at least 2 hours before serving.

grape leaves stuffed with bulgur, apricots, and mint yalancie dolmas

The Turkish word *yalancie* describing these tasty bite-size parcels means "false" because they are not served hot and do not contain meat like traditional stuffed grape leaves. Grape leaves are available packed in jars (a 16-ounce jar contains about 50 leaves) and require rinsing to remove the excess brine that preserves them.

You can prepare these grape leaves up to a day in advance; store them in the refrigerator.

makes 14 dolmas

1 cup water
½ cup coarse bulgur, rinsed and drained
¼ cup red lentils, sorted, rinsed, and drained
3 tablespoons olive oil
1 cup finely chopped red onion
¼ cup raisins
¼ cup (packed) dried apricots, finely chopped
2 tablespoons chopped fresh mint leaves
¼ tablespoon ground cinnamon
¼ teaspoon ground allspice
Salt and freshly ground black pepper to taste
14 grape leaves, rinsed well and patted dry
¼ cup fresh lemon juice
Mint leaves and lemon slices, for garnish

Per *dolma*: 74 calories • 2g protein • 3g fat • 11g carbohydrates • 0 cholesterol • 6mg sodium • 2g fiber

1. In a heavy, medium saucepan, bring the water to a boil. Stir in the bulgur. Reduce the heat, cover, and simmer 15 minutes. Remove from the heat and set aside.
2. Meanwhile, in small saucepan, combine the lentils with enough water to cover by 1 inch. Bring to a gentle boil and cook, reducing the heat if necessary to prevent a full boil, uncovered, until the lentils are tender but still hold their shape, about 15 minutes. Drain well and set aside.
3. In a large skillet, heat 1 tablespoon olive oil over medium heat. Add the onion and cook, stirring often, until soft, about 5 minutes. Remove from the heat and add the raisins, apricots, mint, cinnamon, and allspice. Stir in the bulgur and lentils and season with salt and pepper.
4. To fill grape leaves, place one leaf flat on a work surface with veins facing upward. Place 2 teaspoons of filling in the middle of each leaf close to the stalk end. Fold over the bottom of the leaf and turn each side in to enclose the filling. Roll up firmly toward the tip of the leaf. Place the roll in the palm of your hand and give a slight squeeze to form a firm shape. Repeat the procedure with the remaining leaves and filling.
5. Arrange the stuffed leaves, seam sides down, in a medium skillet. Add the remaining 2 tablespoons oil, the lemon juice, and enough water to cover the leaves. Cover the pan and simmer over low heat for 1½ to 2 hours or until tender. Add extra water to the skillet as needed. Allow the stuffed grape leaves to cool, covered, in the skillet. Transfer to a serving dish and chill in the refrigerator until ready to serve. Serve garnished with lemon and mint if desired.

herb-stuffed grape leaves dolmathakia

A favorite component of Greek *mezze*, what could be more refreshing than grape leaves stuffed with rice, dill, mint, parsley, and sweet, tangy currants? They can also be used to decorate a Greek salad. You might want to try using fresh grape leaves if you grow grapes yourself or happen to be friends with a vintner. Use fresh leaves just as you would those that are jarred. Serve the *dolmathakia* with a dollop of Minty Yogurt Sauce (recipe below).

You can make the grape leaves up to three days ahead. Cover and store them in the refrigerator.

makes 20 servings

For the stuffed grape leaves *(dolmas)*

40 grape leaves (a 16-ounce jar contains about 50 leaves)

1 cup basmati rice

1 can (14½ ounces) vegetable broth, plus enough water to make 2 cups liquid

2 medium onions, chopped

4 garlic cloves, minced

½ cup dried currants, soaked in hot water until softened and drained

¼ cup chopped fresh dill (or 2 tablespoons dried)

¼ cup chopped fresh mint (or 2 tablespoons dried)

¼ cup chopped fresh Italian parsley

½ teaspoon freshly ground black pepper

Several lettuce leaves (optional)

2 cups water

For the minty yogurt sauce

2 cups plain nonfat yogurt

4 scallions, minced

¼ cup chopped fresh mint (or 2 tablespoons dried)

1 garlic clove, minced

1 teaspoon salt

Per serving: 80 calories • 3g protein • 0 fat
• 15g carbohydrates • 1mg cholesterol
• 164mg sodium • 2g fiber

1. In a mixing bowl, pour boiling water to cover the grape leaves and let soak for 1 hour to tenderize them.

2. Meanwhile, in a saucepan, combine the rice and broth/water mixture. Cover, bring to a boil, then reduce the heat to low and simmer for 10 minutes.

3. Stir in the onions and garlic; cover again and simmer 10 minutes more, until all the liquid has been absorbed. Remove the pan from the heat and stir in the currants, herbs, and pepper with a fork, fluffing the rice.

4. Drain the grape leaves and pat them dry with a paper towel; remove the stems. Lay a grape leaf, vein side up with the stem end toward you, on a flat surface. Place a heaping tablespoon of rice filling in the center. Fold over the sides of the leaf, then fold up the bottom and roll closed as tightly as possible. Repeat until you've used all the grape leaves and filling.

5. Line the bottom of a large, heavy saucepan or stockpot with extra grape leaves or lettuce to prevent the stuffed grape leaves from sticking to the pan. Place the filled grape leaves in the saucepan, seam side down, in layers. Pour the water over the leaves and cover them with a heatproof plate set directly on top. Simmer the leaves for 30 to 45 minutes, until tender. It may be necessary to add an additional ⅓ to ½ cup water during cooking to keep the leaves from sticking. Cool to warm or to room temperature, then chill for at least 1 hour before serving.

6. To prepare the sauce, combine all the ingredients in a bowl and stir well. Serve on the side with the grape leaves.

grilled summer vegetable platter

Grilled vegetables are enjoyed especially by Greeks and Italians and are one of the easiest dishes to prepare. Choose fresh seasonal vegetables, grill them, and arrange, spoke-fashion, on a round platter. If you like, garnish with sprigs of fresh rosemary or basil.

Firm vegetables will grill more evenly and quickly if you parboil them first. To do so, plunge the vegetable pieces into boiling water for 1 minute, then immediately drain and immerse in cold water. Pat dry and proceed with the recipe.

You can marinate the vegetables in the dressing up to two days in advance in the refrigerator.

makes 12 servings

3 pounds Japanese eggplants, cut lengthwise or diagonally into ¼-inch-thick strips

2 pounds carrots, cut diagonally into ¼-inch-thick slices, parboiled, and dried

3 pounds zucchini, cut diagonally into ¼-inch-thick slices

2 bunches scallions, trimmed

3 small heads radicchio, separated into leaves

12 jarred roasted red peppers, drained

2 jars (14¾ ounces) marinated artichoke hearts, drained

1½ cups Greek or Italian olives

¾ cup extra-virgin olive oil

Juice of 1 lemon

1 or 2 garlic cloves, minced or passed through a garlic press

Salt and freshly ground black pepper to taste

Sprigs of rosemary and basil for garnish (optional)

Per serving: 173 calories • 3g protein • 7g fat • 24g carbohydrates • 0 cholesterol • 89mg sodium • 8g fiber

1. Preheat the broiler or prepare a grill.
2. Place the eggplant directly on the grill or on a broiler pan in the broiler and cook until soft, about 4 minutes per side; set aside. Grill or broil carrots until tender, about 8 minutes per side; set aside. Grill or broil zucchini for about 5 minutes per side; set aside. Grill whole scallions for about 6 minutes per side, until greens are slightly wilted and whites are tender; set aside. Cook the radicchio for about 1 minute per side, until just wilted but not browned.
3. On serving platters, arrange the cooked vegetables, peppers, artichoke hearts, and olives.
4. In a jar, combine the olive oil, lemon juice, garlic, salt, and pepper. Shake to mix. Pour the dressing over the vegetables. Garnish with the rosemary and basil, if desired. Serve at room temperature.

layered italian torta

Torta, from the French *tarte*, technically means "cake," but that does not begin to describe the many types of dishes that take its name. While most *torti* are sweet confections, there are others that are savory combinations of vegetables and/or cheese. In this piquant version, smooth cream cheese is layered with sun-dried tomatoes and basil. It can be prepared in minutes, and makes enough for a party. Serve it with crackers or good toasted bread.

This *torta* can be refrigerated for up to five days if well wrapped, or frozen for up to three months.

makes 20 servings

½ cup sun-dried tomatoes (dry, not oil-packed)
3 packages (8 ounces each) cream cheese, softened
½ cup (1 stick) butter, cut into thirds and softened
1 container (8 ounces) prepared basil pesto sauce or 1 cup homemade pesto
Freshly ground black pepper, to taste
1 garlic clove
Fresh basil sprigs and toasted pine nuts (see Note, page 153), for garnish

Per serving: 170 calories • 3g protein • 17g fat • 2g carbohydrates • 41mg cholesterol • 126mg sodium • 0 fiber

1. Soak the tomatoes in hot water to cover for 10 minutes.
2. Meanwhile, line an 8-inch round pan with plastic wrap (it should hang over the outside edge of the pan). Set aside.
3. In a food processor, cream together 1 package cream cheese, ⅓ stick butter, the pesto, and pepper until smooth. Place dollops of the pesto mixture in the bottom of the pan; spread into a layer with a spatula. Place the pan in the freezer to firm while making the tomato layer.
4. Drain the tomatoes and puree them in the food processor. Add 1 package cream cheese, ⅓ stick butter, and pepper to taste. Process until smooth. Dollop the tomato mixture over the pesto layer and spread until smooth. Return the pan to the freezer while making the garlic layer.
5. Process the remaining package cream cheese, ⅓ stick butter, and garlic until smooth. Adjust seasonings. Dollop the garlic mixture over tomato layer and spread until smooth.
6. Refrigerate the *torta* until firm, about 6 hours. To serve, invert onto a serving platter and peel off the plastic wrap. Garnish with basil sprigs and pine nuts.

lentil crostini

Crostini roughly means "little crusts" in Italian, an inventive way to use yesterday's bread. This lentil spread looks like mousse and tastes peppery and earthy. Italians like to serve *crostini* with soup, particularly minestrone, and the combination makes for a hearty cool-weather supper.

Often, a variety of *crostini* are served together. If you have the time, try some other *crostini* spreads, too. (Recipes follow.)

You can make the lentil mixture up to two days in advance; store it, covered, in the refrigerator.

makes 8 appetizer servings,
4 main-course servings

1 cup lentils, rinsed, picked over, and stones removed
1 tablespoon balsamic vinegar
½ teaspoon dried thyme
¼ teaspoon freshly ground black pepper
1 small onion, minced
1 loaf Italian bread (or your own Bread for Crostini, page 259)

Per appetizer serving: 121 calories • 7g protein • 0 fat • 43g carbohydrates • 0 cholesterol • 75mg sodium • 3g fiber

1. Preheat the oven to 450°F. In a medium saucepan, simmer the lentils in water to cover until soft, about 20 minutes. Drain; reserve the cooking liquid. Immediately transfer the cooked lentils to a food processor or blender.
2. Add the vinegar, thyme, and pepper to the lentils. Process into a smooth paste, adding the reserved cooking liquid a little at a time, if necessary, to lighten the mixture. It should be somewhat fluffy, not compact.
3. Transfer the mixture to a mixing bowl. Stir in the onion.
4. Slice the bread into ½-inch-thick slices and arrange them on a baking sheet. Toast them lightly in the oven until golden, about 4 minutes, turning once. Spread the toasted bread slices with the lentil mixture.

olive crostini

These two pastes have an intense olive flavor, so a thin layer on each bread slice will suffice. Use the best quality, preferably oil-cured, olives you can find.

You can make the olive pastes up to one week in advance and store them in the refrigerator.

8 ounces green olives, pitted
2 garlic cloves
2 teaspoons dried rosemary
8 ounces black olives, pitted
1 loaf Italian bread (or your own Bread for Crostini, page 259)

Per appetizer serving: 124 calories • 2g protein • 9g fat • 13g carbohydrates • 0 cholesterol • 968mg sodium • 2g fiber

1. Preheat the oven to 450°F. In a blender or food processor, combine the green olives, 1 garlic clove, and 1 teaspoon rosemary; process into a paste. Set aside.
2. Repeat with the black olives and remaining garlic and rosemary.
3. Slice the bread into ½-inch-thick slices and arrange on a baking sheet. Toast lightly in the oven until golden, about 4 minutes, turning once. Spread the toasted bread slices with the different colored olive mixtures, and arrange them in an attractive pattern on a platter, showcasing the two colors.

crostini with pepper spread

The bold color of this spicy pepper spread, served in the center of a deep blue or green platter, makes this dish a vibrant centerpiece in itself.

makes 24 appetizer servings

For the pepper spread

1 tablespoon olive oil

1 small jalapeño pepper, minced

1 teaspoon yellow mustard seeds

12 sun-dried tomato halves (dry, not oil-packed)

½ cup water

2 roasted and peeled red bell peppers, coarsely chopped (see page 63)

3 tablespoons chopped fresh basil

2 tablespoons fresh parsley

Salt and freshly ground black pepper to taste

For the *crostini*

1 loaf Italian bread (or your own Bread for Crostini, page 259)

½ cup minced fresh parsley

⅓ cup extra-virgin olive oil

Coarse salt to taste

Per serving: 217 calories • 6g protein • 6g fat • 33g carbohydrates • 0 cholesterol • 288mg sodium • 4g fiber

1. Preheat the oven to 375°F. In a large skillet over medium heat, warm the olive oil. Add the jalapeño pepper and mustard seeds and sauté until the seeds pop. Add the dried tomatoes and water. Cover the pan and cook for 2 to 3 minutes, until the tomatoes are plump. Remove the pan from the heat.

2. In a food processor, blend the roasted peppers into a rough puree. Add the tomato mixture and process until smooth. Season with the basil, parsley, salt, and pepper. Set aside.

3. Slice the bread into ½-inch-thick slices and arrange them on a baking sheet. Toast them lightly in the oven until golden, about 4 minutes, turning once.

4. In a small bowl, combine the parsley, olive oil, and salt. Drizzle or brush the parsley oil over the toasts. Top with a dollop of pepper spread.

bruschetta with sun-dried tomatoes and rapini

A Tuscan specialty, there are many recipes for *bruschetta*. In this one, slightly bitter rapini (broccoli rabe) is paired with sweet, plump sun-dried tomatoes. It's a striking combination that looks perfect on a holiday buffet or a summer's eve party table.

makes 8 servings

½ cup sun-dried tomatoes (dry, not oil-packed)
2 tablespoons olive oil
2 garlic cloves, minced
4 cups coarsely chopped, packed rapini or spinach
¼ teaspoon crushed red pepper flakes
Salt to taste
1 small loaf crusty Italian country bread (or half of a large loaf)
2 tablespoons freshly grated Parmesan cheese (optional)

Per serving: 127 calories • 4g protein • 5g fat • 18g carbohydrates • 0 cholesterol • 268mg sodium • 2g fiber

1. Preheat the oven to 400°F. Cover the tomatoes with hot water and let soak for 30 minutes; drain and coarsely chop.
2. In a saucepan, heat the olive oil over medium heat; add the garlic and cook, stirring, until lightly golden, about 3 minutes. Stir in the tomatoes, rapini, pepper flakes, and salt and cook, stirring, until the rapini is tender, about 5 minutes more.
3. Slice the bread into 1-inch pieces, cutting large slices in half. Place the bread on a baking sheet and toast in the oven until golden, about 7 minutes, turning once. Top the toast with the rapini mixture. Sprinkle with Parmesan cheese, if desired.

roasted tomato bruschetta

For a taste of harvest time in Italy, this is the simplest of recipes—juicy tomatoes are tossed with fresh basil and a bit of olive oil, then mounded onto toasted bread. Roasting heightens the flavor of out-of-season tomatoes. If you have perfectly ripe ones, you can skip that step.

**makes 8 appetizer servings,
4 main-course servings**

4 pounds beefsteak tomatoes
1 tablespoon extra-virgin olive oil
1 loaf Italian bread
2 garlic cloves, halved

Per appetizer serving: 100 calories • 3g protein
• 2g fat • 18g carbohydrates • 0 cholesterol
• 19mg sodium • 4g fiber

1. Preheat the oven to 500°F. Oil several baking sheets. Cut the tomatoes into ½-inch-thick slices and spread them out in one layer on the baking sheets. Brush the tops with oil. Roast the tomatoes until very soft, about 25 minutes.

2. Meanwhile, cut the bread into 1-inch slices, arrange them on another baking sheet, and lightly toast in the oven until golden brown, about 4 minutes per side. Remove the toast from the oven and rub each slice with the cut side of the garlic cloves.

3. Remove the tomatoes from the pans with a slotted spoon or spatula; distribute them on top of the bread slices. Serve warm or at room temperature.

marinated roasted red peppers

You can buy decent jarred roasted red peppers, but nothing can beat the caramelized, smoky flavor of peppers you roast yourself. If you've got a charcoal grill, use it here; if not, the broiler in your oven will do just fine. You can use the roasted peppers as part of a recipe (and there are many in this book) or let them stand by their sweet selves as an appetizer, served with cheese and crackers or good bread.

You can make the peppers up to a week in advance and store them in the refrigerator.

makes 4 servings

4 to 6 sweet red or yellow bell peppers, or a
   combination of both
2 tablespoons olive oil
2 tablespoons balsamic or red wine vinegar
   (optional)
Salt and freshly ground black pepper to taste
2 garlic cloves, minced
3 tablespoons chopped fresh basil

Per serving: 80 calories • 1g protein • 7g fat
• 4g carbohydrates • 0 cholesterol • 137mg
sodium • 1g fiber

1. Preheat the broiler. Slice the peppers in half and remove the cores and seeds. Flatten the peppers and place onto a greased baking sheet, skin side up. Broil until the peppers are blackened and blistered all over, 5 to 7 minutes. Place the peppers in a large bowl and cover the top of the bowl with a plate or a piece of foil. Let the peppers steam until cool enough to handle, about 20 minutes.
2. To peel the peppers, slip off the charred skin with your fingers. Keep a bowl of warm water nearby to clean your fingers when needed.
3. Cut the peppers into strips and place them in a shallow dish. Add the remaining ingredients, and toss to blend. Serve immediately, or store in the refrigerator.

mouhammara

Originally from Syria, this fiery red dip is served throughout the Mediterranean countries of the Middle East and in Turkey. In it, a puree of succulent roasted peppers is inflamed by the heat of red pepper flakes, then tamed by syrupy sweet and sour pomegranate molasses.

For a variation on this dip or to make a creamy, spicy pasta sauce, mix the *mouhammara* with 8 ounces of softened cream cheese. *Mouhammara* can be made up to a week in advance and stored in the refrigerator.

makes about 2½ cups or
40 tablespoons

6 red bell peppers, roasted (see page 63)
3 tablespoons olive oil
3 tablespoons red wine vinegar
1½ tablespoons pomegranate molasses (available in Middle Eastern groceries or by mail order)
1 teaspoon ground cumin
Dash of crushed red pepper flakes

Per 2 tablespoons: 79 calories • 1g protein • 7g fat • 4g carbohydrates • 0 cholesterol • 3mg sodium • 1g fiber

1. In a food processor, puree the roasted peppers with the other ingredients until smooth.
2. Serve as a dip, pasta sauce, or as a condiment with steamed vegetables, pita bread, humus, or *baba ganoush*.

caponata

Caponata is a traditional thick and hearty Sicilian vegetable spread that almost always includes eggplant. The eggplant for *caponata* is traditionally fried, but grilling or broiling adds an interesting charred taste. *Caponata* can be served either warm or at room temperature, and since it actually tastes better when the flavors have been allowed some time to meld, it is a great make-ahead buffet dish. Serve with plenty of crusty bread.

makes 8 servings

2 medium eggplant, cut lengthwise into ½-inch
slices
Salt
3 tablespoons olive oil
1 small onion, minced
2 celery stalks, chopped
1½ cups Italian canned tomatoes, with juice
¼ cup pitted Italian-style oil-cured olives, chopped
1 tablespoon drained capers
½ cup red wine vinegar
2 teaspoons sugar
¼ cup chopped fresh basil leaves

Per serving: 90 calories • 2g protein • 6g fat
• 10g carbohydrates • 0 cholesterol • 106mg
sodium • 3g fiber

1. Arrange the eggplant slices in a single layer on tea towels or paper towels. Sprinkle both sides liberally with salt; let stand at least 1 hour to allow the bitter juices to drain.
2. Preheat the grill or broiler.
3. Rinse the eggplant slices and pat dry. Brush the slices lightly with 2 tablespoons of the olive oil. Grill or broil the eggplant until soft and slightly charred, about 3 minutes per side; set aside to cool.
4. Heat the remaining 1 tablespoon olive oil in a large skillet over low heat. Add the onion and cook, stirring, for 1 minute. Add the celery; cook, stirring, until soft, about 10 minutes. Add the tomatoes, olives, and capers; increase the heat to medium. Simmer, stirring occasionally, until the tomato liquid has been reduced somewhat and the ingredients are combined, about 7 minutes.
5. Meanwhile, roughly chop the cooked eggplant slices. Add the eggplant to the pan and cook for 1 minute. Add the vinegar and sugar; simmer, stirring occasionally, until most of the liquid has evaporated, about 10 minutes. Remove from the heat; stir in the basil and serve.

Salads

Crisp, cool salads are an integral part of the culinary culture all over the Mediterranean. Since vegetables and grains grow so profusely in the warm climate, the variety of salads offered, sometimes several in one meal, is astonishing. Hearty beans and legumes are boiled until tender and either mashed with garlic and oil or dressed with lemon. Juicy red peppers, fat purple eggplants, zucchini, carrots, mushrooms, onions and garlic, and bunches of verdant lettuces and greens are combined and enriched with olives, capers, cheeses, and fragrant herbs and spices. Different countries have different traditions when it comes to serving salads. In the Maghreb and Levant, salads are served first, with all of the other appetizers. However, they are also often left on the table to accompany the meal. In Europe, specifically France, Italy, and Spain, salads, which are usually made from vegetables and lettuces, are served after the main course, as a palate cleanser before a rich dessert or cheese course. Fresh salads are often made with dark leafy greens straight from the garden, such as watercress, dandelion leaves, arugula, and lettuces. To complement a simple salad of sharp or bitter greens, the cook might add a few slices of sweet juicy orange or some rich nuggets of creamy cheese.

Dressings, not surprisingly, are based on the region's fruity olive oil, and are usually seasoned with lemon or vinegar. ■ The national food of Morocco—couscous—takes center stage in some northern African salads, such as Couscous Salad with Dried Apricots (page 74). Salads made with grains are also popular in the Middle Eastern Mediterranean countries. Tabbouleh is a favorite, made with as much parsley as bulgur, and dressed with lemon and olive oil. Pasta, often left over, is used in some fortifying Italian salads, such as our Tortellini Antipasto Salad (page 96). Legume-based salads, from Italian cannellini beans to ubiquitous chickpeas and lentils, show up on kitchen tables across the Mediterranean, seasoned with the fresh herbs and dried spices favored by the cook. ■ Almost any of the salads in this chapter can be eaten as a meal. Match up several of them to serve together for a healthful, colorful repast.

colorful bulgur salad

When combined with vegetables, bulgur makes a vibrant, filling salad. Try serving any leftovers with Roasted Mediterranean Vegetables (page 231).

(page 231)

makes 6 servings

For the salad

1¼ cups water
1 cup bulgur
1 medium red bell pepper, diced
1 medium zucchini, diced
1 medium yellow squash, diced
½ medium red onion, diced

For the dressing

Juice of 1 lemon
2 tablespoons extra-virgin olive oil
¼ cup minced fresh parsley.
Salt and freshly ground black pepper to taste
¼ cup freshly grated Parmesan cheese (optional)

Per serving: 150 calories • 4g protein • 5g fat • 23g carbohydrates • 0 cholesterol • 6mg sodium • 4g fiber

1. In a small saucepan over high heat, bring the water to a boil. Add the bulgur and boil for 1 minute. Turn off the heat, cover the pan, and let the mixture sit for 15 minutes. Fluff with a fork.
2. In a large bowl, combine the bulgur and remaining salad ingredients, tossing well to mix.
3. In a small bowl, combine the lemon juice, oil, and parsley. Pour the dressing over the salad and toss well. Season with salt and pepper. Garnish with Parmesan cheese, if desired.

eggplant salad with mint and sage

The pine scent of fresh sage marries beautifully with the lively flavor of mint. Here, the two are paired in a vinaigrette that dresses a gorgeous medley of ripe summer vegetables and pasta. If you can get it, use baby eggplant for this recipe. It has a thinner skin and generally fewer seeds. You can prepare this salad up to two days in advance.

makes 6 servings

For the salad

3 tablespoons olive oil

¾ cup diced eggplant

Salt and freshly ground black pepper to taste

½ cup diced yellow squash

½ cup chopped scallions, cut in ½-inch pieces

¼ cup diced yellow bell pepper

¼ cup diced red bell pepper

1½ cups cooked small pasta shells or elbow macaroni

For the dressing

5 tablespoons extra-virgin olive oil

2 tablespoons fresh lemon juice

1 tablespoon white wine vinegar

¼ cup chopped fresh mint

2 tablespoons chopped fresh sage

Salt and freshly ground black pepper to taste

Per serving: 83 calories • 2g protein • 2g fat • 13g carbohydrates • 0 cholesterol • 4mg sodium • 2g fiber

1. In a large skillet, heat the oil over medium heat. Add the eggplant and cook, stirring, until it softens and browns slightly, about 4 minutes. Season with salt and pepper.
2. In a large bowl, combine the eggplant with the remaining salad ingredients. Gently mix.
3. Place all of the dressing ingredients in a blender or food processor and blend or pulse for about 20 seconds. Pour the dressing over the salad and refrigerate the mixture, covered, for at least 30 minutes before serving.

grated carrot-orange salad

There is nothing simpler than this bright, sunset-hued salad. Serve it by itself as a cool side dish or as part of a salad assortment. It can be made up to two days in advance.

makes 4 servings
1 pound carrots, coarsely shredded
Juice of 1 orange
Juice of ½ lemon
1 tablespoon olive oil
¼ cup chopped fresh cilantro
Salt and freshly ground black pepper to taste

Per serving: 83 calories • 1g protein • 3g fat • 12g carbohydrates • 0 cholesterol • 31mg sodium • 2g fiber

In a large bowl, combine all of the ingredients and toss well. Cover the salad and chill for at least 30 minutes before serving.

pasta and vegetable salad

A mélange of vegetables adds brilliant color to this flavorful salad. You can prepare it up to two days in advance, although it is at its best served within six hours of making.

makes 6 servings

½ pound pasta spirals, shells, or wheels
½ cup extra-virgin olive oil
3 tablespoons white wine vinegar
2 teaspoons Dijon-style mustard
2 garlic cloves, minced
Salt and freshly ground black pepper to taste
12 yellow or red cherry tomatoes, halved
1 cup good-quality black olives, pitted and halved
½ cup diced roasted red pepper (page 63)
½ cup mixture of chopped fresh herbs, such as
     parsley, basil, and mint
¼ pound feta cheese, crumbled (optional)
4 scallions, trimmed and sliced
Lettuce, for serving

Per 1-cup serving: 193 calories • 5g protein • 6g fat • 32g carbohydrates • 2mg cholesterol • 420mg sodium • 3g fiber

1. Cook the pasta according to package directions until al dente. Drain well.
2. In a large mixing bowl, whisk together the olive oil, vinegar, mustard, garlic, and salt and pepper. Add the pasta, tomatoes, olives, red pepper, herbs, cheese, if using, and scallions; toss well to mix. Cover the salad and chill for about 1 hour before serving. Serve the salad over a lettuce bed.

greek vegetable salad with curly endive and olives

This colorful cooked vegetable salad becomes a meal in itself when accompanied by crusty bread spread with a soft Greek cheese like *kasseri*. You can serve this salad either hot, warm, or chilled. It can be made up to one day in advance.

makes 6 servings
4 fresh medium beets, peeled and cut into ½-inch dice
2 medium white potatoes, cut into eighths
2 medium carrots, sliced
¼ pound curly endive
6 small zucchini, cut into 1-inch chunks
¾ cup Kalamata olives, pitted and chopped
½ cup capers, rinsed
2 tablespoons red wine vinegar
½ teaspoon salt, or to taste
6 tablespoons extra-virgin olive oil

Per 1-cup serving: 176 calories • 3g protein • 9g fat • 22g carbohydrates • 0 cholesterol • 506mg sodium • 5g fiber

1. Bring a large pot of water to a boil over high heat. Add the beets, potatoes, and carrots and boil for 10 minutes. Reduce the heat and add the endive and zucchini; simmer the vegetables until they are all tender, about 15 minutes longer.
2. Using a slotted spoon, transfer the endive to a large serving platter, then top with the remaining vegetables. Scatter the olives and capers over the vegetables.
3. In a small bowl, whisk together the vinegar and salt with about 1 tablespoon of warm water. While whisking, add the olive oil in a slow stream; mix until the oil is well incorporated. Pour the dressing over the salad.

couscous salad with dried apricots

Dried apricots are often added to savory dishes throughout Turkey, Egypt, and Morocco. They are used to stuff vegetables, added to thick and hearty stews, and included in salads such as this one, where they add a sweet tang and a glowing color.

makes 4 side-dish servings

1¼ cups water

⅔ cup whole wheat couscous

1 small zucchini, diced

½ teaspoon salt

2 tablespoons orange juice

1 tablespoon tahini (sesame paste)

1 cup plain yogurt or soft tofu

½ teaspoon ground cumin

Pinch of ground ginger

½ cup cooked chickpeas (thoroughly rinsed if canned)

½ cup diced apricots

¼ cup chopped fresh cilantro

¼ cup chopped fresh parsley

2 scallions, trimmed and sliced

Per serving: 276 calories • 11g protein • 3g fat • 53g carbohydrates • 1mg cholesterol • 444mg sodium • 7g fiber

1. In a medium saucepan, bring the water to a boil. Stir in the couscous, zucchini, and salt and let the water return to a boil. Cover the pot and turn off the heat. Let sit, covered, until the water has been absorbed, about 15 minutes.

2. Meanwhile, in a small bowl, stir together the orange juice and tahini to make a smooth paste. Place the yogurt or tofu in a large mixing bowl and whisk until light and smooth. Whisk in the tahini mixture, cumin, and ginger. Stir in the chickpeas, apricots, cilantro, parsley, and scallions.

3. Fluff the couscous with a fork to break up any lumps. Stir the couscous mixture into the apricot mixture, mixing well. Cover and refrigerate until chilled through, about 3 hours.

roasted asparagus salad with orange

Roasted vegetables are a Mediterranean favorite, and roasted asparagus makes this an especially tasty salad. When choosing asparagus, look for thin spears whose tips are still closed. Fresh orange and lime juices give this pale green salad a sparkling flavor.

makes 6 servings

1 pound asparagus, trimmed and cut diagonally into ½-inch pieces

3 tablespoons olive oil

Coarse salt to taste

½ cup fresh orange juice

1 tablespoon fresh lime juice

1 garlic clove, passed through a garlic press

Freshly ground black pepper to taste

7 cups chopped romaine lettuce

3 tablespoons pine nuts or slivered almonds, toasted (see Note, page 153)

1 tablespoon minced fresh basil

Per serving: 124 calories • 4g protein • 10g fat • 6g carbohydrates • 0 cholesterol • 16mg sodium • 3g fiber

1. Preheat the oven to 450°F. In a large bowl, toss the asparagus with 1 tablespoon of the olive oil and season with a pinch of salt. Spread the asparagus on a baking sheet in a single layer and roast until tender when pierced with a knife, 10 to 12 minutes. Set aside.

2. In a small bowl, whisk together the orange and lime juices, garlic, remaining 2 tablespoons olive oil, and salt and pepper.

3. Just before serving, arrange lettuce on individual plates or a platter and top with the asparagus. Whisk the dressing and pour it over the salad. Garnish with nuts and basil.

cannellini salad in butter lettuce cups

Cannellini are probably the most popular bean used in the cuisine of central Italy. The little white kidney-shaped beans make this a nutritious, protein-rich salad, which is elegantly served in individual lettuce leaf cups.

makes 6 servings

1 can (15 ounces) cannellini beans (or other white beans), drained and rinsed
Grated zest of 1 lemon
1 cup chopped fresh parsley
1 tablespoon extra-virgin olive oil
3 garlic cloves, minced
2 teaspoons minced fresh rosemary
2 or 3 fresh sage leaves, chopped (optional)
1 to 2 tablespoons Niçoise olives, pitted and chopped (optional)
Salt and freshly ground black pepper to taste
6 leaves butter lettuce

Per serving: 130 calories • 7g protein • 3g fat • 20g carbohydrates • 0 cholesterol • 11mg sodium • 5g fiber

1. In a large bowl, combine all of the ingredients except the lettuce. Toss well. Chill salad for at least 1 hour (or overnight).
2. To serve, place a scoop of bean salad in each lettuce leaf.

riviera salad

The ingredients in this salad have distinctly different flavors and colors that meld together beautifully, making it a vivid accompaniment to any main dish. It will surely transport you to the sandy beaches and turquoise waters of the famous French resort towns.

makes 6 servings

For the salad

1 bunch watercress
1 small head radicchio (or 1 cup finely sliced red cabbage)
1 bunch arugula
2 heads endive
½ head red leaf lettuce
Black olives, sliced radishes, or edible flowers for garnish

For the vinaigrette

3 scallions, sliced
2 to 3 shallots, chopped (or extra scallions)
1 tablespoon Dijon-style mustard
6 tablespoons olive oil
2 tablespoons fresh lemon juice
1 tablespoon red wine vinegar
Salt and freshly ground black pepper to taste
1 tablespoon capers, drained (optional)

Per serving: 132 calories • 1g protein • 14g fat • 2g carbohydrates • 0 cholesterol • 26mg sodium • 1g fiber

1. Carefully wash the salad greens. Dry them in a salad spinner or pat dry with a clean dish towel. Gently tear lettuce into bite-size pieces.
2. Combine the vinaigrette ingredients in a blender or food processor and blend until smooth. Adjust the seasonings to taste. Toss the salad dressing with greens and black olives, sliced radishes, or edible flowers, if desired, just before serving. Add the capers for additional garnish, if desired.

salade niçoise

Traditionally, this salad from southern France is made with anchovies and canned tuna. We've taken some liberties with our version, which is perfect for the vegetarian palate. With the additions of marinated red onion and new potatoes, this salad will satisfy the whole family. Adding slices of tempeh or hard-boiled egg gives the salad enough protein to stand on its own as the perfect light lunch for a hot summer day.

makes 6 servings

2 red onions, thinly sliced
2 celery stalks, sliced
5 tablespoons extra-virgin olive oil
¼ cup minced fresh parsley
3 garlic cloves, minced
2 tablespoons minced fresh basil
1 to 2 tablespoons red wine vinegar
1 teaspoon minced fresh oregano (or ¼ teaspoon dried)
¼ to ½ cup good-quality black olives, whole or pitted
5 small new potatoes, quartered
2 cups string beans, sliced into 1-inch pieces
2 cups wax beans, sliced into 1-inch pieces
Salt and freshly ground black pepper
Red leaf lettuce, radicchio, or Boston lettuce

Additional ingredients of choice

1 cup cooked white beans
½ pound fried tempeh
2 or 3 hard-boiled eggs, quartered
Cherry tomatoes
Sliced avocado

Per serving, without additional ingredients: 189 calories • 3g protein • 14g fat • 16g carbohydrates • 0 cholesterol • 272mg sodium • 4g fiber

1. Combine the onions, celery, olive oil, parsley, garlic, basil, vinegar, oregano, and olives in a dish. Allow the mixture to marinate while you prepare the rest of the salad.
2. Bring a large pot of water to a boil. Add the potatoes and simmer for 5 minutes. Add the beans and simmer until all the vegetables are tender, about 5 minutes longer. Drain well.
3. An hour or so before serving, combine the bean-potato mixture with the marinated vegetables. Season with salt and pepper to taste. Add more olive oil or vinegar if you like and toss well. Serve on a bed of lettuce and garnish with one or more of the additional ingredients.

raw artichoke salad with parmesan

Don't let the simplicity of this traditional recipe mislead you—the flavors are bright and sophisticated. If you aren't accustomed to eating raw artichokes, you're in for a special treat. Choose small
or baby artichokes—they are the most tender. This is a good salad to make ahead since the flavors
develop as the artichokes marinate.

makes 6 servings

12 small, tender artichokes (baby Italian violet
artichokes are best)

½ cup fresh lemon juice (from 4 lemons)

¼ pound Parmesan cheese, sliced very thin, then
cut into small cubes

3 tablespoons extra-virgin olive oil

Salt and freshly ground black pepper to taste

Per serving: 163 calories • 13g protein • 13g fat
• 3g carbohydrates • 15mg cholesterol • 365mg
sodium • 0 fiber

1. Peel away all but the most tender inner leaves of the artichokes. Cut each artichoke in half lengthwise. Remove
and discard the hairy inner chokes. Place the artichokes in
a bowl of water to cover, add all but 2 tablespoons of the
lemon juice, and let soak for 30 minutes.

2. Remove the artichokes from the water, drain, and slice
them into thin wedges. Place the wedges in a serving bowl
along with the remaining 2 tablespoons lemon juice, the
Parmesan cubes, olive oil, and salt and pepper. Let the
salad rest for at least 20 minutes before serving.

caprese salad

Presenting the colors of the Italian flag, this salad from Capri couldn't be prettier to look at or easier to make. Be sure to use vine-ripened tomatoes and fresh mozzarella, not the dry balls of cheese sold in most supermarkets. If you can't find fresh mozzarella, substitute fresh firm goat cheese.

makes 6 servings

2 large, ripe tomatoes, each cut into 6 slices
1 pound fresh mozzarella, cut into 12 slices
12 large fresh basil leaves
1 to 2 tablespoons extra-virgin olive oil
Coarse salt and freshly ground black pepper to
    taste

Per serving: 142 calories • 11g protein • 9g fat
• 4g carbohydrates • 20mg cholesterol • 204mg
sodium • 0 fiber

On a serving platter, arrange overlapping layers of tomato, mozzarella, and basil leaves. Drizzle oil over the top, and sprinkle with the salt and pepper.

moroccan vegetable salad

You can eat this salad before a meal or with a meal, or use it to stuff red or yellow bell peppers or large ripe tomatoes. You can substitute any small white beans, such as cannellini or navy beans, for the European soldier beans.

makes 8 servings
1 cup dried European soldier beans, rinsed
1½ cups vegetable broth
¼ cup plus 1 teaspoon olive oil
1 cup couscous
3 tablespoons white wine vinegar
2 garlic cloves, minced
1 teaspoon freshly grated lemon zest
½ teaspoon ground cumin
¼ teaspoon freshly ground black pepper
½ green bell pepper, finely diced
½ red bell pepper, finely diced
2 slices red onion, finely diced

Per serving: 162 calories • 5g protein • 7g fat • 21g carbohydrates • 0 cholesterol • 4mg sodium • 4g fiber

1. Place the beans in a large saucepan. Pour enough boiling water over the beans to cover them by 2 inches, then cover the pot and allow the beans to soak for 1 hour. (Or soak the beans overnight in tepid water.) Drain the beans, rinse well, then add fresh water to cover by 1 inch. Simmer until the beans are tender but not mushy, about 45 minutes. Drain and reserve.

2. In a small saucepan, heat the vegetable broth with 1 teaspoon of the olive oil until simmering. Remove from the heat and stir in the couscous. Cover and allow to stand for 5 minutes, until the broth is absorbed.

3. In a large bowl, whisk together the remaining ¼ cup oil, the vinegar, garlic, lemon zest, cumin, and black pepper. Add the bell peppers and onion. Stir in the couscous and drained beans, and toss lightly. Let rest for at least 10 minutes before serving.

red and green tabbouleh

Traditionally served as part of a selection of *mezze*, this lemony Middle Eastern bulgur salad made with parsley and tomatoes is both delicious and simple to make. In Lebanon, it is served with lettuce leaves, which are used like pita bread to scoop up the tabbouleh. For a sweeter variation on this basic recipe, substitute 1 cup plumped golden raisins for the tomatoes and add ½ cup slivered almonds.

makes 6 servings

3 cups water
2 cups fine bulgur
2 cups diced tomatoes
2 cups finely chopped fresh Italian parsley
1½ cups diced cucumber (optional)
½ cup trimmed and chopped scallions
½ cup fresh lemon juice
½ cup olive oil
¼ cup chopped fresh mint
Salt and freshly ground black pepper to taste
Romaine lettuce, radishes, and fennel stalks, for
  serving (optional)

Per 1-cup serving: 335 calories • 7g protein
• 19g fat • 40g carbohydrates • 0 cholesterol
• 25mg sodium • 10g fiber

1. In a medium saucepan, bring the water to a boil. In a large heatproof bowl, pour the boiling water over the bulgur. Cover and let sit until all the water is absorbed, about 45 minutes. Fluff the bulgur with a fork.
2. Mix all of the remaining ingredients into the bulgur and let sit at room temperature for 1 hour. If desired, serve with romaine lettuce, radishes, and fennel stalks.

arugula with roasted garlic vinaigrette

Roasting garlic gives it a mellow and surprisingly sweet flavor that is wonderful in a vinaigrette dressing. The tomatoes add color and sweetness, which complement the slightly bitter greens. The vinaigrette will last up to one week in the refrigerator.

makes 8 servings

For the vinaigrette

8 large garlic cloves, unpeeled

¼ cup plus 1 teaspoon olive oil

3 tablespoons balsamic vinegar

Salt and freshly ground black pepper to taste

For the salad

12 cups packed arugula, washed and dried (about 6 bunches)

12 Kalamata olives, pitted and halved

12 yellow or red cherry or teardrop tomatoes

Per serving: 147 calories • 5g protein • 11g fat • 10g carbohydrates • 6mg cholesterol • 134mg sodium • 3g fiber

1. Preheat the oven to 400°F. To make the vinaigrette, place the garlic cloves on a piece of aluminum foil and drizzle with 1 teaspoon of the olive oil. Wrap tightly and bake until the garlic is very tender, about 45 minutes. Cool to room temperature. Squeeze the softened garlic into a small bowl and mash with a fork. Add the remaining ¼ cup oil, the vinegar, and salt and pepper. Whisk until well combined. Transfer to a glass jar or bottle and refrigerate for at least 6 hours.

2. To serve, bring the vinaigrette to room temperature. In a large bowl, mix the greens, olives, and tomatoes. Add the dressing and toss to coat. Serve immediately.

turkish fennel salad

No Turkish meal would be complete without a raw vegetable salad lightly dressed with olive oil and lemon juice. This version uses a flavorful mixture of fresh fennel, cucumber, and radishes. For a less crunchy salad, prepare the dish, cover, and marinate at room temperature for one to two hours.

makes 8 servings

For the salad

1 large fennel bulb, trimmed and thinly sliced, fronds reserved
½ seedless cucumber, halved and thinly sliced
1 bunch radishes, trimmed and thinly sliced
Black olives, for garnish (optional)

For the dressing

3 tablespoons extra-virgin olive oil
3 tablespoons fresh lemon juice
Salt and freshly ground black pepper to taste

Per serving: 56 calories • 0 protein • 5g fat • 3g carbohydrates • 0 cholesterol • 86mg sodium • 0 fiber

1. In a large serving bowl, combine the fennel, cucumber, and radishes.
2. To make the dressing, whisk together the oil and lemon juice in a small bowl. Season with salt and pepper.
3. Pour the dressing over the salad and toss to mix and coat. Serve the salad garnished with the reserved fennel fronds and olives, if desired.

moroccan eggplant salad

In Morocco and throughout much of northern Africa and the Middle East, eggplant salads are common. Baked, boiled, or sautéed mashed eggplant is typically mixed with either sweet or hot pepper, cumin, coriander, and lemon juice, and served either as part of a *mezze* selection or along with other salads for a full meal.

makes 4 servings

2 medium eggplants, peeled and cubed
    (about 1 pound)
1 tablespoon olive oil
2 large tomatoes, chopped (about 1 pound)
1 tablespoon tomato juice
1 teaspoon cayenne pepper, or to taste
1 teaspoon salt

Per serving: 86 calories • 1g protein • 3g fat • 12g carbohydrates • 0 cholesterol • 561mg sodium • 4g fiber

1. Bring a large pot of salted water to a boil. Add the eggplant and cook until very tender, about 30 minutes. Drain well and squeeze out the excess moisture.
2. In a large skillet, heat the olive oil over medium heat. Add the eggplant, tomatoes, tomato juice, cayenne, and salt and cook, stirring, for 5 minutes, mashing with a fork until somewhat smooth. Transfer the mixture to a bowl and let cool. Cover and chill for at least 2 hours before serving.

winter fig salad

This crunchy autumnal salad contains a wonderful mélange of flavors. This is a great salad to make for a holiday feast. Serve it on individual salad plates at each place setting, or arrange it on a large, round tray at the buffet table.

makes 8 servings

For the salad

8 cups torn radicchio, washed and dried

2 cups torn Boston lettuce, washed and dried

4 Bosc pears, cored and thinly sliced

8 dried figs, cut into eighths

1 cup shaved Parmesan cheese

1½ cups chopped toasted walnuts (see page 153)

½ cup chopped fresh Italian parsley

For the vinaigrette

½ cup extra-virgin olive oil

¼ cup white wine vinegar

Salt and freshly ground black pepper to taste

Per serving: 367 calories • 11g protein • 26g fat • 29g carbohydrates • 8mg cholesterol • 199mg sodium • 5g fiber

1. Make an attractive bed of lettuce leaves on salad plates or a large platter. Arrange the pear slices on the lettuce in fan shapes. Scatter the figs and cheese over the pears. Sprinkle the walnuts and parsley over the salad.

2. To make the vinaigrette, place all of the ingredients in a jar and shake well. Just before serving, drizzle the vinaigrette over the salad.

spring salad with goat cheese medallions

Elegant and simple, this salad makes a great starter. The goat cheese lends a creamy texture and subtle flavor to the greens. To save time, you can buy the premixed baby greens called mesclun. Also, the goat cheese medallions can be made up to three days in advance of baking and stored in the refrigerator.

makes 6 servings

8 cups mixed, torn greens such as Bibb, arugula, and endive, washed and dried.
1 log (8 ounces) fresh goat cheese
½ cup olive oil
½ cup plain dry bread crumbs
2 tablespoons red wine vinegar
2 teaspoons Dijon-style mustard
Salt and freshly ground black pepper to taste

Per serving: 307 calories • 9g protein • 27g fat • 9g carbohydrates • 17mg cholesterol • 236mg sodium • 1g fiber

1. Preheat the broiler. Distribute the mixed lettuces equally on 6 salad plates.
2. Cut the goat cheese log into 6 slices. (If they crumble, reshape them with your fingers.) Lightly swish the cheese medallions in a bowl containing the olive oil and then into another bowl with the bread crumbs. Place the medallions on a baking sheet and broil until golden brown and crisp, 1 to 2 minutes per side. Place 1 medallion on top of each plate of lettuce greens.
3. In a jar, combine the remaining oil used for dipping the cheese, vinegar, mustard, and salt and pepper. Shake to combine.
4. Drizzle the dressing over the salads and serve immediately.

chickpea salad with walnuts and tomatoes

Chickpeas are used in salads throughout the Mediterranean. The Lebanese make a lemony chickpea salad called *balilah,* while the French prefer to simmer chickpeas in white wine and herbs and serve them at room temperature. This protein-rich, sweet and tangy salad packs well for picnics. For a main-course salad, add 1 cup cubed pressed tofu, plus more olive oil and lemon juice to taste.

makes 4 servings

4 ounces sun-dried tomatoes (dry, not oil-packed)
⅓ cup golden raisins
1 can (15 ounces) chickpeas, rinsed and drained
½ cup toasted and chopped walnuts
   (see page 153)
⅓ cup crumbled feta cheese
2 tablespoons olive oil
Juice of 1 lemon
Salt and freshly ground black pepper to taste
Lettuce leaves (optional)

Per serving: 356 calories • 11g protein
• 12g fat • 48g carbohydrates • 0 cholesterol
• 22mg sodium • 9g fiber

1. Put the tomatoes and raisins in a shallow dish and add boiling water to cover. Let soak until the tomatoes and raisins are soft and pliable, about 8 minutes; drain well. With a pair of scissors or a sharp knife, cut the tomatoes into slivers.
2. Place the tomatoes and remaining ingredients in a serving bowl and toss well. Serve as an appetizer on individual plates or as a salad on a bed of lettuce, if desired.

panzanella

Stale bread is transformed into a delicious summertime salad in this traditional Tuscan recipe. Use a good-quality, country-style bread with a thick crust for the best texture.

makes 4 servings
6 to 8 thick slices day-old Italian or country-style
  bread
8 plum tomatoes, chopped
2 cucumbers, halved lengthwise, seeded, and
  sliced into crescents
8 scallions, sliced
½ cup shredded and lightly packed fresh basil
  leaves
⅓ cup extra-virgin olive oil
⅓ cup balsamic or red wine vinegar
Salt and freshly ground black pepper to taste

Per serving: 364 calories • 7g protein • 17g fat
• 41g carbohydrates • 0 cholesterol • 554mg
sodium • 7g fiber

Quickly dunk the bread in a bowl of cold water. Squeeze well and tear into bite-size pieces. In a serving bowl, toss the bread with the remaining ingredients. Serve within an hour for the best texture.

greek-style tofu salad

We've replaced anchovies with tofu chunks for a vegetarian twist on the ever-popular traditional Greek salad known as *choriatiki*.

makes 6 servings

¼ cup red wine vinegar

2 tablespoons olive oil

1 tablespoon sliced fresh basil leaves

1 teaspoon kosher or regular salt

½ teaspoon freshly ground black pepper

½ teaspoon dried oregano

1 pound extra-firm tofu, drained and cut into
   ½-inch cubes

2 medium cucumbers, peeled and sliced

1 small red onion, thinly sliced

1 cup good-quality black olives, pitted

¼ cup crumbled feta cheese

Per serving: 136 calories • 7g protein • 10g fat • 7g carbohydrates • 4mg cholesterol • 600mg sodium • 2g fiber

1. In a large bowl, combine the vinegar, olive oil, basil, salt, pepper, and oregano and whisk until slightly thick. Add the tofu cubes and marinate for 1 hour, stirring occasionally.
2. Add all of the remaining ingredients, toss lightly, and serve.

sweet onion and orange salad

Sweet, juicy oranges are often used in Moroccan salads. This colorful, refreshing salad can be served right away or made a few hours ahead, giving it a chance to absorb more of the tangy dressing.

makes 4 servings

5 navel oranges, peeled
1 large Vidalia or red onion, thinly sliced and
    separated into rings
Zest of 1 lemon
¼ cup olive oil
3 tablespoons orange juice
3 tablespoons fresh lemon juice
1 teaspoon Dijon-style mustard
½ teaspoon salt
¼ teaspoon freshly ground black pepper
1 bunch watercress, stems removed
⅓ cup minced fresh mint leaves (optional)

Per serving: 230 calories • 3g protein • 14g fat • 27g carbohydrates • 0 cholesterol • 303mg sodium • 5g fiber

1. Slice the oranges crosswise into ¼-inch slices, reserving as much of the juice as possible. Place the orange slices and juice in a serving bowl. Add the onion rings and sprinkle with the lemon zest.

2. In a separate small bowl, whisk together the olive oil, orange juice, lemon juice, mustard, salt, and pepper. Pour the dressing over the oranges, toss gently, and refrigerate until serving time. Tuck the watercress around the edges of the serving bowl, and sprinkle with mint if desired. Serve chilled.

warm potato salad on bitter greens

In this delightful salad, warm, heartily dressed potatoes are placed on top of a bed of bitter greens, wilting them slightly. The result is a wonderful interplay of textures and flavors. To turn this salad into a main dish, place a generous slice of herbed goat cheese on top of the lettuce before spooning over the warm potato mixture.

makes 4 servings

1 pound red potatoes, cut into ½-inch slices
1 cup vegetable broth
1½ tablespoons olive oil
3 large garlic cloves, minced
2 tablespoons fresh lemon juice
1 tablespoon chopped fresh dill
¼ teaspoon salt
8 cups mixed bitter salad greens, such as arugula, watercress, and endive
Freshly ground black pepper to taste

Per serving: 164 calories • 4g protein • 6g fat • 27g carbohydrates • 0 cholesterol • 420mg sodium • 3g fiber

1. Combine the potatoes and broth in a large, deep skillet. Cover and bring to a boil over high heat. Reduce the heat and simmer until the potatoes are barely tender, about 7 minutes. Add the olive oil and garlic and simmer, uncovered, over medium heat until the potatoes are tender, about 5 minutes. Stir in the lemon juice, dill, and salt and heat through.

2. Arrange the greens on 4 serving plates. Spoon the warm potato mixture over the greens and sprinkle generously with pepper.

spinach salad with pecorino romano–garlic toasts

Crunchy Romano croutons enrich fresh, leafy spinach in this sophisticated salad. Try to find true pecorino (sheep's milk) Romano; it has a nuttier, more complex flavor than the cow's milk variety.

makes 6 servings

12 slices (½ inch thick) French or Italian bread
1 garlic clove, halved
½ cup olive oil
½ cup grated pecorino Romano cheese
2 tablespoons white wine vinegar
Salt and freshly ground black pepper to taste
2 bags (10 ounces each) prewashed ready-to-eat
   fresh spinach, torn
2 scallions, thinly sliced

Per serving: 381 calories • 11g protein • 23g fat • 34g carbohydrates • 8mg cholesterol • 538mg sodium • 4g fiber

1. Preheat the oven to 450°F. Rub the cut side of the garlic clove over both sides of the bread slices, then brush both sides of the bread lightly with some of the olive oil. Place the bread on a baking sheet and top with the cheese. Bake until the cheese is melted and golden, 6 to 8 minutes; set the toasts aside.
2. In a large bowl, whisk together the remaining olive oil, the vinegar, and salt and pepper. Add the spinach and scallions and toss well. Divide the salad among 6 plates and top each serving with 2 pecorino toasts. Serve immediately.

carrot and roasted red pepper salad

Glazed carrots are extremely popular in Morocco, where they may be served hot as a vegetable side dish or cold as an appetizer or in a salad.

makes 4 servings

8 carrots, peeled and cut into 1-inch lengths

3 tablespoons fresh lemon juice

2 teaspoons olive oil

1 garlic clove, minced

½ teaspoon ground cumin

½ teaspoon sweet paprika

½ teaspoon sugar

¼ teaspoon salt

1 roasted red bell pepper (see page 63), cut into medium-size squares

1 to 2 tablespoons chopped fresh parsley

Per serving: 54 calories • 11g protein • 1g fat • 10g carbohydrates • 0 cholesterol • 106mg sodium • 3g fiber

1. Steam the carrots until they are tender, about 10 minutes.
2. In a large mixing bowl, combine the lemon juice, olive oil, garlic, cumin, paprika, sugar, and salt and mix well. Add the carrots and toss to coat them with the dressing. Place the carrots on a serving platter and garnish with the roasted pepper squares and chopped parsley. Serve hot or cold.

triple bean and artichoke salad

The traditional three-bean salad gets a serious makeover in this inventive rendition. Artichoke hearts, a native Mediterranean favorite, and balsamic vinegar offer a twist to this basic dish. This salad is perfect to pack and bring to a picnic.

makes 6 servings

1 can (15 ounces) great northern, cannellini, or other white beans, drained

1 can (15 ounces) chickpeas, rinsed and drained

1 can (15 ounces) black-eyed peas, rinsed and drained

1 can (14 ounces) artichoke hearts, quartered (about 10 hearts)

2 large tomatoes, diced

4 scallions, sliced

3 garlic cloves, minced

3 tablespoons extra-virgin olive oil

3 tablespoons balsamic vinegar

¼ cup chopped fresh parsley

2 teaspoons dried oregano

1 teaspoon ground black pepper

Lettuce, for serving (optional)

Per 1-cup serving: 330 calories • 15g protein • 9g fat • 52g carbohydrates • 0 cholesterol • 449mg sodium • 13g fiber

Combine all ingredients in a mixing bowl and blend thoroughly. Chill for 1 hour before serving to allow the flavors to marry. If desired, serve the salad over a bed of lettuce.

tortellini antipasto salad

For the Italian pasta lovers at your dinner table, serve this easy, make-ahead salad. It is made with tiny cheese-filled tortellini, "tiny cakes," which are said to have been inspired by Venus' navel.

makes 12 servings

2 packages (9 ounces each) fresh cheese tortellini

1 jar (7 ounces) roasted red peppers, drained, rinsed, and cut into short, thin strips

1 can (14 ounces) artichoke bottoms or hearts, drained and quartered

1 cup Kalamata olives, pitted and halved

¼ cup chopped fresh basil leaves

½ cup olive oil

¼ cup fresh lemon juice

1 garlic clove, minced

Salt and freshly ground black pepper to taste

Romaine or red leaf lettuce leaves, for serving

Per ¾-cup serving: 249 calories • 8g protein • 14g fat • 24g carbohydrates • 23mg cholesterol • 416mg sodium • 2g fiber

1. Cook the tortellini according to the package directions until al dente, then drain and rinse with cold water. Combine the tortellini, red pepper strips, artichoke hearts, olives, and basil in a large bowl. Set aside.

2. In a small bowl, whisk together the olive oil, lemon juice, garlic, and salt and pepper. Pour the dressing over the tortellini and toss well. Serve the salad on a lettuce-lined platter.

Soups

Surprisingly, soups, both cold and hot, are almost as popular in the temperate Mediterranean region as they are in the north. While cold soups refresh on a hot summer's afternoon, hot soups fortify the body against the chill winds that blow at night, even in the warmest of climates. In the Levant, lemon, garlic, and olive oil make up the typical soup base, as they do for many of the dishes throughout the region. The flavors match beans and legumes particularly well, and the combination is a favorite. Our Turkish Lentil Soup with Lemon (page 111) is a fine example. In Europe, garlic and olive oil are also prevalent, first sautéed with other aromatic vegetables, then added to a rich, simmering broth. Lightly herbed yogurt soups have a subtle creamy tang and are vastly popular in the eastern Mediterranean countries, where they are generally served well chilled, sometimes garnished with ice cubes. As with all of the area's cooking, the ingredients in Mediterranean soups reflect the changing seasons and the available local produce. Squash and fennel appear in autumn and winter soups, while fresh tomatoes and peppers star in cold summertime soups such as the Garden Gazpacho on page 101. While vegetables and legumes make up the bulk of the vegetarian soups offered, grains also have their place, especially in Italy. Mediterranean Grain Soup on page 103, is rich with chewy spelt. Of course, in Italy pasta is a favorite soup ingredient, often stretching the colorful vegetables already in the broth. Pasta soups are also popular in Greece and Tunisia, where the long-boiled egg noodles practically fall apart in the mouth. ■ In Greece, soups are not usually served as an appetizer or first course. Rather, the Greeks prefer to eat their soup as the main dish, accompanied by a fresh, crusty loaf of bread. Beans, lentils, rice, and pasta, coupled with fresh vegetables in a rich broth, make these soups hearty and nutritious. Similarly, the Lebanese commonly serve their lemony soups as the main course. ■ Sometimes soup takes on meanings that go well beyond nourishing the body. In northern Africa, *harira,* a thick, fragrant, vegetable-based soup, assumes an almost religious significance, since it is traditionally eaten at the end of each day of fasting during the Muslim month of Ramadan. Furthermore, just as we spoon up bowls of steaming hot broth to cure the sniffles, our neighbors across the ocean also believe in the restorative and healing powers of soup.

pasta e fagioli

This recipe makes what seems like a lot, enough to serve 12 people. But the beauty of it is that you can serve it twice: once as a hot, soupy pasta, and then a second time as a chilled pasta salad that has its own, built-in dressing. In the past, Italian peasants would hollow out a loaf of fresh crusty bread and fill it with leftover *pasta e fagioli*. Then they'd spoon out the pasta and beans and eat it with pieces of the bread, which absorbed the dish's robust flavors. You might also want to sprinkle the pasta salad with chopped Italian parsley or chopped fresh basil.

makes 12 servings as soup

1 pound uncooked pasta wagon wheels
1 tablespoon olive oil
2 large onions, chopped
3 garlic cloves, minced
1 can (28 ounces) whole peeled tomatoes in juice
1 teaspoon dried oregano
1 teaspoon dried basil
¼ teaspoon crushed red pepper flakes
2 cups cooked kidney beans or 1 can
   (15 ounces) kidney beans, rinsed and drained
2 cups cooked black beans or 1 can
   (15 ounces) black beans, rinsed and drained
2 cups cooked white beans or 1 can
   (15 ounces) white beans, rinsed and drained
2 cups vegetable broth

Per serving: 300 calories • 14g protein • 2g fat • 58g carbohydrates • 0 cholesterol • 257mg sodium • 9g fiber

1. Cook the pasta according to the package directions until al dente. Drain, reserving 1 cup of the cooking water.
2. Meanwhile, in a large saucepan, heat the olive oil over medium-high heat. Add the onions and cook, stirring, until browned slightly, about 5 minutes. Add the garlic and cook, stirring, until it releases its scent but does not brown, about 2 minutes. Drain the juice from the tomatoes into the pan. Chop the tomatoes coarsely and add to the pan. Add the oregano, basil, and red pepper flakes and cook over medium-heat until the juices are reduced, about 20 minutes. Add the reserved pasta water, beans, and broth and heat through.
3. Combine the bean mixture and pasta, tossing to mix. Divide the mixture in half. Cover and refrigerate one half, serve the other immediately.

moroccan carrot soup

Toasted fennel seeds infuse sweet carrots, apples, and yams with a licorice flavor in this brilliantly colored soup, inspired by the countries of the Maghreb. You can prepare it up to three days ahead, or freeze it for up to a month.

makes 6 servings

1 tablespoon unsalted butter or olive oil
½ teaspoon fennel seeds
1½ pounds carrots, sliced
½ pound sweet potatoes, peeled and cubed
1 large Granny Smith apple, peeled, cored, and diced
5½ cups vegetable broth or water
2 tablespoons white or brown basmati rice (or regular long-grain rice)
¼ teaspoon turmeric or curry powder
1 bay leaf
Salt and freshly ground black pepper
Fresh lemon juice
2 tablespoons minced fresh cilantro or parsley

Per serving: 211 calories • 4g protein • 2g fat • 44g carbohydrates • 6mg cholesterol • 234mg sodium • 4g fiber

1. Warm half of the butter or olive oil in a soup pot over medium heat. Add the fennel seeds and toast until darkened, 2 to 3 minutes. Add the carrots, sweet potatoes, and apple, and cook for about 5 minutes, stirring occasionally. Add the vegetable broth or water, rice, turmeric or curry powder, and bay leaf.
2. Bring the soup to a boil, reduce the heat, cover, and simmer until the rice is done and the vegetables are tender, about 30 minutes.
3. Drain the vegetables and rice, reserving the broth. Discard the bay leaf. Transfer the vegetable-rice mixture and small amounts of the reserved broth in batches to a food processor or blender and puree until smooth. Return the pureed soup and any remaining reserved broth to the soup pot. Simmer for about 5 minutes. Season to taste with salt, pepper, and lemon juice.
4. To serve, drizzle with remaining melted butter or oil and sprinkle with cilantro or parsley.

garden gazpacho

Gazpacho's popularity has spread worldwide from its humble beginnings in Andalusia, Spain. This cooling soup, often called a "liquid salad," is perfect on a scorching day. Fresh tomatoes work best in this recipe, although canned may also be used. Gazpacho is best served within a day of making it.

makes 4 servings
4 ripe plum tomatoes, seeded and chopped
1 small onion, diced
1 green or red bell pepper, diced
1 cucumber, peeled and chopped
1 small jalapeño or serrano pepper, seeded and minced
2 garlic cloves, minced
2 tablespoons minced fresh basil
1½ teaspoons ground cumin
½ teaspoon hot pepper sauce, or to taste
¼ teaspoon salt
¼ teaspoon black pepper
2 cups canned tomato juice
Croutons, for serving (optional)

Per serving: 156 calories • 7g protein • 1g fat • 31g carbohydrates • 0 cholesterol • 361mg sodium • 7g fiber

Place all of the ingredients except the tomato juice and croutons in a food processor fitted with a steel blade. Process for 10 to 15 seconds, forming a mash. Transfer to a large bowl. Blend in the tomato juice. Chill for at least 1 hour before serving. Serve with croutons, if desired.

mediterranean vegetable broth

Saffron, fennel, and red bell peppers give this broth a Mediterranean accent. Use it for dishes of Spanish, Italian, Provençal, and even northern African origin. To make this into a Mediterranean vegetable soup, discard the herb bundle and zest and puree the broth and vegetables in a blender; season with salt and pepper and serve as a first course.

makes 5 servings

4 sprigs fresh thyme (or 1 teaspoon dried)
2 bay leaves
1 teaspoon black peppercorns
About 8 cups water
1 medium onion, coarsely chopped
1 leek, coarsely chopped
6 garlic cloves, coarsely chopped
2 celery stalks, coarsely chopped
2 carrots, coarsely chopped
1 red bell pepper, coarsely chopped
½ small or ¼ large fennel bulb, coarsely chopped
  (or 1 teaspoon fennel seeds)
2 medium tomatoes, coarsely chopped
1 cup dry white vermouth
½ cup orange juice
½ cup fresh basil leaves and stems
½ cup Italian parsley leaves and stems
2 strips orange zest
¼ teaspoon saffron
Salt (optional)

Per 1-cup serving: 131 calories • 3g protein • 1g fat • 16g carbohydrates • 0 cholesterol • 42mg sodium • 4g fiber

1. Tie the thyme, bay leaves, and peppercorns in a cheesecloth bag or place inside a metal tea ball. Combine with all the ingredients except the salt in a large pot and bring to a boil over medium-high heat.
2. Skim the surface, reduce the heat, and simmer the broth, uncovered, until the vegetables are very tender, about 1 hour. Add the water as necessary to keep the vegetables covered, and skim the foam as necessary.
3. Strain the broth, pressing the vegetables with the back of a spoon to extract as much liquid as possible. For a thicker, richer broth, remove the herb bundle and zest and puree the vegetables in a blender or food mill, then strain.

mediterranean grain soup

Zuppa di farro, or grain soup, is a specialty of Apulia in southern Italy. This vegetable-rich, full-bodied version comes from the posh Melograno Hotel in the city of Monopoli on the Adriatic coast.

**makes 8 first-course servings,
4 main-course servings**

1 cup wheat berries
10 cups warm water
Salt to taste
2 tablespoons olive oil
2 medium zucchini, cored and diced
2 carrots, diced
2 celery stalks, diced
1 yellow bell pepper, diced
1 red bell pepper, diced
1 large onion, diced
2 garlic cloves, minced
8 cups Mediterranean Vegetable Broth (page 102)
2 medium potatoes (preferably Yukon Gold), diced
¼ cup chopped fresh Italian parsley
12 basil leaves, thinly slivered
2 bay leaves
1 teaspoon dried or fresh thyme
¼ teaspoon saffron soaked in 1 tablespoon hot
  water
Freshly ground black pepper to taste

Per first-course serving: 299 calories • 8g protein
• 5g fat • 47g carbohydrates • 0 cholesterol
• 73mg sodium • 9g fiber

1. Soak the wheat berries in warm water for at least 2 hours or overnight.
2. Transfer the wheat berries and soaking liquid to a large pot. Simmer, covered, over medium heat, until tender, about 1½ hours. Salt to taste after about 1 hour. Add more water as necessary to keep the grains covered by at least 1 inch. Drain and set aside.
3. Heat 1 tablespoon of the olive oil in a large pot. Add the zucchini, carrots, celery, peppers, onion, and garlic, and cook over medium heat until soft, about 5 minutes, stirring occasionally.
4. Add the wheat berries, broth, potatoes, half of the parsley, half of the basil leaves, bay leaves, thyme, and saffron. Bring to a boil, then reduce the heat to medium and simmer, uncovered, until the vegetables are tender and the soup is well flavored, about 20 minutes. Add more stock as necessary to keep the vegetables covered. Add the salt, pepper, and more thyme and garnish the soup with the remaining parsley and basil.

savory harira soup

This aromatic soup is what Moroccan families traditionally break the fast with each evening during the Muslim month of Ramadan. Spiced with ginger and cinnamon and full of hearty chickpeas and lentils, this soup is definitely restorative. Don't let the long list of ingredients intimidate you; the soup is easy to prepare and the results are well worth it. For a slight variation, add ⅛ teaspoon cayenne pepper or to taste, and a splash of fresh lemon juice.

makes 8 servings

2 tablespoons olive oil

2 cups diced onions

1 celery stalk, diced

6 tablespoons minced fresh parsley

2 tablespoons minced fresh cilantro

2 teaspoons salt

1 teaspoon freshly ground pepper

1 teaspoon turmeric

1 teaspoon paprika

1 teaspoon caraway seeds

½ teaspoon ground ginger

½ teaspoon cinnamon

1 small bay leaf

1½ quarts water or vegetable broth

1 cup cooked chickpeas, rinsed and drained if canned

½ cup dried lentils

1 can (28 ounces) crushed tomatoes

3 tablespoons unbleached all-purpose flour mixed with ½ cup cold water

1 tablespoon tomato paste

8 to 10 lemon slices

Per serving: 166 calories • 7g protein • 4g fat • 28g carbohydrates • 0 cholesterol • 745mg sodium • 5g fiber

1. Heat the olive oil in a large soup pot over medium-low heat. Add the onions, celery, and parsley and cook, stirring, until the onions, are soft, 5 to 7 minutes. Add the cilantro, salt, pepper, turmeric, paprika, caraway seeds, ginger, cinnamon, and bay leaf and stir until mixed. Add the water or broth, chickpeas, lentils, and tomatoes, and bring to a boil. Reduce to a simmer and cook, covered, until the lentils are soft, about 20 minutes.

2. Before serving, add the flour mixture, stirring to avoid lumps. Stir in the tomato paste and cook until heated through, 1 to 2 minutes. Adjust the seasonings to taste. Serve hot with a slice of lemon floating in each soup bowl.

cool cantaloupe soup

The picturesque village of Cavaillion, near the French Mediterranean, is the region's center for growing wonderfully fragrant, sweet melons. Although the French generally prefer their melons served as simply as possible, often just halved and eaten plain or filled with heady port wine, here, we've pureed them into a cool, creamy soup. Serve it for a first course on a hot summer evening, and then savor any leftovers for breakfast the next morning. It's as refreshing as they come.

makes 4 servings

1 ripe medium cantaloupe
1 cup orange juice
2 teaspoons fresh lime juice
1 cup plain yogurt
Fresh mint leaves cut into strips (optional)
Slivers of melon, for garnish

Per serving: 110 calories • 5g protein • 0 fat • 21g carbohydrates • 1mg cholesterol • 61mg sodium • 1g fiber

1. Quarter the melon, remove and discard the seeds, and cut the fruit from the rind. Dice the fruit and place in a food processor or blender. Add the orange and lime juices; puree and set aside.
2. Place the yogurt in a glass mixing bowl and beat with a whisk until light and smooth. Whisk in the melon mixture.
3. Cover the bowl and refrigerate for at least 3 hours, until chilled through and flavors have melded. Serve cold, sprinkled with fresh mint leaves and garnished with slivers of melon, if desired.

creamy spinach soup

This thick and warming soup makes the perfect lunch or first course on a crisp autumn day. Pureed potatoes give it a rich, creamy texture with barely a trace of fat.

makes 4 servings

1 tablespoon olive oil
1 large onion, coarsely chopped
1 garlic clove, minced
Salt and freshly ground black pepper to taste
6 cups water
3 potatoes, peeled and chopped
3 medium zucchini, thickly sliced
2 cups tightly packed fresh spinach leaves
Parmesan cheese, for serving (optional)

Per serving: 123 calories • 3g protein • 0 fat • 27g carbohydrates • 0 cholesterol • 829mg sodium • 3g fiber

1. In a large saucepan, heat the olive oil over medium-high heat. Add the onion and cook, stirring, until tender, about 5 minutes. Add the garlic and cook for 1 minute longer. Season with salt and pepper. Add the water, potatoes, and zucchini, cover the pot, and simmer for 35 minutes.

2. Add the spinach and more salt and pepper. Cook for another 2 minutes. Remove the pan from the heat.

3. Using a slotted spoon, transfer the vegetables to a food processor or blender. Add a little bit of the broth and puree the soup, working in batches if necessary. Return the pureed soup to the pan with the remaining broth. Heat gently for 5 minutes and serve hot, topped with the Parmesan, if desired.

provençal soup with pistou

This is a slightly lighter version of a traditional Provençal combination: vegetable soup enriched with *pistou*. *Pistou*—a pounded, pestolike sauce of nuts, olive oil, garlic, and basil—is unique to the Mediterranean region of France, since tender basil grows well only in temperate climates. It adds both body and an intense, herbaceous flavor to soups and stews.

Simmering the soup with a selection of herbs known as a *bouquet garni* intensifies the flavor. To make a *bouquet garni*, place 1 bay leaf, 4 sprigs of parsley, and 2 sprigs of thyme in a small square of cheesecloth, tie securely, and drop into the soup pot. Discard the bundle before serving the soup.

makes 6 servings

For the soup

1½ tablespoons olive oil
1½ pounds new potatoes, cut into ½-inch cubes
1 pound carrots, cut on the diagonal into
 ¼-inch-thick slices
1 cup diced celery
8 cups water
1 *bouquet garni* (optional, see headnote)
Pinch of saffron threads, crushed (optional)
½ pound green beans, cut into 1-inch pieces
1 pound zucchini, cut into ½-inch cubes
1 cup uncooked elbow macaroni
Salt and freshly ground black pepper to taste
¼ cup chopped fresh parsley

For the *pistou*

½ cup hazelnuts
2 garlic cloves
3 cups lightly packed fresh basil or Italian
 parsley leaves
1 small tomato, peeled, seeded, and chopped
Salt and freshly ground black pepper to taste
½ tablespoon olive oil

Per serving with 1 tablespoon *pistou*: 288 calories • 7g protein • 6g fat • 50g carbohydrates • 0 cholesterol • 445mg sodium • 10g fiber

1. To make the soup, heat 1 tablespoon of the olive oil in a large, heavy-bottomed soup pot over medium heat. Add the potatoes, carrots, and celery and cook, stirring, about 5 minutes. Add the water, *bouquet garni,* and saffron if desired. Bring to a boil, reduce the heat, and gently cook for 10 minutes.
2. Add the green beans and continue to cook until the vegetables are almost tender, about 25 minutes. Add the zucchini and macaroni, and simmer for an additional 10 minutes or until pasta is tender. Season with salt and pepper, stir in the parsley, and drizzle with the remaining ½ tablespoon olive oil. Remove from the heat, cover, and keep warm.
3. To make the *pistou*, heat the hazelnuts in a skillet over medium-high heat and stir until lightly toasted, about 5 minutes. While the nuts are still warm, place in a folded tea towel and rub off their skins. Transfer the nuts to a food processor, add the garlic, and process until finely chopped. Add the basil or parsley and tomato and process, scraping down the work bowl as necessary, until the mixture forms a smooth paste. (Add water to thin as necessary.) Transfer to a bowl, add salt and pepper, and fold in the olive oil. Ladle the soup into shallow soup bowls or transfer to a serving dish. Stir in the *pistou* or pass it separately for guests to stir in a desired amount themselves.

leonardo da vinci's chickpea soup

Who knows if da Vinci invented this flavorful soup, but he probably ate something quite similar to it. Chickpeas are native to the Mediterranean region and are an integral part of savory cuisine.

makes 8 servings

6 cups water

2 cans (17 ounces each) chickpeas, rinsed and drained

1 tablespoon olive oil

2 teaspoons dried sage

2 teaspoons dried rosemary

1 teaspoon ground cinnamon

1 teaspoon salt

½ teaspoon freshly ground black pepper

2 tablespoons finely chopped fresh parsley

Per serving: 104 calories • 3g protein • 4g fat • 14g carbohydrates • 0 cholesterol • 471mg sodium • 3g fiber

1. In a large soup pot, combine all the ingredients except the parsley. Bring the mixture to a boil over high heat, then lower the heat and simmer, partially covered, for 20 minutes.
2. Serve the soup garnished with the parsley.

chilled lemon soup with mint

This luscious soup gains its creaminess from the potato and yogurt, and its body from the egg replacer. It can be made up to one day in advance.

makes 4 servings
1 large potato, peeled and chopped
2½ cups vegetable broth
½ cup water
3 tablespoons fresh lemon juice
Egg substitute equivalent to 1 egg
¾ cup plain nonfat yogurt
2 tablespoons chopped fresh mint
Salt and freshly ground black pepper to taste
Extra mint leaves, for garnish (optional)

Per serving: 77 calories • 3g protein • 0 fat • 17g carbohydrates • 1mg cholesterol • 33mg sodium • 1g fiber

1. In a medium saucepan, simmer the potato in the broth and water until the potato is tender, 10 to 15 minutes. Puree the potato, broth, and water mixture in a blender or food processor.
2. In a medium bowl, whisk together the lemon juice and egg substitute. Gradually add 1 cup hot potato puree, whisking constantly. Transfer the mixture back to the saucepan and heat gently until it thickens slightly, 10 to 12 minutes. Do not let the soup come to a boil.
3. Remove the pan from the heat and let the soup cool. Whisk in the yogurt, mint, and salt and pepper to taste, then chill the soup until it is quite cold, about 3 hours. Garnish with mint leaves before serving, if desired.

tomato and fennel soup

The combination of fennel and tomato is especially popular along the French and Italian Riviera, where the two often meet in soups, stews, and sometimes salads. Here, they are cooked with broth and pureed. Serve this soup as it is or float some Olive Crostini (page 59) on top.

You can make this soup up to three days in advance. It also freezes beautifully for up to two months.

makes 6 servings

2 medium fennel bulbs
2 tablespoons olive oil
1 large onion, chopped
6 garlic cloves, minced
½ teaspoon fennel seeds
Salt and freshly ground black pepper to taste
2 cans (35 ounces each) Italian plum tomatoes
2½ cups vegetable broth

Per serving: 86 calories • 2g protein • 5g fat • 9g carbohydrates • 0 cholesterol • 515mg sodium • 1g fiber

1. Trim the fennel and reserve the fronds. Coarsely chop the fennel bulb.
2. In a large saucepan, heat the olive oil over medium-high heat. Add the onion and chopped fennel and cook, stirring, until the vegetables are quite tender, about 15 minutes. Add the garlic and fennel seeds and cook, stirring, for 5 minutes longer. Stir in salt and pepper.
3. Add the tomatoes and broth to the pan, partially cover, and bring the mixture to a simmer. Reduce the heat to medium-low and simmer the soup for 30 minutes.
4. Working in batches, puree the soup in a blender or food processor, then return it to the pan. Heat the soup gently for 5 minutes, then serve, garnished with the fennel fronds.

turkish lentil soup with lemon

Lemon juice and browned onions enliven this velvety pureed soup. You can serve it as a meal, rounded out by a loaf of bread and a vegetable salad, or as a first course before a light meal.

makes 6 servings

2 cups lentils
2 medium onions
2 quarts vegetable broth
1 large tomato, quartered and seeded
2 garlic cloves, minced
1 tablespoon olive oil
2 tablespoons fresh lemon juice
2 teaspoons ground cumin
1 teaspoon salt
Freshly ground black pepper to taste
2 tablespoons chopped fresh cilantro
1 large lemon, cut into 6 wedges

Per serving: 295 calories • 22g protein • 5g fat • 47g carbohydrates • 0 cholesterol • 1733mg sodium • 21g fiber

1. Rinse the lentils well and place them in a large saucepan. Peel the onions, quarter one, and add it to the pan with the lentils. Thinly slice the other onion and reserve.

2. Add the vegetable broth, tomato, and garlic to the pan with the lentils and bring the soup to a simmer over high heat. Reduce the heat to medium-low and simmer, partially covered, until the lentils are very tender, about 45 minutes.

3. Meanwhile, in a small skillet, heat the olive oil over medium heat. Add the onion slices and cook, stirring, until golden brown, about 15 minutes. Stir in the lemon juice.

4. Using a slotted spoon, transfer the lentils and vegetables to a food processor or blender. Add a little bit of the broth and puree the soup, working in batches if necessary. Return the pureed the soup to the pan and stir in the cumin and salt and pepper. Heat gently for 10 minutes and serve hot, topped with the sautéed onions and cilantro. Serve the lemon wedges on the side and have guests squeeze the juice into the soup to taste.

herbed cucumber yogurt soup

Cold yogurt soup is served throughout the Middle Eastern countries of the Levant, where it makes a delightfully cooling first course. Since the cucumber releases water as it sits, the soup is best prepared the same day you plan to serve it.

makes 4 servings

1 medium cucumber
2 cups plain yogurt
2 teaspoons distilled white vinegar
1 tablespoon minced fresh mint
2 teaspoons minced fresh dill
1 teaspoon extra-virgin olive oil
1 garlic clove, minced
Salt and freshly ground white pepper to taste
4 ice cubes (optional)

Per serving: 85 calories • 7g protein • 1g fat • 11g carbohydrates • 2mg cholesterol • 88mg sodium • 1g fiber

1. Peel the cucumber and slice it in half lengthwise. Scoop out the seeds and grate the cucumber coarsely. Reserve.
2. Put the yogurt in a large bowl and whisk until it is very smooth. Add the vinegar, mint, dill, olive oil, and garlic and whisk well. Add the cucumber and whisk until smooth. Add salt and white pepper.
3. Chill the soup for at least 1 hour before serving. Serve, garnishing each portion with an ice cube, if desired.

eggplant and red pepper soup with roasted garlic toasts

This thick soup, rich with vegetables and topped with sweet garlic toasts, uses a Mediterranean bounty in a new way. You can make the roasted garlic up to five days in advance; store it in the refrigerator.

makes 6 servings

For the toasts
4 heads of garlic, unpeeled
6 tablespoons olive oil
Salt and freshly ground black pepper to taste
Red wine vinegar to taste
1 *baguette*, sliced into ½-inch-thick rounds (about 24 slices)

For the soup
¼ cup olive oil
1 large eggplant, peeled and cubed
Salt and freshly ground black pepper to taste
1 large red bell pepper, chopped
1 large onion, chopped
3 garlic cloves, minced
1 quart vegetable broth
½ teaspoon dried thyme
Pinch of dried rosemary
2 tablespoons chopped fresh basil or mint

Per serving, soup with 2 toasts:
259 calories • 5g protein •
18g fat • 23g carbohydrates •
0 cholesterol • 823mg
sodium • 2g fiber

1. Preheat the oven to 450°F. Prepare the garlic toasts. Slice the tops off the heads of garlic so that the cloves are partially exposed. Place the garlic in a small pan and drizzle each head with 1 tablespoon of the olive oil. Season with salt and pepper. Cover the pan with foil and roast the garlic for 1 hour, or until it is very tender.

2. While the garlic is roasting, place the *baguette* rounds on a baking sheet and brush them on both sides with the remaining oil. Toast the bread until golden, about 4 minutes per side.

3. When the garlic is cool enough to handle, squeeze the garlic cloves out of their papery skins. Put the roasted garlic in a small dish and mash it with a fork until it forms a rough puree. Season it with salt, pepper, and vinegar.

4. To prepare the soup, in a large saucepan, heat 2 tablespoons of the olive oil over medium-high heat. Add the eggplant and cook, stirring, until it is well browned on all sides, about 15 minutes. Season it with salt and pepper and transfer to a paper towel–lined plate; reserve.

5. Add the remaining 2 tablespoons of oil to the pan and heat it for 15 seconds. Add the red pepper and onion and cook, stirring, until they are tender, about 5 minutes. Stir in the minced garlic and cook, stirring, for 2 minutes longer. Add the vegetable broth, thyme, rosemary, and browned eggplant and bring the soup to a simmer. Reduce the heat to low and simmer the soup, partially covered, for 30 minutes.

6. Using a slotted spoon, transfer the vegetables to a food processor or blender. Add a little bit of the broth and puree soup, working in batches if necessary. Return the pureed soup to the pan and heat for 5 minutes. Season with salt and pepper.

7. Spread a thin layer of the garlic puree on the toasts. Serve the soup garnished with the basil or mint and the garlic toasts.

Savory Tarts, Pastries, and Egg Dishes

■ If you were pressed to think of a classic Mediterranean savory pastry, the first image that would probably pop into your mind is *spanakopeta*. These flaky Greek phyllo dough pastries filled with spinach and feta cheese are the quintessential Greek snack and can be found in some sort of variation in most Mediterranean countries. For example, in Lebanon, spinach and spiced, strained yogurt or curd cheese fill dainty pastry crescents, which are then fried in olive oil. Moroccans have their *b'stilla*, which is made with *warkha* pastry layers that are even flakier and finer than phyllo, and filled with almonds, sweet spices, and eggs. Delicious Turkish *boreks* are usually stuffed with savory goat cheese or any number of vegetables. All of these pastries are eaten as often at room temperature as they are hot, which makes them a handy treat to serve any time hunger pangs strike. ■ Egg dishes, with or without flaky crusts, are also extremely popular, including quichelike pies made with spinach, grilled peppers, mint, onions, and eggplant. *Tartas, tortas,* or *tartes*, which resemble quiches but are usually prepared without the custard, are popular in Spain, Italy, and France, where they are made with a variety of regional vegetables including artichokes, fennel, leeks, tomatoes, mushrooms, Swiss chard, and even rice, as in the case of our Sardinian Rice Tart (page 138). Spanish tortillas and Italian *frittatas* are savory omelettes, cooked into a thick cake brimming with potatoes and onions or other vegetables. Traditionally, Spanish farmers and shepherds would bring tortillas to the fields with them to eat cold between two slices of crusty bread as a satisfying midday meal. Now, they are a favorite tapa, nibbled in bars accompanied by cool glasses of nutty, amber-colored sherry. ■ Since many of the traditional pastries and egg dishes of the Mediterranean region are exceptionally rich with butter, eggs, oil, and cheese, we've taken care to reduce the fat wherever it wouldn't change the outcome in a noticeable way. But regardless, all of our pastries, tarts, and egg dishes retain the delectable flavors of those sun-kissed lands.

marinated artichoke heart frittata

Rich and savory, a *frittata* is like a quiche without the crust. While it is at its most delicious when served warm from the oven, it can also be served at room temperature.

makes 12 servings
1 tablespoon olive oil
1 medium onion, finely chopped
2 garlic cloves, minced
1 jar (14½ ounces) marinated artichoke hearts, drained
4 large eggs, beaten
Pinch each of black pepper, dried oregano, dried thyme, ground nutmeg
Dash of hot pepper sauce
2 cups shredded sharp cheddar cheese
3 tablespoons minced fresh parsley

Per serving: 112 calories • 7g protein • 9g fat • 2g carbohydrates • 91mg cholesterol • 145mg sodium • 0 fiber

1. Preheat the oven to 325°F. In a large skillet, heat the olive oil over medium-high heat. Add the onion and cook, stirring, until softened, about 7 minutes. Add the garlic and cook for 1 minute longer.
2. Chop the artichoke hearts and put them in a large bowl. Add the onion mixture and remaining ingredients. Stir the mixture well and pour into a lightly greased, large cast-iron skillet or a 9-by-13-inch baking dish. Bake for 30 minutes, or until the custard is just set. Let the *frittata* cool for 10 minutes, then cut into wedges or squares.

spanakopita

This rich and flaky spinach pie is as well loved in Greece as it is in this country. It is a classic component of hot *mezze* and can also be served as part of a buffet or with a salad, such as Greek-Style Tofu Salad (page 90) for lunch or for a light supper.

makes 20 appetizer-size servings

3 pounds fresh spinach

Pinch of salt

6 tablespoons olive oil

2 large onions, chopped

2 bunches scallions, including 4 inches of green tops, finely chopped

½ cup chopped fresh parsley

½ cup chopped fresh dill (or 3 tablespoons dried)

4 large eggs

½ pound feta cheese, crumbled (about 1½ cups)

1 cup ricotta or cottage cheese

¼ cup melted unsalted butter

16 sheets phyllo pastry

Per Serving: 193 calories • 8g protein • 13g carbohydrates • 65mg cholesterol • 280mg sodium • 2g fiber

1. Remove and discard the coarse spinach stems and wash the leaves well. Sprinkle lightly with salt, stirring to spread the salt evenly, and let stand 10 minutes; rinse off the salt and squeeze out the excess water with your hands. Chop the spinach and drain in a colander for 15 minutes.

2. Meanwhile, in a large skillet, heat 2 tablespoons of the olive oil over medium-high heat and cook the onions and scallions, stirring, until soft but not brown, about 3 minutes. Add the spinach, parsley, and dill, and cook, stirring, until the spinach has wilted, 2 to 3 minutes. Remove from the heat, transfer to a bowl, and let cool.

3. In a separate bowl, lightly beat the eggs. Add the cheeses and spinach mixture and stir well.

4. Preheat the oven to 350°F. In a small bowl, combine the remaining 4 tablespoons olive oil and the melted butter. Lightly grease a shallow 9-by-13-inch baking pan. Take 8 phyllo sheets from the package, keeping the rest covered with a damp cloth so they don't dry out. Center one sheet in the baking pan and brush with the oil-butter mixture. Stack the other 7 sheets one by one on top of the first, brushing each with the oil-butter mixture. The sheets will hang over the sides of the pan. Pour in the spinach-egg mixture and spread evenly. Fold overhanging sides and ends of phyllo over the filling to enclose it. Brush with the oil-butter mixture. Top with the remaining 8 phyllo sheets, brushing each with the oil-butter mixture as you stack them. Tuck the overhanging edges around the inside of the baking pan to seal in the filling.

5. Using the point of a sharp knife, score the surface into 20 rectangles. Bake until golden, about 20 minutes. To serve, cut through the scored lines. Serve warm or cold.

Rapini Pizza (page 267)

White Bean and Rosemary Stew (page 208)

Fava Beans with Pesto Sauce (page 236)

Eggplant Involtini (page 217)

Marinated Pearl Onions with
Tomato-Saffron Sauce (page 244)

Greek Garlic and Potato Dip (page 50) and Marinated Olives (page 51)

Couscous with Turnips and Turnip Greens (page 193)

Vegetable Paella (page 222)

Herb and Walnut Ravioli (page 153)

Penne Niçoise (page 161)

Radiatore Provençal (page 159)

Fusilli with Garlicky
Dandelion Greens
(page 162)

Roasted Asparagus Salad with Orange (page 75)

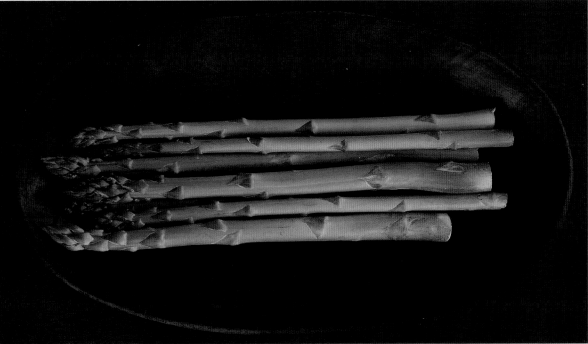

Provençal Soup with
Pistou (page 107)

Raw Artichoke Salad
with Parmesan
(page 79)

Grilled Polenta with Triple-Pepper Sauce (page 187)

Artichoke and Fennel
Tart (page 132)

Eggplant and Red Pepper Soup
with Roasted Garlic Toasts
(page 113)

Rapini Frittata (page 126)

Greek Vegetable Salad with Curly Endive and Olives (page 73)

Olive Crostini (page 59), Crostini with Pepper Spread (page 60), and Roasted Tomato Bruschetta (page 62)

bourekakia

These Greek cheese puffs are similar to Turkish *boreks,* which are little pies traditionally made with eggs, butter, and sheep's milk yogurt, encased in layer upon layer of flaky phyllo. The Greeks traditionally fry *bourekakia,* but we've decided to bake them to cut down on the fat, and they're just as rich and delicious. Serve these puffs as the Greek do, oven-hot as part of *mezze,* along with olives, feta cheese, and fresh vegetables.

The puffs may be frozen before baking. They will keep, well wrapped, in the freezer for about four weeks. When ready to bake, brush the frozen puffs with melted butter and bake in a buttered baking pan at 350°F. until golden, about 30 minutes.

makes 65 appetizers

½ pound feta cheese, crumbled (about 1½ cups)
1 cup ricotta cheese
3 large eggs, lightly beaten
1 tablespoon finely chopped fresh parsley
1 tablespoon dry bread crumbs
1 package (about 1 pound) phyllo pastry
1½ cups melted butter

Per serving: 79 calories • 2g protein • 6g fat • 4g carbohydrates • 25mg cholesterol • 127mg sodium • 0 fiber

1. Preheat the oven to 350°F. In a bowl, mix the cheeses, eggs, parsley, and bread crumbs. Take half of the phyllo sheets from the package; keep the rest covered with a damp cloth and place in the refrigerator to prevent them from drying out. Cut the sheets into strips about 3½ by 12 inches. Use 2 strips at a time, keeping the rest under another damp cloth.
2. Brush one strip with melted butter. Place the second strip on top and brush again. Then place 1 tablespoon of the cheese mixture at one end of the layered strip. Lift a corner of the strip next to the filling and fold it over the filling so that it touches the opposite long side and forms a triangle enclosing the filling. Continue to fold up the pastry, maintaining the triangular shape. Fill and fold the remaining strips in the same way. Take the remaining phyllo sheets from the refrigerator and cut them into strips. Repeat the filling and folding process.
3. Place the puffs on a buttered baking pan and brush with melted butter. Bake until golden, about 20 minutes.

spanish tomato pie

This two-crusted pie has a spicy tomato-pepper filling. It is delicious served hot out of the oven, at room temperature, or even chilled. In fact, the flavors will improve if the pie sits overnight.

makes 6 servings

For the crust

3 cups all-purpose flour
1 teaspoon salt
⅓ cup butter or margarine
½ cup cold water or more as needed

For the filling

3 large red potatoes
1 tablespoon olive oil
1 large Spanish onion, chopped
3 red, yellow, or green bell peppers (or 1 of each), diced
6 large ripe tomatoes, seeded and chopped
1 jalapeño pepper, minced
2 garlic cloves, minced
½ teaspoon dried thyme
½ teaspoon salt
¼ teaspoon freshly ground black pepper
2 tablespoons minced fresh parsley
Egg white (optional)

Per serving: 456 calories • 10g protein • 14g fat • 74g carbohydrates • 0 cholesterol • 755mg sodium • 6g fiber

1. To make the pastry, combine the flour and salt in a large bowl. Cut in the margarine or butter with a pastry blender or 2 knives until the mixture resembles coarse crumbs. Alternately, pulse the mixture in a food processor. Stir in just enough ice water so that the mixture forms a ball and holds together. Flatten the dough into a disk, wrap in plastic wrap, and refrigerate for at least 1 hour.

2. Meanwhile, prepare the filling. Bring a large saucepan full of water to a boil. Add the potatoes and cook until tender, about 20 minutes. Drain and let cool. Cut the potatoes into ½-inch slices.

3. In a large skillet, heat the olive oil over medium-high heat. Add the onion and cook, stirring, for 5 minutes. Add the bell peppers, tomatoes, jalapeño, garlic, thyme, salt, and pepper. Cook over medium heat until the mixture is soft and thick, about 20 minutes. Stir in the parsley.

4. Preheat the oven to 375°F. Divide the dough in half and roll out each piece into a 9-inch circle. Fit one round of dough into a 9-inch deep-dish pie pan or cake pan. Spread on one-third of the vegetable sauce. Top the sauce with one-third of the potato slices. Repeat layering until all the sauce and potatoes are used. Cover the pie with the second pastry circle, crimp the edges to seal, and brush the top with the egg white if desired. Bake the pie for 35 minutes, or until golden brown. Serve hot, at room temperature, or chilled.

pipérade

This Basque specialty is popular on both sides of the rocky Pyrenees, in Spain and in France. It is a hearty baked omelette that can be served for either breakfast or lunch.

makes 4 servings
2 tablespoons olive oil
1 large Spanish onion, thinly sliced
1 red bell pepper, julienned
1 green bell pepper, julienned
2 large ripe tomatoes, seeded and chopped
¼ teaspoon dried marjoram
¼ teaspoon dried thyme
¼ teaspoon dried basil
¼ teaspoon salt
⅛ teaspoon freshly ground black pepper
6 large eggs

Per serving: 221 calories • 10g protein • 13g fat • 9g carbohydrates • 320mg cholesterol • 244mg sodium • 3g fiber

1. In a large, nonstick skillet, heat the olive oil. Add the onion and peppers and cook, stirring, over medium heat until soft, about 15 minutes. Add the tomatoes, herbs, salt, and pepper. Cook, stirring, for 15 more minutes, or until the vegetables are soft and saucelike.
2. Lightly beat the eggs and pour over the vegetables. Cover the pan and cook over medium-low heat until the eggs are set, about 10 minutes.
3. To serve, cut into wedges. Serve hot, at room temperature, or chilled.

spanish tortilla

A Spanish tortilla is not the flat circle of flour or cornmeal found in Mexican cuisine; instead, it's an omelet made with potatoes. This tapa originated in the central and northern region of Castile but is now available in bars all over Spain. Steaming the potatoes and onions produces a lighter dish than the traditional method of frying them in olive oil.

makes 4 servings

2 pounds potatoes, peeled and thinly sliced
   (about 6 cups)
2 large Spanish onions, thinly sliced
6 large eggs
½ teaspoon salt
1 to 2 teaspoon olive oil

Per serving: 362 calories • 15g protein • 9g fat
• 57g carbohydrates • 318mg cholesterol
• 400mg sodium • 6g fiber

1. Steam the potatoes and onions until tender but not mushy, about 10 minutes.
2. Meanwhile, in a bowl, beat the eggs with the salt.
3. Add the potatoes and onions to the eggs and fold to mix. Heat the olive oil in a heavy nonstick skillet. (More oil may be needed for other types of skillets.) Pour in the egg-and-potato mixture and cook over medium heat. When the bottom becomes crisp, 5 to 6 minutes, flip the omelet and cook until crisp on the other side, another 5 to 6 minutes. It's easier to flip the omelet if you slide it onto a plate, then turn it over into the pan.
4. To serve, cut the omelet into wedges. Serve hot, at room temperature, or chilled.

baked vegetable frittata

This baked, tofu-based Sicilian-style *frittata* is commonly served as part of a large antipasto. Consider it a crustless quiche—fancy, flavorful, and relatively low in fat. Sicilians even pack *fritattas*, which can be eaten hot or at room temperature, as a picnic food.

makes 6 servings

2 teaspoons olive oil
1 large onion, chopped
1 large leek, sliced
½ pound mushrooms, sliced (about 2⅓ cups)
6 ounces fresh Swiss chard
1 pound firm tofu
½ cup soy milk or low-fat milk
2 tablespoons arrowroot powder or cornstarch
1 tablespoon minced fresh basil
½ teaspoon freshly grated nutmeg
Salt and freshly ground black pepper to taste
1 small tomato, sliced
Mushroom slices, for garnish (optional)

Per serving: 170 calories • 13g protein • 6g fat
• 14g carbohydrates • 0 cholesterol • 227mg
sodium • 4g fiber

1. In a large skillet, heat the olive oil over medium-high heat. Cook the onion and leek until translucent, about 3 minutes. Add the mushrooms and continue to cook, stirring, until the vegetables are tender, about 5 minutes. Thoroughly wash, dry and chop the chard. Add to the skillet and cook until just wilted, about 4 minutes.
2. Preheat the oven to 350°F. In a food processor or blender, puree the tofu, soy milk, or low-fat milk, arrowroot or cornstarch, basil, and nutmeg. Combine with the cooked vegetables. Season with salt and pepper.
3. Pour the mixture into 6 lightly oiled individual soufflé dishes or a 9-inch quiche dish or round glass dish. Decorate the top with sliced tomatoes and a few extra slices of mushrooms if desired. Bake until puffed, golden brown, and firm to the touch, about 30 minutes for the individual soufflés and 40 minutes for the large one.

zucchini tiropetakia

Tiropetakia literally translates as "three feet" in Greek. It turns out that this triangular-shaped, flaky *mezze* pastry is aptly named. These party-perfect zucchini triangles can be made ahead of time, refrigerated or frozen, brought to room temperature, and reheated.

makes 24 triangles

2 medium zucchini, coarsely shredded

¼ teaspoon salt

½ pound crumbled feta cheese (about 1½ cups)

2 large egg whites

¼ teaspoon freshly grated lemon zest

¼ teaspoon freshly ground black pepper

⅛ teaspoon ground nutmeg

8 sheets frozen phyllo dough, thawed

¼ cup olive oil or olive oil cooking spray

Per triangle: 66 calories • 2g protein • 5g fat • 4g carbohydrates • 8mg cholesterol • 163mg sodium • 0 fiber

1. Preheat the oven to 375°F. Place the zucchini in a colander, sprinkle with ⅛ teaspoon of salt, and let drain for 30 minutes. Rinse the zucchini and squeeze it dry in a clean dish towel.

2. In a medium bowl, combine the zucchini, cheese, egg whites, lemon zest, black pepper, remaining ⅛ teaspoon salt, and nutmeg; mix well.

3. Stack the phyllo dough sheets on a work surface. Cut the sheets lengthwise into 3 strips, about 4½ inches wide by 16 inches long. Remove one strip at a time. (Keep the remaining phyllo covered with plastic wrap to prevent it from drying out.) Lightly brush or spray a strip with oil.

4. Place 1 heaping tablespoon of the zucchini mixture at the bottom of a phyllo strip. Roll up, folding left and right to form a triangle, using the whole strip of dough. Place the triangle on an ungreased cookie sheet. Repeat with the remaining phyllo strips and the zucchini mixture. Lightly brush or spray the tops of the triangles with olive oil.

5. Bake for 14 to 16 minutes or until the pastries are golden brown. Serve warm or at room temperature.

spinach pies with mint

The taste of these small pies is a surprise if you expect the familiar Greek cheese and spinach combination. The addition of mint gives them a refreshing boost of flavor.

makes 12 pies

For the dough

2 large eggs

1 cup milk

½ cup olive oil

1 teaspoon salt

3 cups all-purpose flour

For the filling

2 packages (10 ounces each) frozen chopped spinach, thawed and squeezed dry

¾ pound feta cheese, crumbled (about 2 cups)

¾ cup chopped fresh parsley

6 to 8 scallions, green part only, chopped

2 tablespoons chopped fresh mint

1 garlic clove, minced

Freshly ground black pepper to taste

For the topping

1 egg yolk for brushing crust

Sesame seeds

Per pie: 354 calories • 13g protein • 20g fat • 30g carbohydrates • 93mg cholesterol • 737mg sodium • 2g fiber

1. Preheat the oven to 350°F. To make the dough, place the eggs, milk, olive oil, salt, and 2 cups flour in the bowl of a food processor. Pulse, adding the remaining 1 cup of flour gradually, until the dough is smooth and no longer sticks to the sides of the bowl. Alternatively, mix the dough with a fork in a large bowl. Knead the dough by hand on a floured surface for 4 to 5 minutes more. Cover the dough with a dish towel and let rest until you have prepared the filling.
2. Mix all of the filling ingredients in a large bowl.
3. Separate the dough into 12 equal balls and roll each one out into a 6-inch circle. Place about 3 tablespoons filling in the middle of a circle and close the dough over, sealing it by pressing the edges with a fork. Repeat with each circle.
4. Brush the pies with beaten egg yolk and sprinkle with sesame seeds. Bake until lightly browned, about 20 minutes. Serve hot, warm, or at room temperature.

rapini frittata

Italian *frittatas* are made with eggs and any combination of vegetables that have been sautéed and lightly browned. This recipe calls for rapini (also known as broccoli rabe), an Italian favorite, and is just as satisfying as a main dish as when cut into smaller wedges in an antipasto. You may serve it just out of the oven, or bake it ahead and serve either cold or at room temperature.

If you can't get *ricotta salata*, a delectable, firm ricotta cheese, you can substitute a mild feta.

makes 8 servings

¾ pound rapini (broccoli rabe), trimmed and cut
  into 1-inch pieces
1 tablespoon olive oil
½ cup finely chopped onion
½ cup chopped red bell pepper
2 garlic cloves, minced
4 ounces *ricotta salata* or mild feta cheese,
  crumbled (about 1 cup)
⅓ cup wheat germ
Pinch of crushed red pepper flakes
6 large eggs

Per serving: 189 calories • 12g protein • 13g fat
• 7g carbohydrates • 187mg cholesterol •
414mg sodium • 2g fiber

1. Preheat the oven to 325°F.
2. Steam the rapini until crisp-tender, about 5 minutes. Remove from the heat.
3. In a large skillet, heat the olive oil over medium-high heat. Add the onion and bell pepper and cook, stirring often, until the vegetables are soft, about 5 minutes. Add the rapini and garlic and cook, stirring, for 2 minutes longer.
4. Transfer the vegetables to a large bowl and mix in the cheese, wheat germ, and crushed red pepper.
5. In a separate bowl, beat the eggs until blended. Stir the eggs into the vegetable mixture, then pour the egg mixture into a greased 12-inch quiche dish or round cake pan. Bake until the eggs are set, about 30 minutes. Serve hot, at room temperature, or cold.

zucchini and mozzarella frittata

This is a good brunch or dinner dish, and would work well as a buffet offering. Instead of flipping the *frittata*, you could cook it in an ovenproof skillet. When the underside is done, place the pan in the oven and cook the *frittata* under the broiler until the top is firm to the touch.

makes 6 servings

1½ tablespoons olive oil
1 medium onion, chopped
2 garlic cloves, minced
3 small zucchini, thinly sliced
Salt and freshly ground black pepper to taste
8 large eggs
1 tablespoon minced fresh basil leaves
½ cup shredded fresh mozzarella cheese
2 tablespoons bread crumbs
Lemon wedges

Per serving: 207 calories • 14g protein • 13g fat • 8g carbohydrates • 290mg cholesterol • 194mg sodium • 1g fiber

1. Heat 1 tablespoon of the olive oil in a 12-inch nonstick skillet over medium-high heat. Add the onion and garlic and cook, stirring, until soft, about 5 minutes. Add the zucchini and cook, stirring, until tender, about 5 minutes. Remove the pan from the heat and season with salt and pepper.

2. In a medium bowl, beat the eggs until blended. Stir in the cooked vegetables, basil, cheese, bread crumbs, and more salt and pepper.

3. Place the remaining ½ tablespoon oil in the pan and let it heat up for 15 seconds. Pour in the egg mixture. Cover and cook over medium heat, occasionally uncovering and gently lifting the sides of the *frittata* with a spatula to let the uncooked egg run under the cooked part to set. Continue cooking and lifting the sides until the center is nearly firm, 4 to 5 minutes.

4. Remove the pan from the heat and remove the lid. Cover the pan with a large round plate or pizza pan and carefully flip over the pan and plate together. Remove the pan from the plate and carefully slide the *frittata*, uncooked side down, back into the pan. Cook until the bottom turns golden brown, about 3 minutes. Slide the *frittata* onto a serving platter. Serve immediately, garnished with lemon wedges.

torta rustica

Tortas are Italian "cakes," either sweet or savory. This satisfying, rustic *torta* was originally devised as a way to use up leftovers. Here, a filling of wild mushrooms, Swiss chard, ricotta cheese, and roasted red bell peppers transforms it into a stunning and delicious main-course centerpiece. You can freeze this *torta* for up to one month, and reheat in a 325°F. oven for about 1½ hours.

makes 10 servings

For the pastry

2¼ cups all-purpose flour

½ teaspoon salt

¼ cup (½ stick) unsalted butter or margarine, chilled and cut into pieces

¼ cup vegetable shortening

6 to 7 tablespoons ice water

For the filling

2 tablespoons olive oil

1 cup chopped shallots or onion

2 pounds cremini mushrooms, coarsely chopped

2 pounds Swiss chard, washed, dried, and cut into 1-inch strips

5 garlic cloves, minced

2 tablespoons chopped fresh thyme

¾ teaspoon salt

½ teaspoon freshly ground black pepper

1 container (15 ounces) low-fat ricotta cheese (about 2 cups)

4 large egg whites

¼ teaspoon grated nutmeg

¼ teaspoon crushed red pepper flakes

1 jar (12 ounces) roasted red bell peppers, cut into strips

1 cup freshly grated Parmesan or Asiago cheese

¼ cup fresh Italian bread crumbs, toasted

Per serving: 353 calories • 18g protein • 17g fat • 34g carbohydrates • 14mg cholesterol • 708mg sodium • 5g fiber

1. To make the pastry, combine the flour and salt in a large bowl. Cut in the butter or margarine and shortening with a pastry blender or 2 knives until the mixture resembles coarse crumbs. (Alternatively, pulse everything together in a food processor.) Stir in just enough ice water so that the mixture forms a ball and holds together. Divide the dough in half, flatten each half into a disk, wrap in plastic, and chill while preparing the filling ingredients.

2. In a large skillet, heat the olive oil over medium heat. Add the shallots or onion and cook, stirring often, until soft, about 5 minutes. Add the mushrooms, chard, and garlic and cook, stirring often, until the mushrooms and chard release their liquid and it evaporates, about 10 minutes. Stir in the thyme, salt, and pepper. Remove from the heat and let cool to room temperature.

3. In a medium bowl, mix the ricotta cheese, 3 egg whites, nutmeg, and red pepper flakes until blended. Pat dry the roasted peppers with paper towels.

4. On a lightly floured surface, roll about two-thirds of the dough to a 12-inch circle. Line the pastry along the bottom and sides of a 9-inch springform pan with a removable bottom. Beat the remaining egg white and brush over the pastry, then sprinkle bread crumbs on top.

5. Stir ¼ cup Parmesan or Asiago cheese into the vegetable mixture and another ¼ cup cheese into the ricotta mix-

ture. Spoon the vegetable mixture into the pastry crust and pat it into an even layer. Spread the ricotta cheese mixture evenly over the vegetables. Arrange the roasted pepper strips over the ricotta mixture. Sprinkle the remaining ½ cup Parmesan or Asiago cheese evenly over the peppers.

6. Preheat the oven to 375°F. Roll out the remaining dough into a 10-inch circle. Cut slits attractively in the dough and place over the filling. Trim the edges and fold the top crust under, forming a ridge. Flute the edge attractively. If desired, reroll any pastry scraps, cut into various shapes, brush with cold water, and decorate the top of the pastry with them. (At this point, you can cover the *torta* with plastic wrap, then with foil, and freeze for up to 1 month. Let thaw in the refrigerator for 1 day before baking.)

7. Place the *torta* on a baking sheet. Bake until the crust is golden brown, about 50 minutes. Remove the sides of the pan and bake until the sides of the crust are golden, 10 to 15 minutes more. Transfer to a wire rack and let cool for 10 minutes. Transfer to a serving plate and cut into 10 wedges.

rosemary-scented vegetable phyllo tart

Elegant and sophisticated, this tart makes a showy centerpiece on the buffet table. Rosemary gives it an herbal Provençal flavor. The tart takes some time to make, but there's nothing tricky or complicated about it.

makes 15 servings

6 ounces sun-dried tomatoes (dry, not oil-packed)

2 packages (10 ounces each) chopped frozen spinach, thawed and squeezed dry

6 ounces fresh goat cheese

½ cup skim milk

¼ cup fresh rosemary (or 2 tablespoons dried)

4 scallions, trimmed and minced

3 garlic cloves, minced

1 teaspoon salt

1 teaspoon freshly ground black pepper

1 teaspoon olive oil

½ cup white wine

4 medium zucchini, sliced on the diagonal

2 medium onions, sliced

1 pound mushrooms, sliced

Olive oil spray (or more olive oil)

1 box (about 1 pound) phyllo pastry

8 roasted red peppers, patted dry and cut into long, thick strips (see page 63)

1 jar (14 ounces) marinated artichoke hearts, drained and chopped

¼ cup packed fresh basil leaves, slivered

½ cup pine nuts, toasted (see Note, page 153)

Sprigs of fresh rosemary, for garnish (optional)

Per serving: 281 calories • 11g protein • 9g fat • 37g carbohydrates • 27mg cholesterol • 652mg sodium • 6g fiber

1. Preheat the oven to 375°F. To reconstitute the tomatoes, cover them with boiling water and let sit until the tomatoes are pliable, 7 to 10 minutes. Drain the tomatoes, cut into slivers, and set aside.

2. In a food processor, puree together the spinach, cheese, milk, rosemary, scallions, garlic, salt, and pepper until smooth. If the mixture seems too dry to puree, add a bit more milk. Set aside.

3. In a large nonstick skillet, heat the olive oil over medium-high heat. Add the wine and heat to a simmer. Sauté the zucchini for 5 minutes, then drain on paper towels. Add the onions to the skillet and cook, stirring, for 5 minutes; transfer to paper towels to dry. Add the mushrooms to the skillet and cook, stirring, for 5 minutes; transfer to paper towels to dry.

4. Line a jelly roll pan or large deep-dish pizza pan with foil, leaving the ends of foil sticking up beyond the edge of the pan. Spray the foil with olive oil spray or brush with oil. To form the tart crust, lay down 1 sheet of phyllo and brush lightly or spray with olive oil. Fold down the edges of phyllo that extend beyond the pan. Lay down sheets of phyllo, spraying or brushing each with oil and folding down the edges, until the pan is covered and you've used up all the phyllo.

5. Spread the spinach mixture over the phyllo crust. Arrange the sautéed zucchini, onions, mushrooms,

roasted peppers, artichoke hearts, and sun-dried tomatoes over the spinach mixture and bake the tart for 15 minutes. If the edges of the crust are browning too quickly, reduce the oven heat to 325°F. and bake for 5 minutes more. If the crust is just beginning to turn golden, leave the oven temperature at 375°F. and bake for 5 minutes more, or until the phyllo is golden and crisp and the vegetables are hot.

6. Sprinkle the tart with the fresh basil and toasted pine nuts. Tuck the rosemary sprigs into the folded edges of the crust to garnish if desired, and serve immediately.

artichoke and fennel tart

This tart has an unusual multigrain crust. If you don't have time to roast red bell peppers, you can use the jarred kind.

makes 6 servings

For the crust

⅔ cup millet

1 cup short-grain brown rice

⅓ cup wild rice

3⅓ cups vegetable broth or water

Pinch of salt

For the topping

1 teaspoon yellow mustard seeds

2 teaspoons olive oil

2 medium fennel bulbs, trimmed and chopped (about 3 cups)

3 tablespoons minced fennel fronds

½ cup vegetable broth or water

2¼ cups roasted and diced red bell peppers (see page 63)

1 can (15 ounces) artichoke bottoms, drained, rinsed, and diced

1 tablespoon chopped thyme (or 1 teaspoon dried)

1 tablespoon chopped dill (or 1 teaspoon dried)

2 tablespoons capers, drained and chopped

1 pound firm tofu, drained

2½ tablespoons arrowroot powder or cornstarch

⅔ cup water

1½ tablespoons light miso

2 tablespoons fresh lemon juice

Salt and freshly ground white pepper to taste

Per serving: 296 calories • 15g protein • 9g fat • 37g carbohydrates • 0 cholesterol • 140mg sodium • 6g fiber

1. To make the crust, toast the millet in a heavy saucepan over moderate heat until browned. Add the brown rice, wild rice, broth or water, and salt and bring to a boil. Reduce the heat to low and simmer until the water is absorbed and the rice is very soft, about 50 minutes.

2. While the grains are simmering, warm the mustard seeds and 1 teaspoon of the oil in a large nonstick pan over moderate heat. Cover and cook until the seeds sputter and turn gray. Add the fennel and cook, stirring, for 2 to 3 minutes. Add ¼ cup of the broth or water and cook until it evaporates. Add the bell peppers, artichokes, thyme, dill, and remaining ¼ cup broth or water. Cook until the liquid evaporates. Sprinkle with the capers.

3. Preheat the oven to 375°F. Oil a 10-by-15-by-1-inch baking tray or line it with parchment. Spread the rice mixture evenly over the tray and pack it down with a spatula or spoon.

4. In a food processor, combine the tofu, arrowroot powder or cornstarch, water, miso, lemon juice, and remaining teaspoon oil and process until smooth. Add salt and pepper.

5. Pour the tofu mixture into the artichoke mixture and stir gently to combine. Spread the mixture evenly over the rice crust. Bake for 45 to 50 minutes, or until the topping is firm and browned. Cool 10 minutes before slicing.

leek and onion potato torte

Potatoes make a soft but sturdy base for this wonderful leek and onion pie.

makes 4 servings

For the crust

1 pound Yukon Gold or russet potatoes
  (about 2 large), cooked and mashed
1 large egg, lightly beaten
⅓ cup ricotta cheese
1 tablespoon whole wheat flour

For the filling

1 tablespoon olive oil
2 large leeks, white and light green part only,
  thinly sliced (about 3 cups)
3 medium onions, thinly sliced
Pinch of salt
1 cup skim milk
1 large egg yolk
1 large egg
1 tablespoon all-purpose flour
½ cup sour cream
2 tablespoons minced fresh chives

Per serving: 397 calories • 14g protein • 16g fat
• 52g carbohydrates • 181mg cholesterol
• 127mg sodium • 5g fiber

1. Preheat the oven to 450° F. In a large bowl, mix the mashed potatoes, beaten egg, ricotta cheese, and whole wheat flour until a dough forms. Press the dough into an 8-inch springform pan. Bake until firm but springy, about 20 minutes. Transfer the pan to a wire rack to cool. Leave oven on.
2. Meanwhile, heat the olive oil in a large skillet over medium-high heat. Add the leeks, onions, and salt and cook, stirring, until the vegetables are very soft, about 15 minutes. Set aside.
3. In a mixing bowl, beat together the milk, egg yolk, egg, and flour until smooth.
4. Spread the sour cream over the baked potato crust and sprinkle with chives. Arrange the leek mixture over the chives. Pour in the egg mixture and bake the *torte* until the filling is just set, about 50 minutes. Let rest for 10 minutes before serving.

caramelized onion tart

A variation of this golden tart is sold by the slice all across France, but particularly in the South. In this recipe, we use rich, nutty Swiss cheeses on top—either Gruyère or Emmentaler. You may serve this tart warm or at room temperature.

makes 6 servings

For the dough
½ cup warm water (105° to 115°F.)
½ packet rapid-rising yeast (about 1¼ teaspoons)
1½ cups all-purpose flour
1 teaspoon olive oil
½ teaspoon salt

For the topping
1 teaspoon olive oil
3 large onions, thinly sliced
½ teaspoon sugar
¼ teaspoon dried thyme
¼ teaspoon salt
⅛ teaspoon freshly ground black pepper
½ cup (2 ounces) shredded Gruyère or Emmentaler cheese
¼ cup (1 ounce) freshly grated Parmesan cheese
¼ cup good-quality black olives (optional)

Per serving: 227 calories • 9g protein • 6g fat • 35g carbohydrates • 13mg cholesterol • 389mg sodium • 3g fiber

1. Combine the warm water and yeast in a large bowl and let stand until bubbly, about 5 minutes. Add 1¼ cups of the flour, the olive oil, and salt to form a soft dough. Turn the dough out onto a lightly floured surface. Knead until smooth and elastic, about 5 minutes. Add enough of the remaining flour, 1 tablespoon at a time to prevent the dough from sticking to your hands. Place the dough in a bowl coated with cooking spray, turning the dough to coat with oil. Cover loosely with waxed paper or plastic wrap and let stand in a warm place free from drafts for 40 minutes, or until doubled in bulk.

2. Meanwhile, prepare the topping. Heat the olive oil in a large non-stick skillet over medium-high heat. Add the onions, cover, and cook for 5 minutes or until wilted. Stir well and reduce the heat to medium. Cover and continue to cook for 10 minutes, stirring occasionally. Sprinkle the onions with the sugar and thyme and increase the heat to medium-high. Cook, uncovered, stirring, for 2 minutes or until the onions are golden brown and tender. Stir in the salt and pepper.

3. Punch down the dough and transfer to a lightly floured surface. Press out the dough to a rectangle about 13 by 9 inches. Transfer the dough to a nonstick 15-by-10-inch jelly roll pan. Pinch up the outside edges of the dough on all sides forming a ¼-inch border. Arrange the onions over the dough and sprinkle with both cheeses and the olives if desired.

4. Preheat the oven to 375°F. Let the tart stand in a warm place until the dough rises slightly, about 15 minutes. Bake the tart for 20 to 25 minutes, or until the crust and cheese are golden brown. Cool slightly and cut into squares.

pumpkin flans with olive vinaigrette

Who said flan was just for dessert? These silken, savory flans have a northern African accent, and make a terrific summer luncheon dish or a light Sunday supper. They are best served chilled.

makes 6 servings

For the filling

1 cup solid-pack pumpkin

4 large eggs

4 ounces low-fat cream cheese (Neufchâtel)

½ cup small-curd cottage cheese

1 tablespoon chopped fresh cilantro

½ teaspoon ground coriander

Pinch each of cayenne pepper, ground cinnamon, ground ginger

For the vinaigrette

⅓ cup extra-virgin olive oil

2 tablespoons red wine vinegar

2 tablespoons black olive paste (or 3 tablespoons pitted good-quality black olives, whirled in a food processor)

1 tablespoon water

Salt and freshly ground black pepper to taste

3 cups mixed lettuce leaves

Per serving: 247 calories • 9g protein • 21g fat • 6g carbohydrates • 158mg cholesterol • 237mg sodium • 2g fiber

1. Preheat the oven to 325°F. In a blender or food processor, combine the filling ingredients and puree until smooth.

2. Lightly oil 6 ramekins or custard cups. Divide the pumpkin mixture among them. Set the ramekins in a large baking pan and pour hot water into the baking pan to reach halfway up the sides of the ramekins. Bake until the flans are set and a tester inserted into the center comes out clean, about 35 minutes. Let ramekins cool for 10 minutes, then chill in the refrigerator for at least 1 hour.

3. To make the vinaigrette, in a small bowl, whisk together the olive oil, vinegar, olive paste, water, salt, and pepper. Divide the lettuce equally among 6 plates. Run a thin-bladed knife along the inside of the ramekins to loosen the flans. Carefully unmold the flans onto the lettuce. Spoon the vinaigrette over the flans and lettuce and serve immediately.

asparagus tart

This delicious French tart is traditionally made with the tips of the wild asparagus that grow in the woods and among the olive trees in southern France. Try to use thin, tender asparagus that have firm stems and closed buds. Take this tart along on a picnic or serve it with a green salad for a complete meal. It also makes a great lunch or bridal shower dish.

makes 6 servings

½ pound pencil-thin asparagus, cut into 2-inch pieces
2 tablespoons unsalted butter
1 medium onion, thinly sliced
2 tablespoons all-purpose flour
2 large eggs, lightly beaten
1 cup small-curd cottage cheese
½ cup milk
½ cup grated Swiss cheese
¼ teaspoon nutmeg
½ teaspoon salt
¼ teaspoon freshly ground black pepper
1 frozen 9-inch deep-dish pie crust

Per serving: 317 calories • 11g protein • 19g fat • 22g carbohydrates • 105g cholesterol • 581mg sodium • 2g fiber

1. Preheat the oven to 425°F.
2. Bring a large saucepan of salted water to a boil. Add the asparagus and blanch until crisp-tender, 2 to 3 minutes. Drain and set aside.
3. In a medium skillet over medium heat, melt the butter. Add the onion and cook, stirring, until tender, 4 to 5 minutes. Sprinkle with flour, stir to coat, and transfer the mixture to a bowl. Add the eggs, cottage cheese, milk, Swiss cheese, nutmeg, salt, and pepper, and mix well. Mix in the asparagus. Pour the mixture into the pie crust. Bake until puffy and brown, about 40 minutes. Let stand 10 minutes before slicing. Serve hot or at room temperature.

chickpea b'stilla

B'stilla is a traditional Moroccan savory pastry made with chicken or pigeon and eggs, enclosed by layers of thin *warkha* pastry (which is even thinner and more delicate than phyllo). In this vegan version, chickpeas substitute for the chicken and crumbled tofu replaces the eggs.

makes 8 servings

4 tablespoons olive oil

8 scallions, trimmed and sliced

1 tablespoon ground cinnamon

1 tablespoon paprika

1 pound firm tofu, crumbled

2 cans (15 ounces each) chickpeas, rinsed, drained, and mashed

3 tablespoons chopped fresh cilantro

Salt and freshly ground black pepper to taste

1 cup slivered almonds, toasted (see Note, page 153)

9 sheets phyllo pastry

Per serving: 543 calories • 24g protein • 22g fat • 70g carbohydrates • 0 cholesterol • 671mg sodium • 12g fiber

1. Preheat the oven to 350°F. In a large skillet, heat 2 tablespoons of the olive oil over medium-low heat. Add the scallions, cinnamon, and paprika and cook, stirring, until the scallions are soft and the spices are aromatic, about 2 minutes, being careful not to burn the spices. Add the tofu and cook, stirring, for 5 minutes. Add the chickpeas, cilantro, and salt and pepper and mix well. Remove the pan from the heat and stir in the almonds.

2. Lightly brush a deep dish pie pan or 9-by-13-inch baking pan with oil. Lay 1 sheet phyllo in the pan and brush lightly with oil. Continue layering phyllo and brushing with oil, using 5 sheets total. Spread the chickpea mixture over the phyllo layers. Cover the mixture with 4 additional sheets of phyllo that have been lightly brushed with oil. Gently fold and tuck all layers of phyllo pastry over the filling and into the sides of the pan, securing under the filling.

3. Brush the top of the dish lightly with oil and score into 8 wedges with a sharp knife. Bake until the pastry is golden and crisp, about 20 minutes. Let cool for 10 minutes. To serve, cut into wedges along the score lines.

sardinian rice tart

Redolent of saffron, Italian parsley, and pecorino Romano cheese (sheep's milk Romano), this savory rice tart contains many of the flavors of Sardinia. If you can find sheep's milk ricotta, your tart will be even more authentic; otherwise, regular cow's milk ricotta works perfectly well. Serve this tart still warm from the oven as an entree, or cut it into small squares and pass it around as an hors d'oeuvre.

You can bake the crust (store at room temperature) and make the rice mixture (cover and refrigerate) up to a day in advance, but for the best result, finish preparing the tart just before serving.

makes 6 main-course servings, 24 as an hors d'oeuvre

For the crust

1¼ cups all-purpose flour

2 tablespoons freshly grated pecorino Romano cheese

Pinch of salt

¼ teaspoon freshly ground black pepper

½ cup (1 stick) unsalted butter

3 to 4 tablespoons ice water

For the filling

1 cup vegetable broth or water

Pinch of saffron

½ teaspoon salt

½ cup white rice, preferably short-grain

1 cup ricotta cheese

½ cup freshly grated pecorino Romano cheese

2 large eggs, lightly beaten

½ cup milk

2 tablespoons chopped fresh Italian parsley

Pinch of crushed red pepper flakes

Per main-course serving: 414 calories • 19g protein • 21g fat • 38g carbohydrates • 135mg cholesterol • 733mg sodium • 1g fiber

1. To make the pastry, combine the flour, Romano cheese, salt, and pepper in a large bowl. Cut in the butter with a pastry blender or 2 knives until the mixture resembles coarse crumbs. Alternatively, pulse the mixture in a food processor. Stir in just enough ice water so that the mixture forms a ball and holds together. Flatten the dough into a disk, wrap in plastic, and refrigerate for at least 1 hour.

2. Preheat the oven to 375°F. On a lightly floured surface, roll out the dough into an 11-inch circle. Fit the dough into a 10-inch tart pan with a removable bottom. Alternatively, roll the dough into a 10-by-14-inch rectangle and fit it into a 9-by-13-inch baking pan. Prick the pastry all over with a fork. Line the pan with foil and fill it with pie weights, dried beans, or rice. Bake the crust for 10 minutes, then remove the foil and weights and bake 10 minutes longer, until pale golden brown around the edges. Cool the crust while preparing the filling. Leave the oven on.

3. In a small saucepan, bring the vegetable broth or water, saffron, and salt to a boil. Add the rice and reduce the heat to low. Cover the pan and simmer until all the liquid is absorbed, 17 to 20 minutes.

4. Meanwhile, in a large bowl, mix the ricotta cheese, Romano cheese, eggs, milk, parsley, and crushed red pepper. Mix in the cooked rice. Spread the mixture in the crust and bake the tart until golden brown on top, 25 to 30 minutes. Cool the tart for 10 minutes before serving.

fresh tomato and orange tart

Fresh plum tomatoes and an orange-infused cheese filling makes this sunny tart a delight.

makes 8 appetizer servings

For the crust

1½ cups all-purpose flour

½ teaspoon salt

½ cup (1 stick) unsalted butter

4 to 5 tablespoons ice water

For the filling

8 ounces cream cheese

½ cup heavy cream

¼ cup fresh orange juice

1 large egg

2 tablespoons chopped fresh rosemary

1 tablespoon grated orange zest

1 teaspoon freshly grated lemon zest

1 garlic clove, minced

½ teaspoon freshly ground black pepper

½ teaspoon dried thyme

Salt to taste

For the topping

¼ cup packed basil leaves, slivered

5 ripe plum tomatoes, seeded and cut into ½-inch
cubes

1 tablespoon extra-virgin olive oil

Freshly ground black pepper to taste

Per serving: 326 calories • 6g protein • 24g fat
• 22g carbohydrates • 93mg cholesterol
• 252mg sodium • 1g fiber

1. To make the pastry, combine the flour and salt in a large bowl. Cut in the butter with a pastry blender or 2 knives until the mixture resembles coarse crumbs. Alternatively, pulse the mixture in a food processor. Stir in just enough ice water so that the mixture forms a ball and holds together. Flatten the dough into a disk, wrap in plastic wrap, and refrigerate for at least 1 hour.

2. Preheat the oven to 375°F. On a lightly floured surface, roll out the dough into a 10-inch circle. Fit the dough into a 9-inch tart pan with a removable bottom. Prick the pastry all over with a fork. Line the pan with foil and fill it with pie weights, dried beans, or rice. Bake the crust for 12 minutes, then remove the foil and weights and bake for 10 minutes longer, until pale golden brown around the edges. Cool the crust while preparing the filling. Leave the oven on.

3. In a food processor, combine all the filling ingredients. Pulse until well combined and smooth. Using a large spoon, place dollops of the filling over the crust. Spread the filling into one even layer.

4. Spread the basil over the filling, then top with the tomatoes and drizzle with the olive oil; sprinkle with pepper. Bake the tart until the filling is firm and the tomatoes are heated through, about 30 minutes. Let the tart rest 5 minutes before serving.

provençal mushroom tart

Duxelles is a sauce made from mushrooms that have been sautéed until they give up all their liquid and are reduced to a heady mushroom essence. Here, we flavor the duxelles with *herbes de Provence* and bake up a luscious cream-based tart. Serve it warm or at room temperature.

makes 6 servings

For the crust

1½ cups all-purpose flour
¼ cup freshly grated Parmesan cheese
½ cup (1 stick) unsalted butter
4 to 5 tablespoons ice water
1 tablespoon Dijon-style mustard

For the filling

1 tablespoon olive oil
½ cup minced shallots
10 ounces mushrooms, sliced
3 garlic cloves, minced
½ teaspoon *herbes de Provence*
Salt and freshly ground black pepper to taste
1 cup half-and-half
2 large eggs
2 tablespoons freshly grated Parmesan cheese

Per serving: 319 calories • 10g protein • 19g fat • 29g carbohydrates • 110mg cholesterol • 154mg sodium • 2g fiber

1. To make the pastry, combine the flour and cheese in a large bowl. Cut in the butter with a pastry blender or 2 knives until the mixture resembles coarse crumbs. Alternatively, pulse the mixture in a food processor. Stir in just enough ice water so that the mixture forms a ball and holds together. Flatten the dough into a disk, wrap in plastic, and refrigerate for at least 1 hour.

2. Preheat the oven to 375°F. On a lightly floured surface, roll out the dough into a 10-inch circle. Fit the dough into a 9-inch quiche or springform pan. Prick the pastry all over with a fork. Line the pan with foil and fill it with pie weights, dried beans, or rice. Bake the crust for 12 minutes, then remove the foil and weights and brush the mustard over the crust; bake for 5 minutes longer. Transfer the crust to a wire rack while preparing the filling. Leave the oven on.

3. Heat the olive oil in a large skillet over medium-high heat. Add the shallots and cook, stirring, for 5 minutes, until softened. Stir in the mushrooms, garlic, *herbes de Provence*, and salt and pepper. Cook, stirring, until the mushrooms give up all their liquid and are tender, about 15 minutes. Spread the mushrooms in the bottom of the crust.

4. In a large bowl, beat the half-and-half and eggs until smooth. Pour this over the mushrooms and sprinkle on the Parmesan cheese. Bake the tart until the custard is just set, about 25 minutes. Let the tart rest for 10 minutes before serving.

Pastas

Although the myth persists that pasta came to Italy from China, pasta was actually being boiled up in Italy long before Marco Polo's time. Of course, it continues to be an Italian favorite, and it's probably no surprise to learn that the Italians eat as much as sixty pounds of pasta per person per year! Italian pastas are made primarily from wheat, that bountiful and sustaining grain of the Mediterranean. Finely ground wheat flour is most common, followed by semolina, which is made from more coarsely ground wheat. There are literally hundreds of shapes and sizes of pasta, from flat strips of lasagna to skinny vermicelli, to tiny ear-shaped *orecchiette,* to cheese-filled ravioli. Pasta can also be made with any number of vegetables—such as spinach, tomato, and basil—that stain the noodles with vivid color and add a subtle taste. Unusually shaped or flavored pasta can be found in gourmet or Italian specialty shops and used in many of the recipes in this book. Pasta is as versatile as can be, and may be served as a first course, side dish, or with vegetables and/or beans as a main course. In Italy, vegetables are almost always an integral part of any pasta dish. Spinach, tomatoes, zucchini, and eggplant are only a few of the varieties you might find tangled in your strands of spaghetti.

In the Mediterranean region, pasta sauces are usually light and vegetable based, rather than rich and creamy, as they sometimes are in other parts of Italy. Italians always cook their pasta al dente, or until the pasta is cooked but still firm. And they adamantly refuse to smother their noodles in sauce, so that they can still taste the full flavor of the pasta itself. ■ None of this is to say that pasta is used exclusively in Italy, although among the Mediterranean countries only France, Greece, and Tunisia use it significantly, and then it's usually simmered in soups. France, bordering on Italy, has adopted some of its neighbor's ideas and serves pasta with its own version of pesto—*pistou*—or with a small amount of intense *tapenade* (olive paste). Chopped fresh herbs such as oregano and basil are often strewn on top of bowls of pasta before serving, along with a sprinkling of nutty, freshly grated real Parmesan cheese, which, incidentally, is imported from Italy. ■ In this chapter, many of the recipes are made with homemade pasta. While soft, fresh pasta is easy to make and delightful to eat, factory-made dried pasta also has its place, especially when paired with a robust, chunky sauce. While we've given directions for making pasta from scratch, it is also perfectly fine to buy fresh or dry pasta when time is tight. The important thing is to enjoy preparing these recipes as much as you will enjoy eating them.

fresh pasta dough

Making pasta dough may seem complicated, but with a little practice it's really very easy. Besides, store-bought pasta can't compare in taste or texture. We've provided instructions for making the dough with a food processor and by hand.

makes 6 servings, about 1 pound

About 3 cups unbleached all-purpose flour (see Note)

4 large eggs (or 1 cup egg substitute; or 1 cup hot water) (see Note)

Per serving: 248 calories • 10g protein • 4g fat • 43g carbohydrates • 110mg cholesterol • 36mg sodium • 2g fiber

To make the dough by hand

Pour the flour onto a flat surface, making a mound. Make a well in the center. Crack the eggs into the well and break the yolks with a fork. (Or pour in egg substitute or hot water.) With your fingers, begin drawing in a little bit of flour at a time and mixing it with eggs or water. When the mixture forms a paste, draw in all of the flour. Mix well and begin kneading. Knead for about 8 minutes, until you have a soft but not sticky ball of dough. Wrap the dough in a damp dishtowel and set aside. Go to step 2.

To make the dough in a food processor

1. Insert the metal blade in the processor. Add 1½ cups flour and 2 eggs or half of the egg substitute or water. Process until the dough forms a ball and cleans the sides of the bowl, about 1 minute. Then process for 2 minutes more to knead it. Remove the dough, wrap in a damp dishtowel, and set aside. Repeat the process with the remaining flour and eggs (or egg substitute or hot water). Go to step 2.

2. Remove a piece of dough appropriate for the recipe you are making (an egg-size piece for ravioli or *cappelletti*; a larger piece for tortellini, *tortellacci*, cannelloni, *agnolotti*, and shells). Keep the remaining dough covered with the dishtowel. Roll out the dough with a pasta machine or rolling pin. Cut into shapes needed for the dish you are making and add filling if necessary. Try to use up as much of the rolled-out pasta as possible the first time. (You can

collect the trimmings and roll them again, but rolling too many times toughens the dough.) Repeat with the remaining dough.

3. Bring a large pot of water to a rolling boil and add a large pinch of salt. Add fresh pasta and stir gently. It will begin bobbing to the surface after 1 to 2 minutes, indicating that it's almost ready. Stir and cook another 30 seconds or until it tastes done. Pasta should be served al dente. Do not let fresh pasta overcook, or it will stick together and become sloppy.

Note: The amount of flour you will need can vary greatly, depending on the size of your eggs, the batch your flour comes from, and even the weather. If the dough is wet or sticks to your hands rather than forming a soft ball, add 1 teaspoon of flour at a time, kneading between additions, until the dough reaches the right consistency. If the dough is dry and crumbly, add 1 teaspoon of water at a time, kneading between additions, until it reaches the right consistency.

If you use water instead of egg or egg substitute, the water should be hot but not boiling. Using water will make the dough somewhat stickier than the egg or egg substitute methods, so be extra careful about flouring the rolling pin, work surface, and your hands.

goat cheese and radicchio agnolotti

Agnolotti are simply Piedmont-style ravioli. Although most *agnolotti* today are stuffed with meat, traditionally they were filled with cheese and herbs. Sautéing the radicchio before placing it in these half-moon pasta packets lessens its slightly bitter edge.

You can serve the *agnolotti* with butter, basil, and Parmesan cheese, as directed in the recipe, or with the Herb Pesto on page 291.

makes 6 servings

2 heads radicchio
1 tablespoon olive oil
2 garlic cloves, minced
6 ounces fresh goat cheese, at room temperature
1 recipe Fresh Pasta Dough (page 143) or
  1 pound fresh lasagna sheets
3 tablespoons unsalted butter (optional)
1 cup freshly grated Parmesan cheese (optional)
Shredded fresh basil (optional)
Freshly ground black pepper (optional)

Per serving without sauce: 357 calories

- 13g protein • 13g fat • 45g carbohydrates
- 135mg cholesterol • 155mg sodium • 2g fiber

1. Wash and dry the radicchio. Discard the thick white stems and shred or thinly slice the reddish leaves.
2. In a large skillet, heat the olive oil over medium heat. Cook the radicchio and garlic until the radicchio is wilted, about 4 minutes. Transfer the vegetables to a bowl and add the cheese; mix well.
3. With a pasta machine set on 6 or a rolling pin, roll out a sheet of pasta dough. (You don't need to roll out the pasta if using premade fresh lasagna sheets.) Use a cookie cutter or juice glass to cut the dough into circles about 2½ inches in diameter. Place ¾ teaspoon of filling about ½ inch from the edge of each circle. Fold each circle in half and seal the edges carefully, pressing out the air. Transfer to a floured plate. Repeat with the remaining dough and filling.
4. Bring a large pot of salted water to a boil. Add the pasta and cook until al dente, about 3 minutes. Drain well and serve with butter, Parmesan cheese, basil, and black pepper to taste, if desired.

potato and fennel cappelletti

Their name literally meaning "little hats," these tiny parcels resemble miniature three-corner hats said to be modeled after the headgear of seventeenth-century Spanish invaders. Regardless, they're a perfect autumn dish, filled with fennel, potatoes, and onion.

makes 6 servings

2 medium potatoes, peeled and quartered
1 fennel bulb, trimmed and cut into eighths, fronds
 reserved
1 small white onion, quartered
½ teaspoon salt
1 recipe Fresh Pasta Dough (page 143) or
 1 pound fresh lasagna sheets
Tangy Sun-Dried Tomato Pesto (page 289)

Per serving with ½ cup sauce: 431 calories • 19g protein • 4g fat • 83g carbohydrates • 110mg cholesterol • 800mg sodium • 10g fiber

1. Bring a large pot of water to a boil. Add the potatoes, fennel, and onion and let the water return to a boil. Reduce the heat and simmer until the vegetables can be pierced easily with a fork, 25 to 30 minutes. Drain and allow to cool slightly.

2. Place the vegetables in a large bowl and mash with a fork. Chop the fennel fronds and add to the mixture. Add salt to taste.

3. With a pasta machine set on 7 or a rolling pin, roll an egg-size ball of pasta dough into a rectangle and cut into strips about 2 inches wide and 12 inches long. (You don't need to roll out the pasta if using premade fresh lasagna sheets.) Place 1 strip on a floured surface, and cut it into rectangles approximately 2 inches by 1½ inches. Place ½ teaspoon of filling about ½ inch from a short end of each rectangle. Fold the rectangle in half and press the edges together. Then pick up the rectangle with your index finger and thumb, holding the folded edge up. Pull the 2 folded corners together around your index finger, press together to seal, then flip up the rim. Transfer to a floured plate. Repeat with the remaining dough and filling.

4. Bring a large pot of salted water to a boil. Add the pasta and cook until al dente, about 3 minutes. Drain well and serve with the tomato pesto.

carrot and leek tortellacci

Tortellacci means "big, bad tortellini." These larger pasta packets hold twice as much filling as regular tortellini. Instead of adding a sauce, boil and serve the *tortellacci* in vegetable broth, garnished with basil, mint, and Parmesan cheese.

makes 6 servings

2 teaspoons olive oil
10 small carrots, peeled and cut into matchsticks
4 leeks, white part only, cut into matchsticks
1 shallot, minced
Salt and freshly ground black pepper to taste
1 recipe Fresh Pasta Dough (page 143) or
　1 pound fresh lasagna sheets
2 quarts vegetable broth (optional)
⅓ cup freshly grated Parmesan cheese (optional)
Shredded basil and mint (optional)

Per serving without sauce: 367 calories • 12g protein • 5g fat • 67g carbohydrates • 110mg cholesterol • 272mg sodium • 7g fiber

1. In a large skillet, heat the olive oil over medium heat. Add the carrots, leeks, and shallot and cook, stirring, for 2 minutes. Add enough water to cover the vegetables and braise over medium heat until tender, about 15 minutes. Stir occasionally and add water as needed to keep the skillet from boiling dry. Drain the vegetables in a colander and let cool to room temperature. Season with salt and pepper.
2. With a pasta machine set on 6 or a rolling pin, roll out a sheet of pasta dough. (You don't need to roll out the pasta if using premade fresh lasagna sheets.) Use a cookie cutter or juice glass to cut the dough into circles about 2½ inches in diameter. Place a teaspoon of filling in the center of half of the pasta circles. Top each with a second circle and seal the edges, pressing out any air. Transfer to a floured plate. Repeat with the remaining dough and filling.
3. Bring the broth or a large pot of salted water to a boil. Add the pasta and cook until al dente, about 3 minutes. Serve the pasta in the broth, if using, garnished with the cheese and herbs.

stuffed shells

This is a lighter version of the traditionally hearty Italian dish. To make peeling fresh tomatoes less of a hassle, first cut a small "x" in the bottom of each one. Immerse tomatoes in boiling water for 1 minute, then plunge into ice water and peel with a paring knife.

makes 6 servings

For the sauce

12 ripe plum tomatoes, peeled (or a 28-ounce can whole peeled tomatoes)

1 tablespoon olive oil

2 garlic cloves, minced

Salt and freshly ground black pepper to taste

For the filling and pasta

2 cups part-skim ricotta cheese

⅓ cup freshly grated Parmesan cheese

1 cup diced part-skim mozzarella cheese

⅓ cup chopped fresh Italian parsley

Pinch of ground nutmeg

1 recipe Fresh Pasta Dough (page 143) or a 12-ounce box large pasta shells

Per serving: 412 calories • 23g protein • 12g fat • 53g carbohydrates • 138mg cholesterol • 394mg sodium • 3g fiber

1. To make the sauce, if using fresh tomatoes, remove and discard the seeds, and chop tomatoes coarsely. If using canned tomatoes, chop finely and reserve the liquid.

2. In a large skillet, heat the olive oil over medium-high heat. Add the garlic and cook, stirring, for 1 minute, then add the tomatoes and tomato liquid. Simmer the mixture, uncovered, stirring occasionally, for 20 to 25 minutes. Season with salt and pepper.

3. Preheat the oven to 350°F. To make the filling, combine the cheeses, parsley, and nutmeg in a bowl and mix well. Set aside.

4. If using fresh pasta, use a pasta machine set on 6 or a rolling pin to roll out the dough. Cut the dough sheets into 5-inch squares.

5. Bring a large pot of salted water to a boil and cook the squares of fresh pasta until al dente, about 2 minutes. Drain well.

6. Meanwhile, spread a little bit of sauce on the bottom of a 9-by-13-inch baking pan. When the pasta is done, drain and allow it to cool slightly, then place a square of pasta in your palm and spoon in about 2 teaspoons of the filling. Fold the pasta over slightly without sealing the filling and tuck it into a corner of the pan. Repeat with the remaining squares and filling, placing the shells in the pan until it is full and all of the ingredients are used up. (This placement will keep the dough in a "shell" shape.) Spread the remaining sauce on top, cover with aluminum foil, and bake for 30 minutes. (If using dry shells, cook them in boiling salted water according to the package directions until al dente. Drain and allow to cool slightly. Fill the shells each with 2 teaspoons of the filling, add the sauce and bake as directed.)

pasta and navy beans in tomato sauce

This hearty and economical dish was inspired by *cannolicchi e fagioli,* a pasta and bean combination that is popular in Italy. If you cannot find the short pipe-shaped *cannolicchi pasta,* use the more common penne (tubes).

To make the requisite 2 cups cooked navy beans, bring 1 cup dried navy beans and 4 cups water to a boil. Turn off the heat, cover, and let the beans soak for 1 hour or longer. Return to a boil and simmer, covered, until the beans are tender but not mushy, about 20 minutes. Drain.

makes 5 servings

¾ pound *cannolicchi* or penne pasta
2 tablespoons olive oil
3 garlic cloves, slivered (or to taste)
3 ripe plum tomatoes (or 1 large tomato), seeded and chopped
2 cups jarred tomato sauce
¼ cup water
1 tablespoon chopped fresh parsley, plus extra for garnishing
2 teaspoons dried oregano
2 teaspoon dried basil
2 cups broccoli florets
2 cups cooked dried navy beans (or drained and rinsed canned navy beans)
¼ cup slivered black olives
Salt and freshly ground black pepper to taste

Per serving: 580 calories • 20g protein • 15g fat • 94g carbohydrates • 0 cholesterol • 1151mg sodium • 12g fiber

1. Cook the pasta according to the package directions until al dente. Drain well and reserve.
2. In a large pot, heat the olive oil over medium-high heat. Add the garlic and cook, stirring, until lightly browned, about 2 minutes. Stir in the tomatoes, tomato sauce, water, parsley, oregano, and basil. Cook, uncovered, over medium heat, mashing the tomatoes with a spoon.
3. When the sauce thickens, about 10 minutes, add the broccoli. Simmer, covered, until the broccoli is tender but still crunchy, about 5 minutes. Add the beans and olives and mix well. Simmer, covered, until heated through. Stir in the pasta. Add salt and pepper, sprinkle with parsley to garnish, and serve.

artichoke cannelloni with lemon béchamel

In existence for at least the past 800 years, this indispensable Mediterranean sauce got its current name from Louis de Béchameil, majordomo to Louis XIV. In this dish, the sauce combines with the savory flavor of artichokes and fresh mint, which fill these pasta tubes. If you are using canned artichoke hearts, select those that are not marinated. Make sure to prepare the béchamel at the last minute because it becomes lumpy as it sits.

makes 6 servings

2 lemons

24 baby artichokes (or 24 canned artichoke hearts)

1 recipe Fresh Pasta Dough (page 143) or an 8-ounce package cannelloni

1½ cups diced fresh mozzarella cheese

1 tablespoons chopped fresh mint or basil

1 teaspoon salt

1 cup milk or soy milk

2 tablespoons unsalted butter or margarine

1½ tablespoons all-purpose flour

¼ cup freshly grated Parmesan cheese (optional)

Per serving: 466 calories • 21g protein • 11g fat • 71g carbohydrates • 131mg cholesterol • 531mg sodium • 10g fiber

1. If using fresh artichokes, fill a large bowl with cold water and squeeze the juice of ½ lemon into it. Reserve the squeezed lemon half. Peel away the hard green leaves from each artichoke and slice off the tip of each stem. Cut away the yellow leaves as close to the base as possible, then skin the base and the stem, removing the tough, green outside layer. Cut each artichoke in half and rub the squeezed lemon half over all surfaces. Remove the fuzzy "choke" (center part) with the tip of a knife and discard. Drop the artichokes into the bowl of water.

2. After all the artichokes have been trimmed, drain them, rinse, and place in a pan with enough water to cover. Bring to a boil, then reduce the heat to medium and simmer, covered, until tender, about 12 minutes. Drain and set aside. If using canned artichoke hearts, simply drain thoroughly and set aside.

3. If using fresh pasta, roll out the dough using a pasta machine set on 6 or a rolling pin. Cut the pasta sheets into 5-by-8-inch rectangles. Cook fresh or dry pasta in a large pot of boiling salted water until al dente (about 2 minutes for the fresh pasta; follow package directions for the dry). Drain thoroughly and reserve.

4. Dice the artichokes and combine with the mozzarella. Stir in the mint or basil and ½ teaspoon of the salt.

5. Peel the rind from the uncut lemon, being careful to keep it in one or two large pieces; set the peel aside. Juice this lemon and the remaining ½ lemon; set the juice aside.

6. When the artichoke mixture and pasta are ready, pour the milk into a small pot and add the lemon rind and remaining ½ teaspoon salt. Heat until the milk comes to a simmer, then remove the lemon rind and turn off the heat. In a separate pan, melt the butter or margarine over low heat and whisk in the flour, 1 teaspoon at a time, stirring constantly. When all the flour has been added, continue to cook and stir constantly for 2 minutes. Turn off the heat and slowly add the hot milk, still stirring constantly. Add the lemon juice and reduce the heat to low. Cook, stirring, for 2 minutes, or until the sauce thickens slightly.

7. Preheat the oven to 400°F. Spread a little sauce on the bottom of a 9-by-13-inch baking pan. If using fresh pasta, roll each rectangle around a portion of the artichoke mixture and place in the pan, seam side down. If using packaged cannelloni, stuff each piece with the artichoke mixture and place in the pan. Spread the remaining sauce over the top of the pasta and sprinkle with Parmesan cheese if desired. Cover the pan with aluminum foil and bake for 15 minutes. Uncover and bake for 5 minutes longer, until bubbling and golden on top. Serve immediately.

ravioli with mixed greens

Traditionally, these stuffed square pasta morsels are filled with spinach and ricotta cheese, and served with a light sauce of butter and fresh sage or other herbs. Here, they are stuffed with a zesty combination of bitter and nonbitter greens: rapini and spinach.

Some variations for you to try are using 6 cups of spinach and no rapini; or you can try it with various other types of greens, as long as you don't exceed a 1-to-2 ratio of bitter green (such as collard or mustard greens) to nonbitter greens (such as spinach or Swiss chard).

makes 6 servings

4 cups lightly packed fresh spinach leaves
2 cups lightly packed rapini (broccoli rabe) leaves
¼ cup freshly grated Parmesan cheese (optional)
¼ teaspoon ground nutmeg
Salt and freshly ground black pepper to taste
1 recipe Fresh Pasta Dough (page 143) or
   1 pound fresh lasagna sheets

For the garlic oil (optional)

½ cup extra-virgin olive oil
4 garlic cloves, thinly sliced
Salt and freshly ground black pepper to taste

Per serving without garlic oil: 268 calories • 12g protein • 4g fat • 46g carbohydrates • 110mg cholesterol • 164mg sodium • 4g fiber

1. Rinse the greens, but don't dry them. Place the greens in a dry skillet, cover, and steam them without any additional water until wilted, about 5 minutes. When the greens have cooked, squeeze out as much water as possible and chop into small pieces. Mix with the Parmesan, if desired, and nutmeg; season with salt and pepper.

2. With a pasta machine set on 6 or a rolling pin, roll an egg-size ball of pasta dough into a rectangle or circle and cut into strips about 2 by 12 inches. (If using premade fresh pasta, you don't need to roll it out.) Place one strip on a floured surface, and dot it with single teaspoonfuls of greens about 1 inch apart from each other. Place a second strip of pasta on top. Press down around the portions of filling (forcing out any air), then cut into squares with a knife or pastry crimper. Press the edges together a second time to be sure they stick. Transfer to a floured plate. Repeat with the remaining dough and filling.

3. To make the garlic oil, if using, in a large skillet, heat the olive oil over medium-low heat. Add the garlic and cook, stirring, until it turns golden brown around the edges, about 3 minutes. Turn off the heat and add salt and pepper.

4. Bring a large pot of salted water to a boil and cook the ravioli until al dente, about 3 minutes. Drain well and serve with garlic oil or sauce of choice.

herb and walnut ravioli

The filling in these delicate ravioli is like a cheeseless version of pesto. They are delicious served with your favorite tomato sauce, or with the Spinach and Sun-Dried Tomato Pasta Sauce on page 293.

page 293

makes 6 servings

3 cups lightly packed fresh basil, chopped

3 cups lightly packed fresh Italian parsley, chopped

1 garlic clove

1 cup walnuts, toasted (see Note)

Salt and freshly ground black pepper to taste

1 recipe Fresh Pasta Dough (page 143) or
   1 pound fresh lasagna sheets

Per serving without sauce: 411 calories • 15g protein • 9g fat • 54g carbohydrates • 110mg cholesterol • 139mg sodium • 4g fiber

Note: To toast nuts, preheat the oven to 350°F. Spread the nuts out on a baking tray and toast them in the oven until golden brown, about 8 minutes. For pine nuts, toast 5 minutes. Transfer the pan to a wire rack to cool.

1. Place the basil, parsley, and garlic in a food processor and pulse until finely chopped. Add the toasted nuts and pulse until the nuts are finely chopped. Season with salt and pepper.

2. With a pasta machine set on 7 or a rolling pin, roll an egg-size ball of pasta dough into a rectangle or circle and cut into strips about 2 by 12 inches. (If using premade fresh pasta, you don't need to roll it out.) Place one strip on a floured surface, and dot with single teaspoonfuls of filling about 1 inch apart from each other. Place a second strip of pasta on top. Press down around the portions of filling (forcing out the air), then cut into squares with a knife or pastry crimper. Press the edges together a second time to be sure they stick, then transfer to a floured plate. Repeat with the remaining dough and filling.

3. Bring a large pot of salted water to a boil and cook the ravioli until al dente, about 3 minutes. Drain well and serve with a sauce of choice.

whole wheat lasagna with fresh spinach, ricotta, and olives

Laganon, a flat Greek cake that was served cut into strips, is probably lasagna's ancient ancestor. Whole wheat lasagna has a nutty taste that stands up to the assertive flavor of chopped Greek Kalamata olives. If time is a factor, use frozen chopped spinach instead of fresh and skip the steaming step. If you're not an olive fan, substitute sautéed diced red onions.

For a vegan version, you may substitute firm tofu pureed in a blender or food processor for the ricotta, and mozzarella-style soy cheese for the dairy cheese.

makes 10 servings

2 teaspoons olive oil

2 packaged (10 ounces each) prewashed ready-to-eat salad spinach (about 10 cups)

1 container (15 ounces) ricotta cheese (about 2 cups)

½ cup chopped Kalamata olives

½ teaspoon freshly grated nutmeg

½ teaspoon freshly ground black pepper

1 pound mushrooms, finely chopped (about 4 cups)

Salt to taste

4 cups homemade or prepared tomato sauce

16 whole wheat lasagna noodles

3 cups grated mozzarella cheese

Per serving: 354 calories • 27g protein • 9g fat
• 45g carbohydrates • 17mg cholesterol
• 795mg sodium • 9g fiber

1. Preheat the oven to 350°F. In a large nonstick skillet, heat 1 teaspoon of the olive oil over medium heat. Add the spinach in batches and steam until just wilted (sprinkle water in the pan if needed for moisture). Transfer the cooked spinach to a colander to drain. After all of the spinach is cooked and cool enough to handle, squeeze dry. Roughly chop and return the spinach to the colander to continue draining.

2. Meanwhile, in a medium bowl, mix the ricotta, olives, nutmeg, and pepper. Set aside.

3. Heat the remaining teaspoon oil in the skillet over medium-high heat and cook the mushrooms, stirring, until they give up their liquid and the pan is dry, about 8 minutes. Season with salt and set aside.

4. In a lightly oiled, 9-by-14-by-2-inch deep baking dish, spoon just enough sauce, tilting the sides, to cover the bottom. Fit 4 uncooked lasagna noodles in the bottom of the baking dish and spread with a third of the ricotta-olive mixture. Layer on a third of the spinach, a third of the mushrooms, a quarter of the mozzarella, and a quarter of the sauce. Repeat 2 more layers using ricotta, spinach, mushrooms, mozzarella, and sauce. End with 4 noodles

topped with the remaining sauce spread completely to the edges of the noodles. Sprinkle the sauce with the remaining mozzarella.

5. Lightly oil a 16-inch length of aluminum foil. Cover the pan with the foil, oiled side down, so that it makes a tent above the lasagna surface. Crimp foil around all edges of the pan to seal. Bake for 50 minutes. Using tongs, remove the foil and discard. Using a bulb baster or a spoon, baste the top of the lasagna with sauce from both ends of the pan. Bake for an additional 20 to 30 minutes, until the noodles are tender and the sauce is bubbling. Remove from the oven and let the lasagna cool for 15 minutes. Slice into 10 equal pieces using a serrated knife and serve immediately.

rolled tofu lasagna

By stuffing each lasagna noodle and rolling it in a spiral, you will have an attractive, easy-to-serve entree for a dinner party. Smoked mozzarella provides full-bodied flavor, but regular mozzarella or soy mozzarella can also be used. For another tofu variation, place cooked elbow macaroni or penne pasta in an oiled ovenproof casserole dish and top with tomato sauce, tofu filling, and cheese. Bake until hot, bubbly, and golden, about 35 minutes.

makes 8 rolls

8 lasagna noodles
1 recipe Tofu "Ricotta" Filling (page 295)
1 cup shredded smoked mozzarella, regular mozzarella, or soy mozzarella
4 cups homemade or prepared tomato sauce

Per roll: 303 calories • 12g protein • 17g fat • 26g carbohydrates • 8mg cholesterol • 489mg sodium • 3g fiber

1. Preheat the oven to 350°F. Bring a large pot of salted water to a boil, then add the noodles. Boil until pliable but still firm, about 6 minutes. Drain the noodles and rinse with cold water to stop the cooking. Lay the noodles out on clean dish towels.

2. Divide the tofu mixture among the noodles and spread evenly over the top. Sprinkle each noodle with 2 tablespoons mozzarella. Roll each noodle into a jelly roll shape, being careful to keep the filling in place.

3. Pour 2 cups of tomato sauce in the bottom of a 9-inch square baking pan. Arrange the rolls in the pan so that the spirals are visible, and drizzle with the remaining sauce. Cover the top of the pan with aluminum foil and bake for 45 minutes. Remove the foil and sprinkle on the remaining mozzarella. Bake until golden and bubbly, about 10 minutes.

perfect pastitsio

This big pasta casserole makes a great party dish, and leftovers can be reheated and eaten a day or two later. We've also included a dairy-free, vegan version.

Greek *kefalotiri* is a hard, tangy yellow cheese riddled with tiny holes. Its name literally translates as "head cheese," but only because it is sold in head-shaped lumps. It is usually grated over pasta dishes, or fried and eaten hot. If you can find *kefalotiri* cheese, use it for the most authentic flavor, but if not, Parmesan makes a fine substitute.

makes 10 servings

1 tablespoon olive oil
1 large onion, minced
2 rolls (14 ounces each) meatless beef substitute
½ cup canned tomato sauce
½ cup dry red wine
½ teaspoon ground cinnamon
⅛ teaspoon ground nutmeg or allspice
Salt and freshly ground black pepper to taste
1 pound ziti or elbow macaroni
5 cups milk
5 tablespoons cornstarch
¼ cup water
1 cup freshly grated *kefalotiri* or Parmesan cheese
3 large eggs

Per serving: 365 calories • 26g protein • 5g fat • 40g carbohydrates • 72mg cholesterol • 734mg sodium • 4g fiber

1. Preheat the oven to 350°F. In a large skillet, heat the olive oil over medium-high heat. Add the onion and cook, stirring, until golden brown, about 7 minutes. Add the beef substitute, chopping with a spatula into small bits. Cook until browned, about 5 minutes. Add the tomato sauce, red wine, and spices, stirring to mix. Simmer, uncovered, until the excess moisture has evaporated, about 7 minutes. Season with salt and pepper.

2. Meanwhile, cook the pasta according to the package directions until al dente. Drain and set aside.

3. In a large saucepan, bring the milk to a boil over high heat, then reduce the heat to medium. Dissolve the cornstarch in the water, then add it to the milk in a thin stream, whisking constantly to avoid lumps. Cook, whisking, until the mixture has returned to a boil and is thickened, 2 to 3 minutes. Remove the pan from the heat and stir in ¾ cup of the cheese.

4. In a separate bowl, beat the eggs until light and very frothy. Add to the cheese sauce in a thin stream, whisking constantly. Add salt and pepper to taste. In a large bowl, mix the cheese-egg sauce with the cooked pasta.

5. Lightly oil an 11-by-15-by-2-inch ovenproof casserole dish. Spoon in half of the pasta mixture. Top the pasta

layer with the cheese-egg mixture, then top with the remaining pasta mixture. Sprinkle with the remaining ¼ cup cheese. Bake until the casserole is golden brown and bubbling, about 40 minutes. Let the casserole cool for a few minutes. Slice into 10 rectangles and serve.

Variation: Replace steps 3 and 4 with these directions for a dairy-free sauce:

3. Puree two 10½-ounce packages firm tofu with 2 cups water in a blender or food processor until smooth. (You may have to puree in 2 batches if your processor is small.)

4. Place the mixture in a large saucepan. Add ½ teaspoon salt and ½ teaspoon black pepper. Bring to a boil, stirring constantly, then reduce the heat. Dissolve ¼ cup cornstarch in ¼ cup water. Add it to the tofu mixture in a thin stream, whisking constantly. Cook, whisking, until thickened. Remove from the heat. Add 1 cup grated Parmesan-style soy cheese. Whisk to mix. Proceed with the recipe above, using tofu sauce instead of cheese-egg sauce.

radiatore provençal

The fresh, summertime vegetables in this vivid dish—tomatoes, eggplant, and bell peppers—evoke all the delectable flavors of southern France. Instead of *radiatore* (radiator-shaped) pastas, fusilli or penne pasta would also be good with the chunky sauce.

makes 6 servings

1 pound dried *radiatore* pasta
2 tablespoons olive oil
1 large onion, chopped
1 large green or yellow bell pepper, chopped
2 garlic cloves, minced
1 small eggplant, unpeeled, cut into 1-inch cubes
1 pound ripe plum tomatoes (about 5 medium), chopped
Salt and freshly ground black pepper to taste
¼ cup shredded basil leaves
Sautéed Garlic Crumbs (page 296) (optional)
Freshly grated Parmesan cheese, or Parmesan-style soy cheese (optional)

Per 2-cup serving: 291 calories • 8g protein • 6g fat • 53g carbohydrates • 0 cholesterol • 398mg sodium • 6g fiber

1. Cook the pasta according to package directions until al dente.
2. Meanwhile, in large skillet, heat the olive oil over medium heat. Add the onion, bell pepper, and garlic and cook, stirring often, until soft, about 5 minutes. Add the eggplant and tomatoes and cook, stirring often, until the vegetables are tender and the tomatoes release their juices, about 20 minutes. Season with salt and pepper.
3. Drain the pasta, reserving ½ cup pasta water. Transfer the pasta to a serving bowl. Add the vegetables to the pasta.
4. Add the reserved pasta water to the skillet and cook over high heat, stirring, until reduced slightly. Add it to the pasta and vegetables and toss to combine. Serve the pasta topped with the basil and garlic crumbs, grated Parmesan, or soy cheese, if desired.

whole wheat spaghetti with spinach and feta cheese

Whole wheat pasta and spinach are a great pair. Add feta cheese for its saline richness and you've a meal fit for the best of company. For a vegan version, use oat milk and substitute feta with 1 cup of well-drained, well-pressed, crumbled firm tofu that has been sautéed over high heat with garlic in olive oil.

makes 6 servings

1 pound dried whole wheat spaghetti
1 bag (10 ounces) prewashed, ready-to-eat
   spinach leaves
1 tablespoon olive oil
1 medium onion, finely chopped
2 garlic cloves, minced
1 tablespoon all-purpose flour
1 cup goat's milk, cow's milk, or oat milk
½ teaspoon salt
¼ teaspoon freshly ground white pepper
¼ teaspoon grated nutmeg
1 cup crumbled feta cheese
¼ cup minced fresh dill
Sautéed Garlic Crumbs (page 296) (optional)
Freshly grated Parmesan cheese or Parmesan-
   style soy cheese (optional)

Per ¾-cup serving: 417 calories • 19g protein
• 14g fat • 58g carbohydrates • 42mg cholesterol • 118mg sodium • 10g fiber

1. Bring a large pot of salted water to a boil. Add the pasta and cook until it is al dente, stirring occasionally, about 11 minutes. Stir in the spinach during the last 2 minutes of cooking.

2. Meanwhile, in a medium saucepan, heat the olive oil over medium heat. Add the onion and garlic and cook, stirring often, until the vegetables are soft, about 3 minutes. Add the flour and cook, stirring constantly, for 2 minutes. Remove from the heat. Add the milk all at once. Return to medium heat and cook, stirring constantly, until the sauce begins to boil, 5 to 6 minutes. Remove from the heat and stir in the salt, pepper, and nutmeg.

3. Drain the pasta and spinach and transfer to a serving bowl. Add the sauce, crumbled cheese, and dill and toss to mix. Serve with Sautéed Garlic Crumbs, Parmesan, or Parmesan-style soy cheese, if desired.

penne niçoise

All the vibrant tastes of the traditional French *salade Niçoise* are here in this fish-free vegetarian version. The purple Greek Kalamata olives make a tangy substitute for salty anchovies. In France, *salade Niçoise* is served only in the spring and summer, when seasonal vegetables are readily available, so use the freshest vegetables you can find to make this delicious pasta dish.

makes 8 servings

1 pound green beans, cut into 1-inch lengths (about 4 cups)

1 pound red-skinned potatoes, cut into 1-inch pieces (about 3 cups)

1 pound dried penne pasta

2 tablespoons olive oil

1 medium yellow onion, thinly sliced

2 garlic cloves, minced

1 pound ripe plum tomatoes, chopped (about 3 cups)

1 cup Kalamata olives, pitted and chopped

2 tablespoons balsamic vinegar

½ teaspoon freshly ground black pepper

Salt to taste

Per 2-cup serving: 316 calories • 8g protein • 9g fat • 56g carbohydrates • 0 cholesterol • 502mg sodium • 6g fiber

1. Bring a large pot of salted water to a boil. Add the green beans and potatoes. Return the water to a boil and add the pasta. Cook, stirring occasionally, until the pasta is al dente, about 11 minutes.

2. Meanwhile, in a small skillet, heat the olive oil over medium heat. Add the onion and garlic and cook, stirring often, until the onion is soft, about 5 minutes. Remove from the heat. Stir in the tomatoes and olives.

3. Drain the pasta, beans, and potatoes, reserving ½ cup pasta water, and transfer to a serving bowl. Add the tomato mixture, vinegar, pepper, and salt and toss to mix. If the pasta seems too dry, add the reserved pasta water as needed, a little at a time.

fusilli with garlicky dandelion greens

Dandelion greens, a favorite in Greece, add a goodly amount of beta-carotene and vitamin A to this garlic-laden pasta dish. They have a slightly bitter taste and are a delicious spring treat, but you can substitute almost any leafy green.

makes 5 servings

1 pound dandelion greens
12 ounces dried fusilli
3 tablespoons olive oil
6 garlic cloves, minced
½ cup fresh goat cheese (optional)
Salt and crushed red pepper flakes (optional)

Per 2-cup serving: 354 calories • 11g protein
• 10g fat • 57g carbohydrates • 0 cholesterol
• 536mg sodium • 6g fiber

1. Bring a large pot of salted water to a boil. Add the greens and cook for 3 minutes. Using a slotted spoon, remove the greens to a colander to drain. Return the water to a boil and add the pasta. Cook, stirring occasionally, until al dente, about 10 minutes.

2. Meanwhile, squeeze the excess water from the greens and chop into 1-inch pieces. In a large skillet, heat the olive oil over medium heat. Add the garlic and cook, stirring often, for 30 seconds. Add the chopped greens and cook, stirring often, until heated through, 2 to 3 minutes.

3. Drain the pasta and return to the pot. Add the greens and garlic and toss to mix. Transfer to a serving bowl. Crumble the goat cheese over the pasta and sprinkle with a small amount of salt and crushed red pepper, if desired. Serve immediately.

pumpkin ravioli with leek and sage broth

These unusual ravioli are stuffed with pumpkin and delicately flavored with fennel and nutmeg. If you are adept at preparing homemade pasta, this recipe provides a chance to showcase your talent. Otherwise, purchase fresh pasta sheets from a specialty foods store or Italian market.

You can freeze the ravioli in a sealed plastic bag for up to two months. Cook them, still frozen, as you would fresh ravioli, adding about 30 seconds to the cooking time.

makes 8 servings

For the leek and sage broth

1 tablespoon olive oil

1 large leek, white and light green parts only, thinly sliced (1¼ cups)

1 can (14 ounces) vegetable broth

1 tablespoon chopped fresh sage

⅛ teaspoon ground white pepper

¼ cup water

1 tablespoon cornstarch

For the ravioli

1 can (15 ounces) solid-pack pumpkin

¼ cup freshly grated Parmesan cheese (optional)

½ teaspoon fennel seeds, coarsely crushed

¼ teaspoon salt

¼ teaspoon grated nutmeg

1½ pounds fresh pasta sheets, purchased or homemade (see page 143)

Per serving: • 298 calories • 11g protein • 4g fat • 55g carbohydrates • 62mg cholesterol • 307mg sodium • 2g fiber

1. In a large nonstick skillet, heat the olive oil over medium heat. Add the leek and cook, stirring often, until softened, about 5 minutes. Add the vegetable broth, sage, and pepper and simmer for 5 minutes. In a small cup, mix the water and cornstarch until smooth. Pour into the broth mixture and simmer, stirring often, until thickened slightly, about 3 minutes. Set aside. (The sauce may be prepared up to 2 hours before serving. Just let it stand at room temperature and reheat before serving.)

2. In a medium bowl, mix the pumpkin, cheese, fennel seeds, salt, and nutmeg.

3. Cut the pasta sheets into 2½-by-15-inch strips. Arrange one strip on a lightly floured surface. Spoon the filling by heaping teaspoonfuls down the center of one pasta sheet, making 6 mounds per strip, spaced about 1 inch apart. Using a pastry brush dipped in water, wet the edges of the pasta around the mounds. Place another pasta strip on top and press firmly around the filling, forcing out any air. Cut into squares around the filled areas and crimp the edges of each ravioli firmly to seal. Transfer to a dry kitchen towel or sheet of waxed paper. Repeat with the remaining pasta strips and filling.

4. Bring a large pot of salted water to a boil. Add the ravioli and cook until the pasta is al dente, 5 to 8 minutes, depending on the thickness of the dough. Drain well and transfer to a shallow serving bowl. Top with the warm leek and sage broth.

pasta wedges with fennel and tomato

The licorice taste of fennel paired with juicy ripe tomatoes may just convince you that you're enjoying a sunset summer meal in the heart of Provence, even when you're right at home.

makes 6 servings

For the pasta wedges

½ pound angel-hair pasta

3 tablespoons minced fresh basil or parsley

1 tablespoon olive oil

Salt and freshly ground black pepper to taste

2 tablespoons freshly grated Parmesan cheese or Parmesan-style soy cheese (optional)

2 tablespoons chopped fresh cilantro or basil

For the vegetable sauce

2 teaspoons olive oil

½ tablespoon cracked coriander seeds

½ teaspoon fennel seeds

1½ cups chopped fennel bulb

1½ cups chopped celery

1½ cups chopped carrot

1½ cups chopped parsnips

1½ cups chopped red bell pepper

¼ cup chopped fresh dill or parsley

4 cups water

2 cups diced tomatoes or tomato sauce

Salt and freshly ground black pepper to taste

Per serving: • 157 calories • 4g protein • 4g fat • 26g carbohydrates • 0 cholesterol • 76mg sodium • 7g fiber

1. Cook the pasta according to the package directions until al dente. Drain well. Toss with the basil or parsley, ½ tablespoon of the olive oil, and salt and pepper. Line a 9-inch round cake or pie pan with plastic wrap. Distribute the pasta evenly on top of the plastic wrap. Cover with a second sheet of plastic wrap and nestle a second cake or pie pan over the pasta. Place a weight (such as a can) in the top pan. Refrigerate for at least 8 hours.

2. To make the vegetable sauce, heat the olive oil in a large saucepan over medium-high heat. Add the coriander and fennel seeds and toast until fragrant, about 2 minutes. Add the fennel bulb, celery, carrot, parsnips, bell pepper, and dill or parsley. Cook, stirring, until the vegetables are slightly soft, about 5 minutes. Add the water and cook over moderate heat for 20 minutes. Stir in the tomatoes or tomato sauce and cook for another 10 to 15 minutes or until thickened. Season with salt and pepper.

3. Preheat the broiler. Warm the pasta to room temperature. Cut into 6 wedges. Place the wedges on a nonstick or oiled baking tray. Drizzle with the remaining ½ tablespoon olive oil and sprinkle with Parmesan if desired. Broil until lightly browned, about 4 minutes.

4. To serve, place a pasta wedge in a shallow soup bowl and sprinkle with cilantro or basil. Pour the vegetable sauce around the pasta wedge.

tuscan-style spelt rotini

This pasta dish, combining hearty spelt *rotini* with tender white cannellini beans, needs only a tossed salad and perhaps some crusty Italian bread to complete the meal. Spelt pasta is generally available in gourmet or natural food stores. Use nutritional yeast, which imparts a cheesy flavor, in place of Parmesan for a dairy-free alternative.

makes 4 servings

½ pound spelt *rotini, rotelli,* or other spiral pasta

1 bag (10 ounces) prewashed, ready-to-eat fresh spinach leaves, rinsed but not dried.

2 tablespoons olive oil

1 small red bell pepper, cut into ¼-by-2-inch strips

2 garlic cloves, minced

1 can (15 ounces) great northern or cannellini beans, drained and rinsed

1 can (14 ounces) plum tomatoes, chopped, with liquid

¼ cup oil-packed sun-dried tomatoes, minced

1 teaspoon dried oregano

½ teaspoon crushed red pepper flakes, or to taste

Salt and freshly ground black pepper to taste

Freshly grated Parmesan cheese or nutritional yeast flakes (optional)

Per serving: • 385 calories • 17g protein • 3g fat • 73g carbohydrates • 0 cholesterol • 65mg sodium • 12g fiber

1. Cook the pasta according to the package directions until al dente.

2. Meanwhile, place the spinach in a large saucepan, covered, and steam, without adding any additional liquid, until wilted, about 3 minutes. Drain and squeeze out excess liquid. Chop finely, then separate chopped leaves with your fingers.

3. In a large skillet, heat the olive oil over medium heat. Add the red bell pepper and garlic and cook, stirring, for 2 to 3 minutes, or until the garlic is golden. Add the beans, both tomatoes, oregano, and crushed red pepper and bring to a gentle simmer. Stir in the spinach and simmer for another minute. Remove from the heat.

4. When the pasta is done, drain well and combine it in a large serving bowl with the tomato mixture. Toss well. Season with salt and pepper and sprinkle with cheese or yeast flakes if desired.

orzo pilaf with lemon and mint

This sprightly pilaf, made with a combination of orzo (a tiny, rice-shaped pasta), and rice, makes a wonderful accompaniment to the Grilled Summer Vegetable Platter (page 56). The pilaf can be stored in the refrigerator in a covered container for up to four days.

makes 6 servings

4 cups vegetable broth or water
2 cups converted or white rice
½ pound orzo
Freshly grated zest of 1 lemon
⅓ cup packed minced fresh mint leaves

Per serving: • 269 calories • 6g protein • 1g fat • 59g carbohydrates • 0 cholesterol • 7mg sodium • 1g fiber

1. In a medium saucepan, bring the broth or water to a simmer over high heat. Add the rice and reduce the heat to low. Cover the pan and cook the rice for 20 minutes, or until the liquid has been absorbed and the grains are tender.

2. Meanwhile, rinse the orzo. Bring a large pot of salted water to a boil. Add the orzo and cook, stirring occasionally, until al dente, about 5 minutes. Drain, then stir the orzo into the rice along with the zest and mint. Serve warm or at room temperature.

linguine with pine nuts, roasted garlic, and capers

The delicate pink and white flowers of the wild caper plant make them easy to spot as they blossom out from the cracks between ancient stones of Italian castles and churches. The edible caper is actually the unopened flower bud, which is harvested and cured before it blooms. In this marvelous pasta dish, the capers lend a salty bite to the nutty, mellow flavors of roasted garlic and toasted pine nuts.

makes 6 servings

2 whole heads of garlic, unpeeled
¾ cup pine nuts
12 ounces linguine
¼ cup extra-virgin olive oil
¼ cup coarsely chopped fresh parsley
2 tablespoons balsamic vinegar
2 tablespoons capers, drained
2 garlic cloves, minced
¼ teaspoon salt
Freshly ground black pepper to taste
⅓ cup freshly grated Parmesan cheese (optional)

Per serving: 289 calories • 6g protein • 20g fat • 19g carbohydrates • 0 cholesterol • 105mg sodium • 4g fiber

1. Preheat the oven to 350°F. Slice off the top ¼ inch of the garlic heads. Wrap the garlic in foil and bake until very soft, about 1 hour. Remove the garlic from the oven and let cool. Squeeze the garlic from the cloves, mash it with a fork, and set aside.
2. Meanwhile, spread the pine nuts in a shallow baking pan and toast in the oven until golden, about 5 minutes. Transfer to a wire rack to cool.
3. Cook the pasta according to the package directions until al dente. Drain well.
4. In a large bowl, combine the olive oil, parsley, vinegar, capers, garlic, salt, pepper, and ½ cup of the nuts. Add the linguine and mix thoroughly. Garnish with the remaining nuts and cheese, if desired.

pasta and vegetables with basil-marjoram pesto

Pesto (*pistou* in French) translates literally as "pounded" in Italian, and refers to any food that is traditionally mashed with a mortar and pestle, but more specifically to a sauce made with fresh basil leaves, olive oil, pine nuts (or walnuts), garlic, and Parmesan or pecorino cheese. Our vegan version uses miso instead of cheese and introduces the flavor of marjoram.

makes 4 servings

For the pesto

6 to 7 cups loosely packed basil leaves
½ cup loosely packed fresh marjoram leaves
½ cup loosely packed fresh Italian parsley leaves
¼ cup extra-virgin olive oil
4 tablespoons lightly toasted pine nuts or chopped walnuts (see Note, page 153)
3 garlic cloves, minced
1 tablespoon fresh lemon juice
2 to 3 teaspoons dark barley miso, or to taste
2 to 4 tablespoons vegetable broth

For the pasta

12 ounces fettucine or other long pasta
1 tablespoon extra-virgin olive oil
2 cups green beans, sliced diagonally into 1½-inch-long pieces
2 small green zucchini, halved lengthwise and sliced diagonally into 1½-inch-long pieces
2 small yellow summer squash, halved lengthwise and sliced diagonally into 1½-inch-long pieces
Salt and freshly ground black pepper to taste
Fresh lemon juice to taste (optional)
Freshly grated Parmesan cheese (optional)

Per serving: • 632 calories • 23g protein • 18g fat • 92g carbohydrates • 0 cholesterol • 22mg sodium • 8g fiber

1. To make the pesto, combine the basil, marjoram, ¼ cup parsley, olive oil, 2 tablespoons of the nuts, garlic, lemon juice, and 2 teaspoons of the miso in a food processor or blender. Blend, stopping to scrape down the sides several times, until the mixture forms a smooth paste. Blend in the broth a tablespoon at a time, until the mixture reaches a saucelike consistency. Add the remaining nuts and pulse briefly. Taste and blend in more miso and/or broth if necessary.

2. Cook the pasta according to the package directions until al dente. Drain well and toss with the oil.

3. Meanwhile, in another pot, bring 4 quarts of water to a boil. Add the green beans and cook until tender, about 4 minutes. Using a slotted spoon, transfer the beans to a colander. Add the zucchini and squash to the pot and cook until tender, about 2 minutes. Using a slotted spoon, transfer the vegetables to the colander with the beans. Drain the vegetables well and place them in a bowl. Season with salt, pepper, and a little lemon juice, if desired.

4. Divide the pasta among 4 large plates. Scatter the vegetables on top and drizzle with the pesto sauce. Serve immediately, garnished with the remaining ¼ cup chopped parsley leaves and grated cheese, if desired.

cavatelli with garden vegetables and herbs

Somewhere between a hearty soup and a pasta, the bright combination of vegetables—including asparagus, red pepper, yellow squash, and fennel—makes this tasty dish both healthful and beautiful. Sharp, straw-colored Asiago cheese (the unaged predecessor of pecorino) may be grated on top.

makes 6 servings

12 ounces *cavatelli* or *orecchiette*

2 tablespoons olive oil

6 ounces (about 10) fresh asparagus spears, diagonally sliced into 1-inch pieces

2 medium yellow squash, halved lengthwise and cut into ½-inch pieces

1 small fennel bulb, trimmed and very thinly sliced

1 red bell pepper, sliced into thin strips

3 garlic cloves, minced

2 cups vegetable broth

⅓ cup chopped assorted fresh herbs, such as mint, thyme, chives, and basil

Salt and freshly ground black pepper to taste

½ cup grated Asiago cheese (optional)

Per serving: 297 calories • 10g protein • 6g fat • 52g carbohydrates • 0 cholesterol • 209mg sodium • 5g fiber

1. Cook the pasta according to the package directions until al dente.
2. Meanwhile, heat the olive oil in a large saucepan over medium heat. Add the asparagus, squash, fennel, red bell pepper, and garlic and cook, stirring, until the vegetables soften slightly, about 5 minutes. Add the broth and bring the mixture to a boil over high heat. Reduce the heat and simmer, uncovered, stirring occasionally, until the vegetables are crisp-tender, about 3 minutes.
3. Drain the pasta and return it to the pot along with the herbs, vegetables, and broth, tossing well. Season with salt and pepper. Serve in shallow soup bowls and sprinkle with cheese if desired.

ziti with fresh tomato-olive sauce

A home-cooked meal doesn't get any easier than this. This Greek-style pasta dish is tossed with fresh tomatoes, olives, balsamic vinegar, and seasonings, and takes only 25 minutes from kitchen to table.

makes 8 servings

8 ounces ziti or *mostaccioli* pasta
½ cup pitted Kalamata olives
⅓ cup packed shredded fresh basil leaves
2 tablespoons extra-virgin olive oil
2 tablespoons balsamic vinegar
3 garlic cloves, minced
1 tablespoon capers, drained (optional)
½ teaspoon crushed red pepper flakes
1¾ pounds ripe tomatoes, halved crosswise
 (about 4 large)
4 ounces goat cheese or feta, crumbled, or ¼ cup
 freshly grated Parmesan cheese (optional)
Salt and freshly ground black pepper to taste

Per serving: 163 calories • 5g protein • 4g fat
• 27g carbohydrates • 0 cholesterol • 305mg
sodium • 2g fiber

1. Cook the pasta according to the package directions until al dente.
2. Meanwhile, in a large serving bowl, combine the olives, basil, olive oil, vinegar, garlic, capers if desired, and red pepper flakes. Place a strainer over the serving bowl and squeeze juice from the tomato halves into the strainer. (Push on the seeds with the back of a wooden spoon to extract the tomato liquid.) Discard the seeds. Coarsely chop the tomatoes and add them to the olive mixture, tossing well.
3. Drain the pasta and add it to the bowl, tossing well. Sprinkle with cheese if desired. Season with salt and pepper.

linguine with caramelized onions and pine nuts

Caramelized onions, sautéed in olive oil and herbs and cooked with white wine, make this dish sweet and rich. Toasted pine nuts add a lovely, nutty flavor.

makes 6 servings

3 tablespoons olive oil

4 large red or yellow onions, thinly sliced

1 bay leaf

1 teaspoon chopped fresh rosemary (or 2 table-spoons chopped fresh Italian parsley)

½ teaspoon salt

¼ teaspoon freshly ground black pepper

2 garlic cloves, minced

½ cup dry white wine

1 cup water or vegetable broth

⅓ cup pine nuts

1 pound linguine

Freshly grated Parmesan cheese (optional)

Fresh rosemary, for garnish (optional)

Per serving: 466 calories • 14g protein • 13g fat • 73g carbohydrates • 0 cholesterol • 373mg sodium • 5g fiber

1. In a large skillet, heat the olive oil over medium-high heat. Add the onions and cook, stirring, for 3 minutes. Reduce the heat to low and add the bay leaf, rosemary, salt, and pepper. Cook, stirring often, until the onions are golden brown, about 15 minutes.

2. Add the garlic and wine to the skillet and increase the heat to medium. Cook for 4 to 5 minutes, or until the wine is reduced by about half. Add the water or broth and cook, uncovered, until the liquid is reduced by about a third, about 7 minutes.

3. Meanwhile, place the pine nuts in a skillet over medium-high heat. Toast by shaking the pan and stirring often, until the nuts are golden and fragrant, 2 to 3 minutes. Immediately transfer the nuts to a plate to stop the cooking.

4. Cook the pasta according to the package directions until al dente. Drain and transfer to a serving bowl along with the pine nuts. Pour the onion sauce over the pasta and pine nuts, and toss well. Sprinkle with Parmesan and garnish with rosemary, if desired.

asparagus and olive tortellini

Asparagus is cultivated throughout the Mediterranean and is even found growing wild in the olive groves and woods of southern France. Choose the thinnest stalks of asparagus that you can find, making sure that the tips are closed and the stems are firm.

makes 4 servings

1 package (12 ounces) frozen or fresh cheese or spinach tortellini

1 tablespoon plus 1 teaspoon olive oil

1 large red onion, very thinly sliced

1 pound asparagus spears, cut into 2-inch pieces

¼ pound Greek-style oil-cured black olives, pitted and coarsely chopped

Salt and freshly ground black pepper to taste

½ cup plain yogurt or 2 tablespoons freshly grated Parmesan cheese (optional)

Per serving: 227 calories • 9g protein • 9g fat
• 29g carbohydrates • 18mg cholesterol
• 532mg sodium • 5g fiber

1. Bring a large pot of salted water to a boil. Add the tortellini and cook until al dente, 8 to 10 minutes. Drain, then transfer the pasta to a bowl and toss with a teaspoon of the olive oil. Keep warm.

2. Heat the remaining tablespoon of oil in a large nonstick skillet over medium-high heat. Add the onion and cook, stirring, until softened, 5 to 6 minutes. Add the asparagus and olives and cook, stirring, until the asparagus is crisp-tender, about 4 minutes. Add the tortellini and salt and pepper and stir to mix. Transfer the mixture to a serving platter and top with yogurt or cheese, if desired.

pasta with fennel and saffron

This classic Sicilian dish is served in almost every restaurant on the island. Wild fennel, which has a more distinct flavor than cultivated fennel, is commonly used in Sicily. Here, we've combined easily available cultivated fennel with fennel seeds to boost the flavor.

makes 4 servings

1 medium bulb fennel with fronds
12 ounces spaghetti
2 tablespoons olive oil
1 small yellow onion, chopped
¼ teaspoon fennel seeds
¼ teaspoon ground saffron threads
1 tablespoon warm water
2 tablespoons currants or raisins plumped in warm
   water and drained
1 tablespoon pine nuts

Per serving: 440 calories • 13g protein • 10g fat • 76g carbohydrates • 0 cholesterol • 21mg sodium • 5g fiber

1. Bring a large pot of salted water to a boil.
2. Meanwhile, wash and trim the fennel, discarding the stems but reserving the fronds and bulb. Chop the fronds and set aside. Add the fennel bulb to the boiling water and cook for 10 minutes. Remove the fennel bulb with a slotted spoon, leaving the water in the pot.
3. When the water returns to a boil, add the pasta and cook according to package directions until al dente. Drain the pasta, reserving ½ cup of the cooking water.
4. In a large skillet, heat 1 tablespoon of the olive oil over low heat. Add the onion, fennel seeds, and fennel fronds and cook, stirring, until the onion is soft, about 5 minutes. Dissolve the saffron in the warm water and add the mixture to the pan. Dice the cooked fennel bulb and add it to the pan. Cook, stirring, until the fennel is golden and very tender, about 5 minutes. Add the currants and pine nuts. If the mixture seems dry, add spoonfuls of the reserved pasta cooking water to moisten it. Add the cooked pasta and remaining fennel fronds to the pan. Cook, stirring, for 1 minute over medium heat. Drizzle with the remaining olive oil before serving.

pasta with fava beans and peas

Fava beans are one of the earliest recorded Sicilian foods. For generations, many Sicilian laborers survived on a diet consisting mainly of *maccù*, a fava bean mush flavored with wild fennel. In Italy today, beans, especially heavy ones like favas, are used sparingly in pasta dishes. You may wish to add more favas and peas to this entree. French fava beans are sold in their pods, and are often available fresh and frozen in Italian and Middle Eastern groceries. Do not use dried fava beans in this recipe.

makes 4 servings

1 pound shells or other pasta
1 tablespoon extra-virgin olive oil
6 scallions, sliced (white part only)
¼ cup shelled fresh or frozen fava beans (do not use dried)
¾ cup shelled fresh or frozen peas
½ cup water
1 to 2 tablespoons white wine vinegar
¼ cup loosely packed mint leaves
2 tablespoons toasted bread crumbs (see Note), for garnish

Per serving: 547 calories • 20g protein • 5g fat • 103g carbohydrates • 0 cholesterol • 248mg sodium • 9g fiber

Note: To toast bread crumbs, place them in a dry skillet over medium heat. Cook, stirring, until golden brown, about 4 minutes.

1. Cook the pasta according to package directions until al dente. Drain well.

2. In a large skillet, heat the olive oil over medium heat. Add the scallions and cook, stirring, for 1 minute. Add the fava beans and peas and cook, stirring, for 2 minutes, taking care not to brown the scallions. Add the water. Simmer the vegetables until most of the water evaporates and they are tender. Taste the vegetables and add additional ¼ cupfuls of water to cook as needed.

3. When the beans and peas are cooked but still moist, stir in the vinegar and cook for 1 minute. Scatter on the mint leaves and remove the pan from the heat. Add the pasta to the bean mixture. Toss briefly over low heat, allowing the pasta to absorb the remaining moisture. Garnish with the bread crumbs and serve immediately.

pasta with wild mushroom tomato sauce

Wild mushrooms have always been an important ingredient to the people of the Mediterranean, often serving as a meat substitute. In this country, the supermarket selection of fresh mushrooms has exploded in recent years, and many varieties are available already cleaned and sliced. Three or four varieties of mushrooms give this sauce a hearty, robust taste. A sprinkling of fresh herbs enlivens the sauce at the last moment.

makes 6 servings

2 tablespoons olive oil
8 ounces white mushrooms, sliced
6 ounces portobello mushrooms, sliced
4 ounces fresh oyster or shiitake mushrooms, sliced
7 garlic cloves, minced
¼ cup water or red wine
1 can (14 ounces) stewed tomatoes
1 can (14 ounces) tomato puree
2 teaspoons dried basil
2 teaspoons dried oregano
¼ teaspoon crushed red pepper flakes
½ teaspoon salt
12 ounces dried linguine or spaghetti
¼ cup packed fresh basil, arugula, or parsley leaves, chopped
Freshly grated Parmesan or Romano cheese (optional)

Per 1-cup serving: 200 calories • 8g protein • 6g fat • 32g carbohydrates • 0 cholesterol • 483mg sodium • 5g fiber

1. In a large skillet, heat the olive oil over medium heat. Add the mushrooms and cook, stirring frequently, until tender and golden, about 7 minutes. Stir in the garlic and cook, stirring, for 2 minutes longer. Add the water or wine and cook, stirring, until the liquid is evaporated. Stir in the tomatoes, tomato puree, and dried seasonings. Reduce the heat to low and simmer the mixture for 20 minutes, stirring occasionally.

2. Meanwhile, cook the pasta according to package directions until al dente. Drain and transfer to warm serving plates.

3. Remove the sauce from the heat and stir in the fresh herbs. Spoon the sauce over the pasta. Serve with freshly grated Parmesan or Romano cheese, if desired.

Grains

Nutty, healthful grains are as important a part of the Mediterranean diet as vegetables themselves. What would Moroccan cuisine be without couscous, or Italy without polenta, or the Middle East without bulgur? Grains are as much the staff of life as bread. In terms of healthfulness, grains, along with pasta, bread, and legumes, form the wide base of the Mediterranean diet pyramid and are key to the healthful eating pattern of all Mediterranean peoples. Wheat, whether in the form of couscous, pasta, bread, or bulgur, has been the cornerstone of the Mediterranean diet for thousands of years. Couscous originated with the nomadic Berbers of northern Africa and is made from cracked durum wheat or semolina. One may justly say that couscous, served almost every day, is to northern Africans what pasta is to the Italians. Traditionally it is steamed—as many as seven times—and mixed with butter, broth, or olive oil. (Here, we've streamlined the recipes and simmer the couscous instead.) Then, it is mixed into colorful vegetable salads, used as a bed for savory stews, or sweetened with spices and dried fruit and served for dessert. Bulgur is the wheat preparation of choice in the Middle East. To prepare bulgur, whole wheat kernels are steamed, dried, and then coarsely ground. Bulgur can be made into savory, parsley-based salads such as tabbouleh, used in soups and stews, or cooked with beans to make Vegetable and Bulgur Kibbeh in Yogurt Sauce (page 228). It can also take the place of rice in a warming, oniony pilaf. ■ Contrary to what most people picture when pilafs come to mind, they can be made from any number of grains (not just rice) that have been sautéed in oil or butter and then cooked in broth. Seasonal vegetables, herbs, and spices are other usual additions. Rice pilafs are generally more common in northern Africa and the European countries whereas bulgur dominates in Turkey and the Middle East. Lentils, eggplant, pine nuts, tomatoes, and caramelized onions are all used in various pilafs. Another rice dish, risotto, is an Italian favorite and is made from stubby short-grained rice. Risotto is cooked slowly and stirred constantly while adding water or broth and white wine little by little until the rice is just done. Bright yellow, saffron-enriched Spanish paella is also made from short-grained rice and is usually served with seafood or vegetables. Valencians eat rice almost every day and will heatedly assert their expertise and that their version of paella is *the* version of paella. ■ Polenta, milled from dried corn kernels, is a relatively new addition to the Mediterranean culinary lexicon, since corn was brought over from the New World in the early seventeenth century. Before that, Italians made their soft, puddinglike dish from spelt, an ancient form of wheat. Now, polenta is commonly molded into a loaf, sliced, and served with a sauce or stew. Soft polenta—that is, polenta that has not been molded—is also popular, topped with creamy mascarpone cheese, earthy wild mushrooms, or a light sauce of wine, vegetables, herbs, and spices.

zucchini stuffed with dilled barley salad

This tantalizing dish is extremely low in fat, but tastes so good you'll hardly notice. Stuffed zucchini boats are a great make-ahead dish because they can be prepared and stored in the refrigerator for up to 3 days.

makes 6 servings

6 medium zucchini

1½ cups cooked barley

⅓ cup diced green bell pepper

⅓ cup diced red bell pepper

⅓ cup diced yellow bell pepper

⅓ cup trimmed and chopped scallions

¼ cup chopped fresh dill

3 tablespoons white wine vinegar

1 tablespoon fresh lemon juice

1 teaspoon extra-virgin olive oil

Salt and freshly ground black pepper to taste

Per serving: 86 calories • 3g protein • 1g fat • 18g carbohydrates • 0 cholesterol • 6mg sodium • 4g fiber

1. Trim the zucchini, then slice them in half lengthwise. Using a teaspoon or melon baller, scoop out the insides of the zucchini halves, leaving a ¼-inch border. Slice off enough of the rounded (uncut) side of the zucchini halves so that they sit on the platter without falling over. Set aside.

2. In a mixing bowl, combine the barley, diced bell peppers, and scallions. In a separate bowl, combine the dill, vinegar, lemon juice, olive oil, and salt and pepper. Add the dressing to the barley mixture and toss well to coat. Spoon the barley filling into the zucchini, cover with plastic wrap or waxed paper, and refrigerate until serving time.

herb and rice stuffed peppers

Fresh and colorful, these zesty stuffed peppers are both hearty and healthful. If you don't have a microwave, you can steam the peppers until nearly tender, about 5 minutes. Keep in mind that the amounts of nuts and Parmesan you add depend on your personal taste; the more you add of either, the higher the fat content will be.

makes 4 servings

4 green bell peppers
2 cups water
1 cup uncooked brown rice
¼ cup white wine
½ cup dried currants
¼ to ½ cup pine nuts
3 to 5 tablespoons freshly grated Parmesan cheese
2 tablespoons chopped fresh parsley
2 tablespoons chopped fresh basil
2 tablespoons chopped fresh mint
1 teaspoon chopped fresh sage
1 teaspoon salt
1 teaspoon freshly ground black pepper

Per stuffed pepper: 320 calories • 10g protein • 8g fat • 55g carbohydrates • 3mg cholesterol • 659mg sodium • 3g fiber

1. Cut off the tops of the peppers and remove the seeds and membranes. Place the peppers in a shallow glass baking dish filled with ½ inch of water. Microwave the peppers on high for about 3 minutes, or until barely tender. Set aside to cool.

2. In a saucepan, combine the water and rice. Cover, bring to a boil, then reduce the heat to medium-low. Simmer for 50 minutes, or until the rice is tender.

3. Meanwhile, in a small skillet, heat the wine to a simmer over medium-low heat, then add the currants. Simmer until the currants are softened, about 1 minute. Remove from the heat.

4. Preheat the oven to 350°F. In a mixing bowl, stir together the hot rice, wine mixture, Parmesan, herbs, salt, and pepper. Taste and adjust the seasonings as desired. Stuff the peppers, pressing the filling into all cavities. Bake the stuffed peppers for 10 to 15 minutes, or until the filling is thoroughly hot and the peppers are tender.

bulgur and goat cheese–stuffed frying peppers

This hearty dish uses the light yellowish-green Italian frying peppers; they have fewer seeds to fuss with and a perfectly shaped cavity that lets little of the delicious stuffing escape.

makes 4 main-course servings

8 side-dish servings

1½ cups water

1 cup coarse bulgur

8 Italian frying peppers, each 5 to 6 inches long

1 tablespoon olive oil

1 medium onion, diced

2 garlic cloves, minced

2 cups diced broccoli florets

½ cup crumbled goat or feta cheese

2 tablespoons finely chopped fresh parsley

2 scallions, trimmed and chopped

1 teaspoon ground cumin

1 teaspoon ground coriander

Salt and freshly ground black pepper to taste

Per main-dish serving: 272 calories • 11g protein • 10g fat • 39g carbohydrates • 27mg cholesterol • 127mg sodium • 11g fiber

1. Bring the water to a boil in a medium saucepan. Stir in the bulgur. Reduce the heat to medium-low and simmer gently, covered, until water is absorbed, about 40 minutes. Remove from the heat and set aside.

2. Meanwhile, slice off the very tops of the frying peppers, then carefully cut away the seeds, leaving the peppers whole. Set the seeded peppers aside.

3. In a small skillet, heat the olive oil over medium-high heat. Add the onion and garlic and cook, stirring, until the onion becomes translucent, about 5 minutes. Lower the heat to medium low, add the broccoli and cook, covered, until crisp-tender, about 3 minutes longer.

4. Preheat the oven to 350°F. In a large mixing bowl, combine the bulgur, broccoli mixture, cheese, herbs, spices, and salt and pepper. Stuff the mixture into the peppers, and arrange them in a shallow, lightly oiled casserole dish. Cover the dish with foil and bake until the peppers are tender, 30 to 40 minutes. Serve immediately.

polenta squares

Polenta is an Italian cornmeal dish that is cooked with water into a puddinglike mixture. Before corn came to Italy from the Americas in the early seventeenth century, the Romans had been making a similar dish using spelt. Although usually made as a savory dish, in some regions of Italy polenta is cooked with milk and eaten for breakfast.

Look for polenta in either the bulk section or packaged grains section of your grocery or specialty foods store. You could also substitute coarsely ground cornmeal. Serve the polenta squares with tomato sauce, ratatouille, or one of the sauces on pages 285–286.

makes 9 servings

2½ cups water
2½ cups vegetable broth
¼ teaspoon freshly ground black pepper
1 cup polenta or coarse-ground yellow cornmeal
2 teaspoons butter or olive oil
⅓ cup freshly grated Parmesan cheese or soy
  Parmesan cheese

Per square: 114 calories • 4g protein • 4g fat • 16g carbohydrates • 6mg cholesterol • 525mg sodium • 1g fiber

1. In a large, heavy-bottomed saucepan over medium-high heat, combine the water, vegetable broth and black pepper. Bring the mixture to a boil.
2. Reduce the heat to low and slowly add the polenta in a fine stream, stirring constantly with a wire whisk to prevent lumps from forming. Simmer, stirring constantly, until the mixture becomes very thick, about 10 minutes.
3. Stir in the butter or olive oil and all but 2 tablespoons of the cheese. Spoon the polenta into a lightly oiled 9-inch square baking dish and smooth it evenly to fill the dish. Sprinkle the remaining cheese on top.
4. Let cool until the polenta sets, at least 30 minutes. You may reheat it in the microwave before serving if desired. Cut into 3-inch squares and serve, either plain or topped with sauce.

grilled polenta with minted eggplant topping

Polenta is a traditional Italian dish that dates back to Caesar's time. Our recipe combines a savory eggplant topping with coarsely ground cornmeal that is simmered in water, then cooled and sliced into wedges. Comforting and filling, polenta can be eaten plain or made into a fancy and elegant dish.

makes 6 servings

For the polenta

4 cups water

½ teaspoon salt

½ teaspoon freshly ground black pepper

1 cup coarse-ground cornmeal

For the topping

¼ cup olive oil

2 large eggplant, cut into 1-inch cubes

½ small onion, minced

4 garlic cloves, minced

3 tablespoons chopped fresh mint

1 tablespoon minced fresh parsley

2 teaspoons balsamic vinegar

Salt and freshly ground black pepper to taste

Per serving: 189 calories • 3g protein • 10g fat • 23g carbohydrates • 0 cholesterol • 210mg sodium • 4g fiber

1. In a heavy saucepan over high heat, combine the water, salt, and pepper. When the water comes to a boil, add the cornmeal in a steady, thin stream, stirring constantly with a wooden spoon. Reduce the heat to low and continue cooking for 20 minutes, stirring frequently. The polenta will be very thick.

2. Spoon the polenta onto a sheet of waxed paper. With a wet spatula, spread the polenta until it is ½ inch thick. Set aside.

3. While the polenta cools, prepare the topping. In a medium skillet, heat the olive oil over medium heat. Add the eggplant, onion, and garlic and cook, stirring, until the eggplant is very soft, about 20 minutes. Stir in the herbs and vinegar and season with salt and pepper.

4. Cut the polenta into 6 squares and put them on a lightly oiled baking sheet. Broil on both sides until golden-brown spots appear. Spoon the topping over the squares and serve immediately.

polenta with rapini

This wonderfully healthful polenta recipe features rapini (also known as broccoli rabe or rape), a cruciferous vegetable high in calcium, and plenty of immunity-boosting garlic. Substitute fresh broccoli florets if rapini is unavailable.

makes 8 servings

5 cups water

1 teaspoon salt

1½ cups coarse-ground yellow cornmeal

1 bunch broccoli rabe (about ¾ pound), tough stems removed

1 tablespoon olive oil

8 garlic cloves, minced

Per serving: 114 calories • 3g protein • 3g fat • 21g carbohydrates • 0 cholesterol • 311mg sodium • 3g fiber

1. In a large, heavy saucepan, bring the water to a boil. Reduce the heat to low and add salt. Pour in the cornmeal in a fine stream, stirring constantly to prevent clumping. Keep stirring until evenly thickened and soupy, about 5 minutes. Adjust the heat to the lowest setting so the polenta barely bubbles. Cook for 30 minutes, stirring every few minutes to prevent sticking.

2. Meanwhile, bring 3 quarts of salted water to a boil. Add the rapini and cook until tender, about 5 minutes. Drain, squeeze out any excess water, and chop into 1-inch pieces.

3. In a large skillet, heat the oil over medium heat. Add half of the garlic to the pan and cook, stirring, until fragrant, about 1 minute. Add the rapini and cook, stirring, 4 minutes longer. Add the remaining garlic to the cooked polenta and stir to blend. Pour half of the polenta mixture into an 8-inch square baking dish. Arrange the rapini in an even layer over the polenta, then pour the remaining polenta over the rapini layer. Let stand at room temperature until set, at least 30 minutes.

4. To serve, heat the polenta in a 300°F. oven for 15 minutes or in the microwave on high power for 2 to 3 minutes. Cut into 8 squares with a sharp knife.

quick layered polenta and red sauce

If you're looking for something fabulous (besides pasta) to serve with red sauce, try this rustic polenta dish. It's extremely fast and easy to make, and the polenta can be made up to three days ahead.

makes 8 servings

6½ cups water

2 teaspoons salt

1½ cups polenta or coarse-ground yellow cornmeal

¾ cup freshly grated Parmesan cheese

¾ cup grated pecorino Romano cheese

3 cups Roasted Red Sauce (page 297)

Per serving: 160 calories • 9g protein • 7g fat • 13g carbohydrates • 16mg cholesterol • 984mg sodium • 1g fiber

1. Lightly grease a 9-by-5-inch loaf pan. In a large saucepan, bring the water to a boil and add the salt. Remove from the heat and pour in the polenta in a thin, even stream, stirring to prevent clumping. Return the saucepan to medium-low heat and cook, stirring constantly with a wooden spoon, for 5 minutes, until the polenta is thick and soft. Pour the polenta into the prepared pan and let cool completely (place the pan in the refrigerator if you want to speed up the cooling time).

2. Preheat the oven to 375°F. Lightly grease an 8- or 9-inch square baking dish. In a small bowl, mix the Parmesan and Romano cheeses. Cut the cooled polenta into ¼-inch-thick slices.

3. Arrange a single layer of polenta over the bottom of the dish. Cover the polenta layer with about 1 cup of the sauce, and ¼ cup of the cheese mixture. Repeat these layers 2 more times, then end with a layer of the polenta. Sprinkle the remaining cheese on top. Cover loosely with foil and bake 20 minutes. Remove the foil and bake until the polenta and sauce are bubbling hot, about 10 more minutes. Let stand for 5 minutes before serving.

polenta fava bean loaf

Fava beans add a garden-fresh flavor and an extra moist texture to this hearty polenta loaf. Serve slices of it with Roasted Mediterranean Vegetables (page 231) or with your favorite tomato sauce. You can buy frozen cooked fava beans in Middle Eastern grocery stores. Otherwise, use the canned variety (rinse them well).

makes 8 servings

½ cup sun-dried tomatoes (dry, not oil-packed)
¼ cup boiling water
5 cups water or vegetable broth
1 tablespoon olive oil
1 teaspoon salt
2 cups polenta or coarse-ground yellow cornmeal
1 cup cooked fava beans
¼ cup freshly grated Parmesan cheese (optional)

Per serving: 82 calories • 4g protein • 2g fat
• 10g carbohydrates • 2mg cholesterol
• 463mg sodium • 2g fiber

1. In a small bowl, combine the sun-dried tomatoes and boiling water; let soak until the tomatoes are soft, about 15 minutes. Drain the rehydrated tomatoes and slice them into thin strips.
2. In a large saucepan, bring 5 cups of water or broth to a boil over high heat and add the oil and salt. Pour in the polenta in a thin stream, whisking to prevent clumping. Cook the polenta, stirring constantly, until it thickens, 3 to 5 minutes.
3. Add the fava beans, rehydrated tomatoes, and cheese. Whisk until the mixture comes away from the sides of the saucepan. Turn the mixture into an oiled 9-by-5-by-3-inch loaf pan. Refrigerate the loaf for about 2 hours.
4. Cut the loaf into ½-inch-thick slices and serve cold, warmed, or grilled.

grilled polenta with triple-pepper sauce

Here are a few helpful hints for cooking with polenta. For a nuttier flavored dish, try lightly toasting the cornmeal in a dry, heavy-bottomed skillet before stirring it into boiling water. If you are short on time, make the polenta in the morning or the night before, cover, and refrigerate—it will firm up during the day. Finally, for the quickest of meals, substitute ready-made polenta, which is available in large supermarkets and health food stores.

makes 4 generous servings

For the polenta

3 cups water

¼ teaspoon salt

1 cup polenta or coarse-ground yellow cornmeal

1 cup cooked or frozen corn kernels

Olive oil for grilling or broiling

For the pepper sauce

2 teaspoons olive oil

1 medium onion, thinly sliced

6 garlic cloves, minced

1 large green bell pepper, cut into 1½-inch-long slivers

1 large red bell pepper, cut into 1½-inch-long slivers

1 large orange or yellow bell pepper, cut into 1½-inch-long slivers

½ teaspoon dried marjoram

¼ cup vegetable broth

¼ cup cooked white beans, rinsed and drained

½ teaspoon freshly grated lemon zest

Salt and freshly ground black pepper to taste

2 to 3 tablespoons coarsely chopped Italian parsley leaves, for garnish

Per serving: 223 calories • 5g protein • 3g fat • 44g carbohydrates • 0 cholesterol • 146 mg sodium • 7g fiber

1. Lightly grease a glass or ceramic 8-inch square or 9-inch round baking dish.
2. To prepare the polenta, in a large saucepan, bring the water to a boil and add the salt. Pour in the cornmeal in a fine stream, whisking constantly to avoid lumps. Reduce the heat to low and/or place the pot on a heat diffuser. (You also can use a double boiler, but allow for extra cooking time.) Cook, stirring often with a wooden spoon, until the polenta is thick yet still smooth, 20 to 30 minutes.
3. Add the corn kernels to the polenta mixture and cook for 5 minutes longer. Spread the mixture evenly into the prepared pan and set aside until cool and solid, about 30 minutes.
4. To prepare the pepper sauce, heat the olive oil in a skillet over medium heat. Add the onion and cook, stirring, for about 2 minutes. Stir in the garlic and bell peppers. Cook, stirring, until the vegetables are tender, about 5 minutes. Stir in the marjoram and cook, stirring constantly, for about 30 seconds. Stir in the vegetable broth, white beans, and lemon zest. Cook until the mixture is heated through, adding salt and pepper to taste.
5. Preheat the grill or broiler. Cut the polenta into 4 equal squares or wedges. Arrange on a nonstick or lightly greased baking sheet and brush the tops lightly with olive oil. Grill or broil, turning once, until light brown on both sides. Serve the polenta immediately, topped with the pepper sauce and garnished with fresh parsley.

polenta with three-mushroom sauce

A trio of flavorful mushrooms, plus shallots, tomatoes, garlic, and thyme, is the topping for this vibrant polenta dish. And not only does this dish taste wonderful but it's also quick and easy to make since we've given simple directions for cooking the polenta in a microwave oven. Or, if you prefer, cook it on the stove as you would any of the polenta recipes in this book.

makes 4 servings

2 cups vegetable broth

1¾ cups water

1 cup polenta or coarse-ground yellow cornmeal

2 tablespoons olive oil

¼ cup minced shallots or onion

2 garlic cloves, minced

4 ounces fresh cremini or button mushrooms, sliced

4 ounces fresh shiitake mushrooms, caps sliced thinly (stems discarded)

4 ounces fresh oyster mushrooms, halved lengthwise if large

2 large ripe tomatoes, seeded and coarsely chopped

1 tablespoon chopped fresh thyme leaves (or 1 teaspoon dried)

Salt and freshly ground black pepper to taste

Freshly grated Parmesan cheese (optional)

Per serving: 308 calories • 8g protein • 8g fat • 56g carbohydrates • 0 cholesterol • 181mg sodium • 7g fiber

1. In a 3-quart microwave-safe bowl or casserole, whisk together the broth, water, and cornmeal. Cover loosely with waxed paper and microwave on high for 6 minutes. Whisk carefully (the mixture will be hot), then cover and return to the microwave. Cook until the polenta is very thick, 4 to 5 minutes. Whisk again, cover, and let stand until cooled to room temperature.

2. Heat the olive oil in a large nonstick skillet over medium heat. Add the shallots and garlic and cook, stirring, for 1 minute. Add the mushrooms and continue cooking, stirring occasionally, until the mushrooms are tender, about 5 minutes.

3. Add the tomatoes and thyme to the mushroom mixture. Cook until heated through, stirring occasionally, for 3 to 4 minutes. Season with salt and pepper and remove from the heat.

4. Spoon the polenta onto 4 warmed serving plates and top with the mushroom mixture. Sprinkle freshly grated Parmesan cheese on top if desired.

mozzarella polenta casserole

The flavors of woodsy fresh rosemary, salty Greek Kalamata olives, and creamy mozzarella cheese add a special Mediterranean taste to this dish. Serve it with a large green salad and a warm loaf of crusty country bread.

makes 8 servings

For the filling

½ cup sun-dried tomatoes (dry, not oil-packed)

2 medium zucchini, sliced lengthwise ½ inch thick

1 medium red onion, sliced ¼ inch thick

1 teaspoon olive oil, plus more for brushing

5 garlic cloves, minced

2 teaspoons chopped fresh rosemary leaves

½ cup chopped pitted Kalamata olives

Salt and freshly ground black pepper to taste

4 ounces fresh mozzarella cheese, thinly sliced

For the polenta

5 cups water

2 ½ cups polenta or coarse-ground yellow corn-meal

2 tablespoons butter or margarine (optional)

¼ cup freshly grated Parmesan cheese

Salt to taste

Per serving: 243 calories • 8g proteins • 6g fat • 40g carbohydrates • 7g cholesterol • 332mg sodium • 5g fiber

1. Soak the sun-dried tomatoes in hot water to cover until softened, about 30 minutes; drain and slice into slivers.

2. Preheat the grill or broiler. Brush the zucchini and onion slices with olive oil and grill or broil until charred and soft, about 4 minutes per side. Set aside the zucchini and coarsely chop the onion slices.

3. Heat 1 teaspoon of the olive oil in a small sauté pan over medium-low heat. Cook the garlic, stirring, until fragrant, about 2 minutes. Add the grilled onion, rosemary, olives, rehydrated tomatoes, and salt and pepper. Remove from the heat and set aside.

4. To prepare the polenta, bring 5 cups salted water to a boil. Add the polenta in a thin stream while stirring constantly with a wooden spoon to prevent clumping. Cook the polenta for 20 minutes, stirring often. Add the butter or margarine (if desired), all but 2 tablespoons of the Parmesan cheese and the salt, stirring with a wooden spoon until the ingredients are incorporated and the polenta is thick and creamy. Remove from the heat.

5. Preheat the oven to 350°F. Brush the inside of a 9-inch square shallow baking dish with olive oil. Pour half of the polenta into the dish and smooth the surface. Arrange the zucchini slices over the polenta then top with the onion mixture. Layer the mozzarella cheese over the onion mixture. Pour the remaining polenta on top and smooth the surface. Sprinkle the remaining Parmesan cheese on top. Bake for 20 to 30 minutes, or until warmed through. Let cool for 5 minutes before serving.

traditional couscous

Couscous, the Arab equivalent of the Italian's beloved pasta and the Spaniard's adored rice, is a widely used staple that can be made into dishes with seemingly unending variations. Couscous is made from cracked semolina wheat and is traditionally steamed two or three times (and sometimes as many as seven!) before being mixed with olive oil or *smen* (clarified butter).

Although it takes more time to make, we guarantee that you will never mistake traditional couscous for the kind cooked according to package directions.

makes 8 servings

2 cups couscous

7 cups water

Vegetable broth (the amount will depend on the size of your steamer/pot)

2 teaspoons salt

1 or 2 tablespoons butter (optional)

Per ¾-cup serving: 133 calories • 4g protein • 0 fat • 28g carbohydrates • 0 cholesterol • 539mg sodium • 2g fiber

1. Place the couscous in a large bowl and cover with 6 cups cold water. Swirl the grains with your hand 2 or 3 times, then drain the excess water from the bowl (the couscous should be very wet). Smooth the couscous out on a baking sheet, leaving the grains to swell for about 10 minutes.
2. With wet, cupped hands, work the grains by lifting and breaking apart any lumps, then letting them fall back onto the baking sheet. Rake the couscous with your fingers to circulate the grains.
3. In a large pot with a steamer attachment, bring the vegetable broth to a simmer. There should be ample liquid in the bottom of your pot but it should not come too close to the bottom of the steaming basket. Place the couscous in the steamer (uncovered for conventional metal steamers, covered for bamboo steaming baskets) and steam for 20 minutes.
4. Dump the couscous back onto the baking sheet and spread out the grains with a large spoon. Sprinkle the remaining 1 cup water and the salt over the grains. Lightly oil your hands and rework the grains, breaking up any lumps. Smooth out the couscous and allow it to dry for 10 minutes. (If you are preparing ahead, you may let the couscous dry, covered with a damp towel, for up to several hours.)
5. Finally, wet your hands and break up any lumps that may have formed as the couscous dried. Return the couscous to the steamer over simmering broth and steam once more (uncovered for conventional metal steamers, covered in bamboo steaming baskets) for 20 minutes.
6. To serve, remove the couscous to a warm serving dish, make a well in the center and add the butter, if desired.

quick couscous

If you need to make dinner in a hurry, follow the directions on the box, or, if you buy in bulk, use the chart and quick-cooking directions that follow. One-half cup of dry couscous will make two to four servings.

couscous	water
½ cup	¾ cup
1 cup	1½ cups
1½ cups	3 cups

Per ¾-cup serving: 133 calories • 4g protein • 0 fat • 28g carbohydrates • 0 cholesterol • 6mg sodium • 2g fiber

In a saucepan, bring the desired amount of water to a boil. Add the corresponding amount of couscous and stir. Return the mixture to a boil, then reduce the heat to a low simmer. Cover the saucepan and cook over low heat until the water is absorbed, 1 to 2 minutes. Remove from the heat, fluff with a fork, and let stand, covered, for 5 minutes. Fluff the couscous again just before serving.

israeli couscous with chunky tomato sauce

Couscous was brought to Israel in the 1950s by northern African Jews and has been given a place of honor at Israeli tables ever since. Try using whole wheat couscous or a blend of half whole wheat and half regular couscous for a boost of nutrition and flavor. This well-seasoned sauce can be used to top your favorite pasta and polenta dishes, too.

makes 4 servings

1 ¾ cups vegetable broth
1 cup couscous
Pinch of saffron, crushed
1 tablespoon pine nuts, toasted
   (see Note, page 153)
3 scallions, trimmed and thinly sliced
1 small onion, diced
2 garlic cloves, minced
1 can (28 ounces) whole plum tomatoes
2 tablespoons chopped fresh basil
1 tablespoon fresh thyme, chopped
¼ teaspoon crushed red pepper flakes
Salt and freshly ground black pepper to taste

Per serving: 265 calories • 10g protein • 2g fat • 50g carbohydrates • 0 cholesterol • 869mg sodium • 5g fiber

1. In a small saucepan, heat 1½ cups of the broth until simmering. Stir in the couscous and saffron. Remove the couscous from the heat, cover, and let sit until all the liquid is absorbed, about 5 minutes. Transfer the couscous to a baking dish and stir in the pine nuts and scallions. Cover with foil to keep warm and set aside.

2. Heat the remaining ¼ cup broth in a medium saucepan over medium heat and cook the onion and garlic until tender, about 5 minutes. Roughly chop the plum tomatoes and add them to the saucepan with their juice. Add the basil, thyme, and red pepper flakes. Cook over medium heat, stirring occasionally, until thickened, about 20 minutes.

3. Season the sauce with salt and pepper. Pour over the couscous and serve immediately.

couscous with turnips and turnip greens

Make sure to buy small, tender turnips with fresh, bright-looking greens for this tasty dish. If you can find them, pink turnips have a delightfully subtle flavor.

makes 6 servings

2 ½ cups vegetable broth
3 tablespoons olive oil
1 ¼ cups whole wheat or regular couscous
1 bunch baby turnips with greens
½ teaspoon whole cumin seeds
1 garlic clove, minced
½ medium onion, finely chopped
Salt and freshly ground black pepper to taste

Per serving: 235 calories • 7g protein • 5g fat • 36g carbohydrates • 0 cholesterol • 454mg sodium • 4g fiber

1. In a medium saucepan, bring the broth and 2 tablespoons of the olive oil to a boil. Add the couscous, cover the saucepan, and remove from the heat. Set aside and let stand for 5 minutes.
2. Cut the turnips away from the greens and wash them well. Wash the turnip greens, trimming away any wilted leaves. Cut the turnip greens into 1-inch pieces. Trim the turnips and cut them in half.
3. Heat the remaining tablespoon of oil in a large skillet over medium-high heat. Add the cumin and toast it, shaking the pan, until fragrant, about 1 minute. Add the garlic and cook, stirring, for 1 minute. Add the onion and cook, stirring, until soft, 3 to 4 minutes. Add the turnips (not the greens) and cover the pan. Cook, shaking the pan occasionally, until the turnips are crisp-tender, 3 to 4 minutes. Add the turnip greens and salt and pepper, and cook, uncovered, until the greens wilt, about 2 minutes.
4. Transfer the couscous to a serving bowl, add the cooked vegetable mixture, and fluff with a fork. Serve immediately.

warm couscous tabbouleh

This recipe is a twist on a traditional Middle Eastern tabbouleh salad, usually made with bulgur, parsley, and lemon. Our quick and tangy version can be served warm or chilled as a main dish or first course.

makes 6 main-dish servings

1½ cups boiling water
1 cup couscous
1 can (15 ounces) chickpeas, rinsed and drained
10 to 12 yellow or red cherry tomatoes, halved
8 scallions, trimmed and chopped
1 small cucumber, peeled, seeded, and diced
¼ cup chopped fresh parsley
Juice of 1 large lemon
3 tablespoons olive oil
2 tablespoons chopped fresh mint (optional)
½ teaspoon freshly ground black pepper
¼ teaspoon salt

Per 1-cup serving: 263 calories • 8g protein • 8g fat • 42g carbohydrates • 0 cholesterol • 315mg sodium • 5g fiber

1. Combine the boiling water and couscous in a small mixing bowl. Cover and let sit for 10 minutes.
2. Meanwhile, in a medium mixing bowl, combine the remaining ingredients. When the couscous is ready, remove the lid and fluff with a fork. Add the couscous to the vegetables and toss thoroughly. Serve warm or chilled.

chickpea-couscous croquettes

No eggs or bread crumbs are needed for these mouth-watering croquettes. Serve them in a sandwich, as an appetizer, or as a main dish accompanied by pasta and tomato sauce. You can bake these flavorful croquettes ahead of time, simply wrap them well and refrigerate. Reheat the croquettes just before serving.

makes 24 croquettes

⅔ cup hulled, raw sunflower seeds (optional)
2 cups cooked and drained chickpeas
1 cup couscous
½ cup tomato juice
½ cup dry red wine
3 tablespoons minced fresh parsley
3 tablespoons soy sauce
2 tablespoons Dijon-style mustard
2 tablespoons red wine vinegar
3 or more garlic cloves, minced
2 teaspoons dried rosemary
1 teaspoon dried thyme
½ teaspoon freshly ground black pepper
1 tablespoon olive oil

Per 2-inch croquette: 48 calories • 2g protein •
1g fat • 8g carbohydrates • 0 cholesterol •
164mg sodium • 1g fiber

1. If using sunflower seeds, preheat the oven to 350°F. Spread the seeds on a baking tray. Remove any shells or discolored seeds. Bake for 5 to 7 minutes, until the seeds smell nutty and darken slightly. Grind the seeds in a food processor for 30 seconds or until coarsely chopped. Add the chickpeas and process until well mixed. Leave the mixture in the food processor and set aside.

2. In a heavy, 1-quart saucepan, combine the couscous, tomato juice, and red wine. Stir and bring the mixture to a boil. Lower the heat, cover the pot, and let simmer for 2 to 3 minutes, until the couscous has absorbed all of the liquid. Remove the pot from the heat and let sit for 5 more minutes.

3. Add the cooked couscous to the chickpea mixture along with the remaining ingredients, except for the olive oil. Mix well, stopping the processor and scraping down the sides once or twice, until smooth.

4. Lightly oil your hands. Shape 2 to 3 tablespoons of chickpea mixture to form a ball. Repeat with remaining mixture until you have 24 balls. Flatten each ball to form a croquette about 2 inches wide and ½ inch thick. Brush each croquette with olive oil and place on a lightly oiled baking tray. Bake croquettes for about 15 minutes, turn them over, brush with oil and bake for another 10 to 12 minutes. Serve immediately.

lentil bulgur pilaf

Pilafs are found all over the world in some form or another—they are simply any of a vast array of dishes usually made with rice and one or more additional ingredients. This dish is from Turkey, where bulgur is actually used more often than rice and at one time was seen as a luxury import, as it is not grown there. You may substitute basmati rice for the bulgur if you wish.

makes 6 servings

1 ½ cups brown lentils
4 ½ cups vegetable broth
2 tablespoons olive oil
3 large onions, thinly sliced
Salt and freshly ground black pepper to taste
1 ½ cups fine bulgur
1 tablespoon tomato paste
1 cup packed spinach leaves, tough stems removed
¼ teaspoon crushed red pepper flakes, or to taste

Per serving: 387 calories • 21g protein • 6g fat • 67g carbohydrates • 0 cholesterol • 774mg sodium • 24g fiber

1. In a large saucepan over high heat, combine the lentils and 3 cups of the broth. Bring the mixture to a boil, skim the surface, then reduce the heat to medium-low and simmer the mixture, partially covered, until the lentils are tender, about 40 minutes.

2. Meanwhile, in a large skillet, heat the olive oil over medium heat. Add the onions and cook, stirring often, until tender and golden, 12 to 15 minutes. Season with salt and pepper and set aside.

3. When the lentils are tender, add the remaining 1½ cups of stock, the bulgur, and tomato paste to the pan. Bring the mixture to a simmer and cook, stirring occasionally, until the bulgur is tender, about 15 minutes. Stir in the spinach, cover the pan, and let the spinach wilt for 2 minutes.

4. Uncover the pan and fluff the pilaf with a fork. Taste and season with red pepper flakes and salt and pepper. Transfer to a warmed serving dish and top with the onions; serve immediately.

pilaf with golden onions and pine nuts

Here's another pilaf recipe, this one using long-grain basmati rice. Since its flavor depends a good deal on the intensity of the caramelized onions, make sure to cook them until they are a deep-golden brown, but not at all burnt.

makes 8 servings

1 tablespoon olive oil
3 cups chopped onions
1½ cups basmati rice
2½ cups vegetable broth or water, heated to
  boiling
Salt and freshly ground black pepper to taste
⅓ cup chopped fresh cilantro or parsley
2 tablespoons pine nuts, toasted
  (see Note, page 153)

Per serving: 159 calories • 4g protein • 4g fat • 28g carbohydrates • 0 cholesterol • 318mg sodium • 2g fiber

1. In a deep saucepan, heat the olive oil over medium heat. Add the onions and cook, stirring often, until dark golden, 10 to 15 minutes. Add the rice and stir to coat, then cook, stirring, for 1 minute. Add the boiling broth or water and stir well. Cover and cook until the rice is tender and all the liquid has been absorbed, 18 to 20 minutes. Season with salt and pepper. Remove from the heat and let stand for 5 minutes, covered.

2. Fluff the rice with a fork and transfer to a warmed serving dish. Sprinkle with cilantro or parsley and pine nuts. Serve immediately.

saffron risotto with almonds

Rice was brought to Italy from Asia during the Crusades, but it did not become popular until the mid-sixteenth century. Now rice, often made into risotto, is a great Italian favorite. Arborio rice, a plump, short-grain variety, is the best choice for making risotto, although if you can't find it, any short-grain type will do.

makes 4 main-dish servings

1 tablespoon unsalted butter
½ cup slivered almonds
4 cups low sodium vegetable broth
1 tablespoon olive oil
3 shallots, chopped
2 garlic cloves, minced
1 cup Arborio rice
Pinch of saffron
½ cup dry white wine
½ teaspoon dried thyme

Per serving: 426 calories • 8g protein • 15g fat • 57g carbohydrates • 8mg cholesterol •87mg sodium • 3g fiber

1. In a small saucepan, melt the butter over medium heat. Add the almonds and cook, stirring, until toasted and golden brown, about 4 minutes. Remove from the heat and reserve.

2. In a medium saucepan, bring the broth to a boil. Keep it hot over very low heat.

3. Meanwhile, heat the olive oil in a heavy-bottomed non-stick saucepan over medium-low heat. Add the shallots and garlic and cook, stirring constantly, until soft, about 2 minutes. Add the rice and saffron and cook for another minute or two, stirring constantly. Add the wine and stir gently until absorbed. Add the simmering broth about ½ cup at a time, stirring continually until each addition is absorbed. Continue cooking, stirring, and adding broth until the rice is tender yet al dente, moist but not soupy, 20 to 25 minutes. You may not need to add all of the broth.

4. Stir in the thyme and almonds and serve immediately.

risotto with artichokes

Artichokes endow this classic risotto rendition with a wild and earthy Mediterranean flavor, while asparagus adds its savory taste and crisp texture. For an herbal nuance, sprinkle chopped fresh parsley or basil over the risotto at the last minute.

makes 6 servings

1 tablespoon olive oil
10 to 12 white button mushrooms, sliced
10 to 12 asparagus spears, trimmed and cut into
   1-inch sections
1 medium red onion, diced
4 garlic cloves, minced
1½ cups Arborio rice
4½ cups very hot water
½ cup dry white wine
½ teaspoon salt
½ teaspoon white pepper
1 can (14 ounces) artichoke hearts, rinsed and
   coarsely chopped
½ cup freshly grated Parmesan cheese

Per serving: 289 calories • 9g protein • 5g fat • 48g carbohydrates • 25mg cholesterol • 489mg sodium • 2g fiber

1. Heat the olive oil in a large saucepan over medium heat. Add the mushrooms, asparagus, onion, and garlic. Cook, stirring, for about 6 minutes. Add the rice and cook, stirring, for 2 minutes longer. Add 2 cups of the hot water, the white wine, and seasonings. Bring the mixture to a simmer and cook, uncovered, over medium-low heat for about 8 to 10 minutes, stirring frequently.

2. Once the liquid has been absorbed, stir in more water, about ½ cup at a time, stirring continually until each addition is absorbed. Continue cooking, stirring, and adding water until the rice is tender yet al dente, moist but not soupy, about 20 minutes. You may not need to add all of the water. Fold in the artichoke hearts and Parmesan cheese and serve.

lemon-basil risotto with ricotta salata

This rather piquant risotto uses *ricotta salata*, a semifirm, salted ricotta cheese, in place of the ubiquitous Parmesan. You can buy it in large supermarkets and Italian specialty stores.

makes 4 side-dish servings,
2 main-course servings

For the broth

4 cups water

1 cup white wine

2 celery stalks

2 carrots, peeled and chopped

2 garlic cloves

1 large onion, quartered

4 whole peppercorns

1 bay leaf

¼ teaspoon salt

For the risotto

1 tablespoon unsalted butter

1 small white onion, finely chopped

⅔ cup Arborio rice

½ cup crumbled *ricotta salata* cheese (or use a
  mild feta cheese, preferably from France)

¼ cup minced fresh basil

½ teaspoon finely grated lemon rind

Per side-dish serving: 295 calories • 8g protein
• 7g fat • 40g carbohydrates • 24mg cholesterol
• 71mg sodium • 4g fiber

1. In a large saucepan, combine the water, wine, celery, carrots, garlic, onion, peppercorns, and bay leaf. Bring to a boil, cover, lower the heat, and simmer for about 1 hour.
2. Strain the broth into another large saucepan, stir in the salt, and keep warm over low heat.
3. Melt the butter in a medium saucepan. Add the chopped onion and cook, stirring, until soft and translucent, about 7 minutes. Add the rice and stir to blend. Add the simmering broth about ½ cup at a time, stirring continually until each addition is absorbed.
4. Continue cooking, stirring, and adding broth until the rice is tender yet al dente, moist but not soupy, 20 to 30 minutes. You may not need to add all of the broth.
5. Add the cheese, basil, and grated lemon rind to the pan and stir well. Remove the risotto from the heat and serve immediately.

Vegetable Entrees

■ Vegetables are truly the cornerstone of all Mediterranean menus, where they are consumed every single day. Chock-full of vitamins and minerals, fresh vegetables are grown in backyards and fields throughout the region, where they sometimes travel no more than a few steps to the kitchen and straight into the pot. ■ Hearty vegetable stews are popular throughout this vast and diverse area. Here, we provide two versions of French ratatouille, made with the traditional combination of tomatoes, zucchini, peppers, and eggplant. Every country seems to have its own variation on a classic vegetable stew, which appears in northern Africa as the generously spiced Moroccan and Algerian *tagine* made with fresh vegetables, dried fruits, and chickpeas. *Tagine*s simmer slowly all day in the earthenware pots that share the same name and have specially designed conical lids that capture and retain the steam as the stew simmers. Hearty Eastern European–inspired Israeli *cholent*s, laden with potatoes, barley, and legumes, are also slow-cooking stews that warm and satisfy the whole family each Sabbath. And in Spain, quickly cooked summer vegetable stews are fortified with garlic toast, eggs, or potatoes. ■ But vegetables are not just stewed when made into a main course. They are also sautéed, baked, roasted, and formed into patties. Our Italian Tofu and Spinach Patties (page 226) are mixed with smoked mozzarella cheese, then pan-fried to golden perfection. And our Vegetable and Bulgur Kibbeh in Yogurt Sauce (page 228) is a tasty twist on a traditional Middle Eastern spiced and stuffed meatball. And there are endless variations on *kibbeh,* the renowned centerpiece of the Middle Eastern table, which incorporates ingredients such as rice or bulgur, spinach, pumpkin, lentils, chickpeas, potatoes, and even pomegranate. Good *kibbeh* has the reputation of being moist, light, and well seasoned, and while *kibbeh* may be fried, poached, steamed, baked, or grilled, ours are baked until crisp, then served with a tangy spiced yogurt sauce. ■ Out of all the vegetables available in the Mediterranean region, eggplant is probably one of the most popular on which to base a meatless main course. Here, we have no less than six recipes starring eggplant, and not one uses an excessive amount of oil, despite eggplant's unctuous reputation. Tomatoes, combined with cheese, other vegetables, pasta, bread, or grains, can also take center stage, as can rich, woodsy mushrooms and sweet-fleshed winter squash. In fact, given the proper attention, even such pantry staples as canned white beans or chickpeas can be turned into simple, flavorsome Mediterranean entrees worthy of even your most discerning guests.

hearty root vegetable and bean stew

Any variety of white beans, including cannellini, will work in this colorful and hearty winter stew.

makes 6 servings

1 small butternut squash, halved, seeds discarded
1 medium sweet potato
2 red or white new potatoes
24 peeled baby carrots
2 cups broccoli or cauliflower florets
2 parsnips, peeled and diced
2 tablespoons olive oil
2 tablespoons flour
1½ cups vegetable broth
1 teaspoon chopped fresh thyme
  (or ½ teaspoon dried)
1 teaspoon chopped fresh rosemary
  (or ½ teaspoon dried)
Salt and freshly ground black pepper to taste
1 can (15 ounces) white beans, rinsed and drained
½ pound spinach, chard, or kale leaves, cut into
  ribbons
3 tablespoons fresh minced herbs (use a combination which may include basil, cilantro, marjoram,
  sage, parsley, oregano, rosemary and thyme)

Per serving: 393 calories • 11g protein • 4g fat
• 79g carbohydrates • 10mg cholesterol • 210mg
sodium • 13g fiber

1. Preheat the oven to 425°F. Prick the squash, sweet potato, and white potatoes in several places with a fork. Place them on a baking sheet and bake until tender, about 30 minutes.

2. Meanwhile, place the carrots, broccoli or cauliflower florets, and parsnips in a steamer insert set over 1 inch of boiling water and steam until tender, about 5 minutes. Reserve ½ cup of the steaming water.

3. Cool the squash, sweet potato, and white potatoes slightly, then peel. Cut the squash into 1-inch pieces; cut the sweet potato and the white potatoes into ¾-inch pieces.

4. In a Dutch oven, heat the olive oil over medium-high heat. Add the flour and cook, stirring, for about 1 minute. Whisk in the reserved steaming water, vegetable broth, thyme, rosemary, and salt and pepper. Bring the mixture to a simmer over medium heat and cook for 3 minutes. Stir in the beans and cook for 1 to 2 minutes longer to heat them through. Add the greens and cook over low heat for 4 to 5 minutes more, until slightly wilted. Stir in the herbs and serve immediately.

quick cassoulet

Carcassonne, in the Languedoc region of France, is home to the *cassoulet,* a savory baked white bean dish flavored with herbs and meats. Here's a quick, one-pot vegetarian version. It's perfect when you're short on time.

makes 4 servings
1 teaspoon olive oil
2 parsnips or rutabagas, chopped
2 carrots, diced
1 medium onion, diced
4 garlic cloves, minced
½ pound seitan or firm tofu, cubed
2 cups cooked white beans
1 tablespoon prepared mustard
½ teaspoon salt
½ teaspoon dried thyme
½ teaspoon dried basil
½ teaspoon dried marjoram
½ teaspoon dried rosemary
½ teaspoon white pepper
About 2 cups water or Mediterranean Vegetable
  Broth (page 102)
Chopped fresh parsley or sliced scallions, for
  garnish

Per serving: 311 calories • 20g protein • 7g fat
• 47g carbohydrates • 0 cholesterol • 375mg
sodium • 11g fiber

1. Preheat the oven to 350°F. In a heavy ovenproof pot or casserole dish, heat the olive oil over medium-high heat. Add the parsnips or rutabagas, carrots, onion, and garlic and cook, stirring, for about 5 minutes. Add the seitan or tofu, beans, mustard, salt, thyme, basil, marjorm, rosemary, and pepper. Add enough water or broth to just barely cover the mixture.
2. Cover the *cassoulet* and bake for 45 minutes. Stir just before serving and adjust seasonings to taste if necessary. Garnish with fresh parsley or scallions and serve.

garbanzo cassoulet

Cassoulet is a peasant bean stew from southern France. Farm women used to prepare these stews in enormous quantities and let them simmer all day in an earthenware pot, or *cassole*. Today, *cassoulet* is served in homes and restaurants all over France. Each cook has his or her own version, but all *cassoulets* contain beans and lots of fresh herbs. This version calls for chickpeas, a favorite in the Mediterranean region of France.

makes 6 servings

For the beans

1½ cups dried chickpeas

4 whole cloves

1 small onion, peeled but left whole

1 cup cubed carrots

2 garlic cloves, minced

2 sprigs fresh parsley

For the sauce

2 tablespoons olive oil

1 cup chopped onion

1 tablespoon finely minced garlic (or to taste)

6 plum tomatoes (or 3 medium tomatoes), chopped

2 cups purchased or homemade Mediterranean Tomato Sauce (page 298)

1 tablespoon chopped fresh basil (or 1 teaspoon dried)

1 tablespoon chopped fresh thyme (or 1 teaspoon dried)

Salt and freshly ground black pepper to taste

For the topping

2 tablespoons olive oil

2 cups dry bread crumbs (see Note)

½ cup chopped fresh parsley

Per serving: 487 calories • 16g protein • 17g fat • 72g carbohydrates • 0 cholesterol • 837mg sodium • 9g fiber

1. In a large, deep pot, soak the chickpeas in water to cover overnight. Rinse the chickpeas, then add more water to the pot so that the chickpeas are covered by an inch or two. Stick the cloves into the whole onion and add it to the pot along with the carrots, garlic, and parsley sprigs. Bring the mixture to a boil, then reduce the heat, cover, and simmer for about 45 minutes or until the beans and carrots are tender. Drain, reserving the cooking liquid. Discard the onion with cloves and the parsley sprigs. Set the bean mixture aside.

2. To make the sauce, in a large skillet, heat the olive oil over medium-high heat. Add the onion and garlic and cook, stirring, until the onion becomes translucent, about 5 minutes. Stir in the fresh tomatoes. Add the tomato sauce, 1½ cups of the reserved bean cooking liquid, basil, and thyme. (If using fresh herbs, do not add until the last 15 minutes of cooking.) Bring the sauce to a boil. Reduce the heat and simmer, covered, for about 45 minutes. Add salt and pepper. Remove the pan from the heat and set the sauce aside.

3. To prepare the topping, in a medium skillet, heat the olive oil over high heat. Add 1 cup of the bread crumbs and the fresh parsley and cook, stirring, until golden, about 1 minute. Remove the pan from the heat, transfer to a bowl, and mix in the remaining 1 cup of bread crumbs. Set the topping aside.

4. Preheat the oven to 350°F. Combine the bean mixture and sauce in a deep oven-proof casserole or baking dish. Sprinkle ⅓ of the bread crumb mixture on top. Bake for 15 minutes, then push the bread crumb layer down into the beans with the back of a spoon and sprinkle another ⅓ of the bread crumb mixture on top. After another 15 minutes of baking, repeat the procedure and add the remaining bread crumb mixture. Bake for 10 minutes longer, then place the *cassoulet* under a broiler for about 5 minutes or until lightly browned on top. Serve immediately.

Note: You can make your own bread crumbs by cutting fresh bread into cubes and baking it at 350°F. until crisp, 15 to 20 minutes. Then process the cubes in a blender or food processor until finely crumbed.

catalán garbanzos

This fragrant dish can be served in wide soup plates and eaten with bread or rice. A tossed green salad completes the meal.

makes 6 servings
2 tablespoons olive oil
4 large ripe tomatoes, peeled and chopped
1 green bell pepper, diced
4 garlic cloves, minced
½ teaspoon salt
¼ teaspoon freshly ground black pepper
¼ teaspoon dried thyme
Pinch of ground nutmeg
Pinch of ground cinnamon
3 cups canned chickpeas, drained

Per serving: 210 calories • 7g protein • 6g fat • 34g carbohydrates • 0 cholesterol • 548mg sodium • 6g fiber

1. Preheat the oven to 325°F. In a medium skillet, heat the olive oil over medium-high heat. Add the tomatoes, bell pepper, garlic, salt, pepper, thyme, nutmeg, and cinnamon. Stir the mixture and cook, stirring, for 3 minutes. Lower the heat, cover the skillet, and simmer for 10 minutes.
2. Place the chickpeas into a 2-quart baking dish and top with the tomato mixture. Cover the dish and bake for 1½ hours, stirring every 30 minutes.

white bean and rosemary stew

White cannellini beans with roasted peppers and rosemary make a hearty Italian stew. This simple dish may be served with crusty Italian rolls and a spinach salad. If you use jarred roasted peppers, you can have dinner in less than 20 minutes.

makes 4 servings

2 tablespoons olive oil

1 medium sweet or yellow onion, chopped

2 garlic cloves, minced

1 can (14 ½ ounces) vegetable broth

1 can (19 ounces) cannellini beans, rinsed and drained

1 ½ teaspoons chopped fresh rosemary (or ½ teaspoon crushed dried)

½ teaspoon black pepper

1 large red bell pepper and 1 large yellow bell pepper, roasted (page 63) and julienned (see Glossary), or 2 jars (6 ounces each) roasted red peppers, julienned

1 tablespoon balsamic vinegar

Per serving: 246 calories • 11g protein • 6g fat • 39g carbohydrates • 0 cholesterol • 43mg sodium • 8g fiber

In a large saucepan, heat the olive oil over medium heat. Add the onion and garlic and cook, stirring, until tender, about 5 minutes. Stir in the vegetable broth and bring the mixture to a boil over high heat. Stir in the beans, rosemary, and black pepper. Reduce the heat to medium-low and simmer, uncovered, for 10 minutes, stirring occasionally. Stir in the roasted peppers and vinegar and cook for 3 minutes more. Ladle the stew into shallow bowls and serve.

tuscan cannellini supper

White, kidney-shaped cannellini beans are used in many Tuscan dishes. Try this easily prepared cold bean dish as a summertime entree or as an accompaniment to Riviera Salad (page 77).

(page 77)

makes 4 main-course or 8 side-dish servings

2 pounds plum tomatoes, diced

Pinch of salt

3 tablespoons red wine vinegar

1 tablespoon olive oil

¼ teaspoon black pepper

⅛ teaspoon crushed red pepper flakes, or to taste

2 garlic cloves, minced

2 cans (15 ounces each) cannellini beans, rinsed and drained

½ cup chopped firmly packed fresh basil

½ cup diced onion

Salt to taste

Per serving: 334 calories • 15g protein • 5g fat • 60g carbohydrates • 0 cholesterol • 365mg sodium • 13g fiber

1. Place the diced tomatoes in a colander or strainer over a bowl or the sink, sprinkle with a pinch of salt, and leave to drain for 15 minutes.

2. Meanwhile, in a large mixing bowl, combine the vinegar, olive oil, black pepper, red pepper flakes, and garlic and beat lightly. Add the tomatoes, beans, basil, and onion. Toss to combine, adding salt to taste.

stuffed baby eggplant

Imam bayaldi, the Turkish name of this renowned dish, means "the priest fainted." There are two thoughts on how this name was derived. The first is that the priest fainted with pleasure after savoring a bite of this luscious eggplant dish. However, the second is that he fainted owing to the copious amount of oil traditionally used to create this recipe. In any case, we greatly reduced the oil but retained the exceptional flavor.

makes 12 servings

6 baby eggplant
3 tablespoons olive oil
1 large onion, quartered and thinly sliced
2 garlic cloves, crushed
1 can (14 ounces) diced tomatoes in juice, drained
    and juice reserved
½ cup chopped fresh parsley
½ teaspoon ground cinnamon
1 bay leaf
Salt and freshly ground black pepper to taste
¼ cup fresh lemon juice
½ teaspoon sugar
Chopped parsley, for garnish (optional)

Per serving: 68 calories • 1g protein • 4g fat • 8g carbohydrates • 0 cholesterol • 176mg sodium • 1g fiber

1. Cut the baby eggplant in half lengthwise. Using a melon baller or a small spoon, carefully scoop out flesh, leaving about a ⅛-inch wall and keeping the skin of the eggplant intact. Finely chop the eggplant flesh and set aside.

2. Arrange the eggplant shells, cut side up, in a large skillet that will hold them snugly. In a medium saucepan, heat 1 tablespoon of the olive oil over medium heat. Add the onion and cook, stirring often, until it softens and begins to brown, about 10 minutes. Add the garlic and cook, stirring, 1 minute more. Add the tomatoes, reserved eggplant flesh, parsley, cinnamon, and bay leaf. Season with salt and pepper. Cook, stirring occasionally, until the eggplant is soft and most of the liquid has been absorbed, about 10 minutes. Remove the saucepan from the heat and discard the bay leaf. Gently spoon the mixture into the eggplant shells (they will be very full).

3. In a small bowl, mix the remaining oil, the lemon juice, reserved tomato juice, and sugar. Pour this dressing over the stuffed eggplant. Cover the skillet and cook the eggplant over low heat until tender, about 30 minutes. Remove from the heat and allow the eggplant to cool slightly in the skillet.

4. Carefully transfer the eggplant to a serving platter, reshaping if necessary. Spoon the pan juices over and around the stuffed eggplant. Serve warm, at room temperature, or cover and chill to serve cold. Sprinkle with chopped parsley, if desired.

eggplant with yogurt-walnut sauce

This robust, Lebanese-inspired dish is chock-full of chunky walnuts, tender eggplant, and soft, earthy chickpeas. A pale, mint and garlic-flavored yogurt sauce crowns the top.

makes 6 servings

For the sauce

3 cups plain yogurt

¼ cup packed mint leaves, finely chopped

2 garlic cloves, minced

Salt to taste

1 tablespoon unsalted butter

½ cup coarsely chopped walnuts

For the vegetables

3 tablespoons olive oil

2 large eggplant, cut into 1-inch cubes

1½ cups cooked chickpeas, rinsed and drained if canned

½ teaspoon salt, or more as needed

½ teaspoon ground cinnamon

1 whole wheat pita bread, split open

Per serving: 353 calories • 12g protein • 21g fat • 35g carbohydrates • 21mg cholesterol • 284mg sodium • 7g fiber

1. To prepare the yogurt sauce, in a medium bowl, combine the yogurt, mint, and garlic and stir well. Add salt and set aside.

2. In a small skillet, melt the butter over medium-high heat. Add the walnuts and toast them until golden brown, about 3 minutes. Set aside and keep warm.

3. To prepare the vegetables, in a large skillet, heat the olive oil over medium heat. Add the eggplant and cook, stirring occasionally, until it is golden brown on all sides and tender within, about 7 minutes. Add the chickpeas, salt, and cinnamon and cook, stirring, until heated through, about 5 minutes. Taste and add more salt, if desired.

4. Toast the pita bread halves in a toaster oven or conventional toaster. Place them on a serving platter. Top with the eggplant mixture, then with the yogurt mixture, and then with the toasted walnuts. Serve immediately with rice.

classic ratatouille

Ratatouille is a rich and hearty mélange of favorite Mediterranean ingredients. Don't be shy about using lots of garlic and herbs—the long cooking mellows their flavors. This dish is extremely versatile and can be served hot or cold, as an hors d'oeuvre, side dish, or as part of the entree. Some say it tastes better reheated, so you might want to prepare it a day or two ahead to let the flavors have a chance to meld.

makes 6 servings

2 tablespoons olive oil
8 garlic cloves, minced
3 pounds tomatoes, cored and diced
1 pound zucchini, sliced
2 large eggplant, cubed
2 large Spanish onions, chopped
1 cup dry red wine or water
Salt and freshly ground black pepper to taste
Pinch of crushed red pepper flakes, or to taste
1 cup packed chopped fresh basil leaves

Per serving: 211 calories • 4g protein • 6g fat • 31g carbohydrates • 0 cholesterol • 34mg sodium • 9g fiber

In a large, heavy skillet or stockpot, heat the olive oil over medium-high heat. Add the garlic and cook for 1 minute. Add all the remaining ingredients except for the fresh basil. Cook over medium heat about 30 minutes, stirring occasionally, until the liquid has evaporated and the mixture resembles a stew. Add the fresh basil and cook for 5 minutes longer.

grilled ratatouille

Grilled ratatouille is even richer tasting than the traditional sautéed version. If you decide to serve your ratatouille cold, stir in 1 teaspoon of olive oil and the juice of half a lemon just before serving.

makes 4 servings

12 cherry tomatoes

2 large zucchini, sliced 1 inch thick

2 medium onions, quartered

1 large eggplant, sliced ¼ inch thick and quartered

1 recipe Mediterranean Marinade (page 287)

1 large red bell pepper, cut in ½-inch slices

1 large yellow or orange bell pepper, cut in ½-inch slices

6 whole unpeeled garlic cloves

12 fresh whole basil leaves, minced

Per serving with 1 tablespoon marinade: 193 calories • 6g protein • 10g fat • 25g carbohydrates • 0 cholesterol • 66mg sodium • 7g fiber

1. In a large bowl, combine the tomatoes, zucchini, onions, eggplant, and marinade. Cover the bowl and refrigerate for at least 30 minutes and up to 8 hours.
2. Soak 8 wooden skewers in water to cover at least 30 minutes before cooking.
3. Preheat the grill or broiler. Thread each wooden skewer with a single type of vegetable, using all the vegetables including the garlic. Brush the kebabs with marinade and grill or broil, turning often, until the vegetables are lightly charred. Remove the vegetables from the skewers (making sure to squeeze roasted garlic cloves from their skins), and toss together in a large bowl. Sprinkle with the basil and serve.

spanish-style vegetable stew

Similar to French ratatouille, this Spanish stew calls for potatoes instead of eggplant. It is traditionally served with four soft-boiled eggs on top of the mixture and extra olive oil for drizzling. Though still a filling and hearty dinner, this lighter version omits the eggs and extra oil.

makes 6 servings

3 tablespoons olive oil
2 large Spanish onions, chopped
6 garlic cloves, minced
8 medium tomatoes, chopped
4 green bell peppers, diced
3 medium zucchini, sliced into rounds
2 medium potatoes, peeled and chopped
1 tablespoon red wine vinegar
½ teaspoon salt
¼ teaspoon freshly ground black pepper

Per serving: 189 calories • 4g protein • 8g fat • 29g carbohydrates • 0 cholesterol • 201mg sodium • 5g fiber

1. In a large, deep skillet with a lid, heat the olive oil over medium heat. Add the onions and garlic and cook, stirring, for 3 minutes. Add the tomatoes, peppers, zucchini, and potatoes. Reduce the heat to medium-low, cover, and cook for about 20 minutes, stirring occasionally, until the vegetables are soft.
2. Remove the lid and simmer for another 10 minutes, or until the mixture becomes thick and stewlike. Stir in the vinegar, salt, and pepper and serve.

pisto manchego

This simple Spanish stew is similar to the preceding recipe, except that instead of being made with potatoes, it is served with thick slices of golden, garlic-fried bread.

makes 6 servings
4 tablespoons olive oil
2 large onions
2 garlic cloves, 1 minced, 1 smashed
2 green bell peppers, diced
1 red bell pepper, diced
3 medium zucchini, sliced
2 large tomatoes, seeded and cubed
1 tablespoon chopped fresh parsley
Salt and freshly ground black pepper to taste
6 thick slices country bread

Per serving: 218 calories • 5g protein • 10g fat • 28g carbohydrates • 0 cholesterol • 186mg sodium • 4g fiber

1. In a large skillet, heat 2 tablespoons of the olive oil over medium-high heat. Add the onions and minced garlic and cook, stirring, until softened, about 5 minutes. Add the bell peppers and cook, stirring, until the peppers begin to soften, about 10 minutes longer. Add the zucchini and tomato and cook the mixture, stirring occasionally, until the tomatoes are broken down and saucelike and the vegetables are tender, about 20 minutes. Stir in the parsley and salt and pepper.

2. In another large skillet, heat the remaining 2 tablespoons oil over medium heat. Add the smashed garlic and cook until it browns around the edges, 2 to 3 minutes. Discard the garlic. Add the bread slices and cook until they are golden brown on both sides, about 2 minutes per side. Season with salt and pepper. Serve the bread alongside the stew.

eggplant and tomato gratin

This is a filling entree for lunch or dinner. Other vegetables, such as zucchini, yellow squash, or peppers, can be used as well.

makes 4 servings
One 1-pound eggplant, thinly sliced on a diagonal
1 tablespoon plus 1 teaspoon olive oil
¼ cup vegetable broth
2 garlic cloves, minced
1 tablespoon balsamic vinegar
½ teaspoon salt
½ teaspoon freshly ground black pepper
1 medium tomato, thinly sliced
½ pound fresh mozzarella cheese, thinly sliced
¼ cup packed fresh basil leaves, julienned

Per serving: 235 calories • 17g protein • 15g fat • 10g carbohydrates • 31mg cholesterol • 571mg sodium • 3g fiber

1. Preheat the broiler. Spread the eggplant slices on a baking sheet. Combine the olive oil, broth, garlic, vinegar, and ¼ teaspoon each of the salt and pepper in a small bowl and whisk well. Brush the eggplant slices with the oil mixture on both sides. Broil 4 inches from the heat for 6 minutes per side.

2. Transfer the eggplant to a baking dish and lower the oven temperature to 375°F. Lay the tomato slices alternating with the cheese slices on top of the eggplant; sprinkle with the remaining salt and pepper. Bake until heated through and bubbling, about 15 minutes. Garnish with fresh basil and serve.

eggplant involtini

These Italian-style eggplant rollups can serve as an antipasto appetizer or main course. In our version, the filling is sweet and nutty, but another option is to make a stuffing using olives and capers. *Involtini* can be served immediately at room temperature, placed in a lightly oiled baking dish and heated before serving, or placed in a lightly oiled baking dish, covered, and refrigerated, then heated and served the next day.

makes about 20 *involtini*

2 medium eggplant, cut lengthwise into ¼-inch slices
Salt
2 tablespoons olive oil
1 cup dry bread crumbs
¼ cup chopped fresh parsley
2 tablespoons plumped, drained, and chopped raisins
1 tablespoon chopped pine nuts
2 garlic cloves, minced
¼ cup orange juice

Per *involtino*: 49 calories • 1g protein • 2g fat • 7g carbohydrates • 0 cholesterol • 48mg sodium • 1g fiber

1. Preheat the grill or broiler. Lay the eggplant slices in a single layer on a clean tea towel or paper towel. Sprinkle both sides liberally with salt and let stand for at least 1 hour to allow the bitter juices to drain. Rinse the eggplant slices under cold water and pat dry. Brush the slices with 1 tablespoon olive oil and grill or broil until soft and slightly charred, about 3 minutes per side.

2. Combine the bread crumbs, parsley, raisins, nuts, and garlic. Add the remaining 1 tablespoon olive oil and the orange juice and mix well.

3. Place 1 cooked eggplant slice on a flat surface. Place about ½ tablespoon of filling at one end of the slice. Flatten the filling slightly with the back of your spoon. Roll the slice starting at the stuffing end and place the roll seam side down on a warmed serving plate. Repeat the procedure with the remaining slices and filling.

eggplant and walnut ragout

This is a pleasantly spicy union of tender eggplant, crunchy nuts, and aromatic spices. It can be served with rice pilaf, pasta, or couscous, and garnished with some plain yogurt if desired. Reheated leftovers taste just as good the next day.

makes 6 servings

2 tablespoons olive oil

1 medium eggplant, coarsely chopped (about 4 cups)

2 celery stalks, chopped

1 medium onion, diced

1 red bell pepper, seeded and diced

3 garlic cloves, minced

1 can (28 ounces) crushed or stewed tomatoes

1 can (14 ounces) crushed or stewed tomatoes

⅓ cup water

1 tablespoon dried oregano

½ teaspoon ground cumin

½ teaspoon freshly ground black pepper

½ teaspoon salt

¼ teaspoon cayenne pepper

½ cup coarsely chopped walnuts, toasted (see Note, page 153)

¼ cup chopped fresh cilantro

Per serving: 175 calories • 4g protein • 11g fat • 18g carbohydrates • 0 cholesterol • 576mg sodium • 4g fiber

1. In a large saucepan, heat the olive oil over medium heat. Add the eggplant, celery, onion, bell pepper, and garlic and cook, stirring, until the vegetables are tender, 8 to 10 minutes.
2. Stir in the tomatoes, water, oregano, cumin, black pepper, salt, and cayenne and cook over medium-low heat for 20 minutes, stirring occasionally. Stir in the walnuts and cilantro and let stand for about 5 minutes before serving.

vegetable tagine with olives and prunes

In Morocco and Algeria, deliciously spiced *tagines* simmer all day in special earthenware pots called by the same name. You can serve the stew with the Fennel Sesame Bread on page 260 or with Traditional Couscous (page 190) or Quick Couscous (page 191).

makes 6 servings

2 tablespoons olive oil

4 shallots, coarsely chopped

1 celery stalk, diced

2 garlic cloves, slivered

1 cinnamon stick

1½ teaspoons paprika

1½ teaspoons ground cumin

1½ teaspoons ground coriander

1 teaspoon salt

1 teaspoon freshly ground black pepper

⅛ teaspoon cayenne pepper, or to taste

1 can (32 ounces) crushed or diced tomatoes (see Note)

⅓ pound string beans, cut into 1-inch lengths

1 small butternut squash or sweet potato, peeled and cut into 1-inch chunks

½ head cauliflower, cut into florets

½ fennel bulb, trimmed and cut into ½-inch chunks

1 large carrot, peeled and sliced into ¼-inch-thick rounds

Vegetable broth or water as needed (see Note)

¼ teaspoon crushed saffron

1 cup canned chickpeas

½ cup whole pitted Kalamata olives

½ cup halved pitted prunes, diced

3 tablespoons chopped fresh parsley

Per serving: 271 calories • 10g protein • 7g fat • 49g carbohydrates • 0 cholesterol • 1,075mg sodium • 10g fiber

1. Preheat the oven to 350°F. In a Dutch oven, heat the olive oil over medium-low heat. Add the shallots, celery, garlic, and cinnamon stick and cook, stirring, until the shallots and celery are soft, about 7 minutes.

2. Add the paprika, cumin, coriander, salt, black pepper, and cayenne. Cook, stirring, until the spices are fragrant, about 1 minute.

3. Stir in the tomatoes, string beans, squash or sweet potato, cauliflower, fennel, and carrot. Add additional vegetable broth or water as needed to cover the vegetables. Add the saffron and stir well.

4. Cover the pot and bake until the vegetables are tender, 40 to 45 minutes. About 5 minutes before the stew is done, stir in the chickpeas, olives, and prunes. Garnish with parsley just before serving.

Note: The type of tomatoes used will determine the amount of broth or water that will be needed to cook the vegetables. Crushed tomatoes will require the addition of about 1 cup water. Stovetop cooking may require slightly more water. Diced tomatoes may not require quite as much water. The finished stew should be somewhat dry, not soupy, and the vegetables should be tender but shapely, not soggy.

moroccan stew

This stew is simple to make and is full of delicious northern African spices. It tastes even better reheated the next day. The Berber spice mixture may be refrigerated in a sealed jar for up to two weeks or stored in the freezer for up to three months. It is also excellent as a spice rub for grilled eggplant, zucchini, and tofu.

makes 6 servings

For the Berber spice mixture (makes extra)

2 tablespoons cumin seed (or 1 teaspoon ground cumin)

½ tablespoon fennel seeds

1 tablespoon whole black peppercorns

1 tablespoon whole allspice berries

3 whole cloves

½ tablespoon coriander seeds

Pinch of saffron

2 tablespoons sweet paprika

½ teaspoon ground cinnamon

½ teaspoon turmeric

For the stew

2 tablespoons olive oil

3 cups peeled and chopped potatoes

2 cups peeled and chopped carrots

2 cups chopped tomatoes

1½ cups chopped onions

1 small butternut squash, peeled, seeded, and chopped

1 cup chopped green bell pepper

1 cup chopped red bell pepper

3 garlic cloves, minced

4 cups water or vegetable broth

Salt to taste

¼ cup minced fresh parsley

Per serving: 170 calories • 3g protein • 5g fat • 31g carbohydrates • 0 cholesterol • 403mg sodium • 7g fiber

1. To make the Berber spice mixture, simply combine all of the ingredients. Set aside.
2. To make the stew, in a large saucepan or Dutch oven, heat the olive oil over medium heat. Add the vegetables, 1½ tablespoons of the spice mixture, and the garlic. Cook, stirring occasionally, for 5 minutes. Add the water or broth, cover, and simmer for 20 to 25 minutes, or until the vegetables are tender. Add salt and garnish with parsley before serving.

mushroom pot pie with polenta crust

Made with both cremini and porcini mushrooms, this dish will impress your guests with its exotic and robust flavors. Because the crust is made of polenta, and not pastry, prep time in the kitchen is greatly reduced, as is the fat content.

makes 4 servings

For the filling

½ ounce dried porcini mushrooms

¾ cup hot water

1 tablespoon plus 2 teaspoons olive oil, plus more as needed

2 pounds new potatoes, cubed

1 medium onion, diced

4 garlic cloves, crushed

1 pound cremini mushrooms, sliced

1 teaspoon dried thyme

⅛ teaspoon cayenne pepper

1½ tablespoons flour

1 cup frozen green peas, thawed

For the crust

3 cups water

¼ teaspoon salt

¾ cup polenta or coarse ground yellow cornmeal

Per 1-cup serving: 427 calories • 12g protein • 5g fat • 86g carbohydrates • 0 cholesterol • 154mg sodium • 9g fiber

1. Soak the porcini in the hot water for at least an hour. Remove the rehydrated mushrooms from the water and, depending on their quality, either discard or reserve the mushrooms for another use. Strain the soaking water through cheesecloth, a fine sieve, or a coffee filter. Set aside the soaking water.
2. Preheat the oven to 425°F. Lightly oil a roasting pan large enough to hold the potatoes in one layer with 1 teaspoon of the oil. Roast the potatoes in the oven, stirring once or twice to prevent sticking and to brown evenly, until tender, about 35 minutes. (The potatoes can be roasted several hours in advance or even the preceding day.)
3. While the potatoes are roasting, in a nonstick skillet, heat 1 teaspoon of the olive oil over medium-high heat. Add the onion and garlic and cook, stirring, until the onion is soft, about 5 minutes. Add the fresh mushrooms, thyme, and cayenne and cook until the mushrooms soften and shrink to about half their original size, about 15 minutes.
4. In a separate skillet, heat the remaining tablespoon of olive oil. Make a roux by adding the flour and stirring until the flour begins to brown. Add the roux and reserved porcini water to the fresh mushroom mixture and cook over medium heat until the liquid reduces by about a third, about 5 minutes.
5. Remove the roasted potatoes from the oven and reduce the oven temperature to 350°F. Combine the mushroom mixture, potatoes, and peas in an oiled 9-by-9-inch baking pan. Set aside and make the polenta crust.
6. For the polenta crust, in a medium saucepan, bring the water and salt to a rolling boil. Add the polenta in a fine stream, stirring constantly to avoid clumping. Turn the heat down to medium, and stir constantly until the mixture thickens and begins to pull away from the sides of the saucepan, about 10 minutes.
7. Spread the polenta over the vegetable and mushroom mixture and bake until the polenta begins to brown, about 15 minutes. Remove from the oven and let sit for 15 minutes before serving.

vegetable paella

Traditional Spanish paella is made with Valencia short-grained rice, but Italian Arborio rice (used for risotto) also works well. It is important to cook the rice uncovered, which prevents it from steaming.
Look for small glass vials of saffron threads (which keep longer than ground saffron) in the spice section of large supermarkets, gourmet specialty stores, or Italian or Spanish groceries.

makes 12 servings

3 tablespoons olive oil

1 large fennel bulb, trimmed, feathery fronds reserved for garnish, bulb chopped

1 large onion, chopped

5 garlic cloves, minced

2 cups Valencia or Arborio rice

1 can (16 ounces) stewed tomatoes

1 can (14 ½ ounces) vegetable broth

1 cup dry vermouth

2 teaspoons dried thyme

½ teaspoon saffron threads (or ¼ teaspoon ground)

¼ teaspoon cayenne pepper

1 can (14 ounces) artichoke hearts, drained and cut into ½-inch wedges

1 large yellow or red bell pepper, cut into 1-inch chunks

1½ cups frozen peas

¼ cup chopped fresh cilantro

Per 1-cup serving: 204 calories • 5g protein
• 4g fat • 35g carbohydrates • 0 cholesterol
• 327mg sodium • 1g fiber

1. In a Dutch oven, heat the olive oil over medium heat. Add the fennel, onion and garlic and cook, stirring, for 5 minutes, stirring frequently. Stir in the rice and cook for 1 minute. Add the tomatoes with their juice, vegetable broth, vermouth, thyme, saffron, and cayenne and bring the mixture to a boil. Stir in the artichoke hearts and bell pepper and return the mixture to a boil. Cover and simmer over low heat for 20 minutes or until most of the liquid has been absorbed.

2. Stir in the peas, cover, and continue to simmer for 2 minutes longer. Remove the pan from the heat and let stand, covered, for 5 minutes or until the liquid has been absorbed. (At this point, the paella may be cooled, covered and refrigerated for up to 24 hours before serving. To serve, reheat until hot, adding additional vegetable broth or water as necessary.)

3. Transfer the paella to a serving dish, sprinkle with fresh cilantro and reserved chopped fennel fronds, and serve.

saffron-flavored stew à la marseilles

The addition of saffron will impart a glowing golden-yellow color to this delicious vegetable stew. If you wish you may garnish each bowl with a teaspoon of Aïoli à la Estella (page 284) before serving.

To easily peel and seed tomatoes, start by cutting a small "x" on the bottom of each one. Drop them in a small pot of boiling water for 1 to 2 minutes, until the skins begin to loosen. Drain and rinse the tomatoes under cold water. Use a small paring knife to remove the skins. Slice each tomato in half through the middle and scoop out the seeds with a small spoon.

makes 4 servings

1 cup dried navy beans or small lima beans
3 cups water
1-by-2-inch piece of orange peel
2 or 3 sprigs of fresh parsley
1 bay leaf
1 sprig of fresh thyme (or ¼ teaspoon dried)
1 small piece of cheesecloth
1 teaspoon olive oil
1 large onion, diced
2 medium leeks, diced
2 to 3 celery stalks, diced
1 large carrot, diced
1 to 2 small new potatoes, diced (optional)
3 to 4 garlic cloves, minced
½ teaspoon dried thyme
½ teaspoon dried basil
½ teaspoon white pepper
1 teaspoon fennel seeds
¼ teaspoon saffron
Pinch of salt
2 cups water or Mediterranean Vegetable Broth (page 102)
2 large tomatoes, peeled (see headnote), seeded, and chopped
Salt and freshly ground black pepper to taste

Per serving: 267 calories • 14g protein • 2g fat • 51g carbohydrates • 0 cholesterol • 52mg sodium • 15g fiber

1. Rinse the beans and remove any tiny stones. Rinse again and place in a large saucepan. Add water to cover the beans by 1 inch and bring to a boil over high heat. Reduce the heat to medium-low and simmer the beans for 5 minutes. Cover the pot, remove from the heat, and let the beans soak for at least 20 minutes.

2. Meanwhile, make a *bouquet garni* by wrapping the orange peel, parsley, bay leaf, and thyme in a piece of cheesecloth and tying tightly with kitchen string to close. Set aside.

3. Drain and rinse the beans and return them to the pot. Add enough water to cover them by 2 inches, and drop in the *bouquet garni*. Bring the beans to a boil, then lower the heat and simmer for 45 minutes, or until the beans are very soft. Drain and discard the *bouquet garni*.

4. In a large skillet, heat the olive oil over medium-high heat. Add the onion, leeks, celery, carrot, potatoes if desired, and garlic. Cook the vegetables, stirring, for 3 to 5 minutes. Stir in the thyme, basil, pepper, fennel seeds, saffron, and salt. Add water or broth and bring to a simmer. Cook for 15 minutes. Stir the beans into the vegetable mixture and add tomatoes. Return the stew to a simmer, and cook for 10 to 15 minutes more. Season with salt and pepper.

mushroom tagine in winter squash

This hearty Moroccan *tagine* is perfect for a festive autumnal meal. Cooked in and served from a whole squash, it is both stunning to look at and scrumptious to eat. Serve it over couscous, if desired.

makes 6 servings

1 *kabocha* squash or sugar/pie pumpkin (5 to 6 pounds)
2 teaspoons olive oil
2 large yellow or red onions, chopped
1 pound mushrooms, halved
1 small zucchini, cut into ½-inch slices
1 small turnip, diced
¼ cup all-purpose flour or whole wheat pastry flour
2 cups dry red wine, plus more if needed
¼ cup water
2 to 3 cubes vegetable bouillon (optional)
4 garlic cloves, minced
3 tablespoons fresh lemon juice
2 tablespoons chopped fresh cilantro
1 tablespoon honey
½ teaspoon ground coriander
¼ teaspoon ground cinnamon
¼ teaspoon cayenne pepper
Pinch of ground nutmeg
Freshly ground black pepper to taste

Per serving: 157 calories • 3g protein • 0 fat • 19g carbohydrates • 0 cholesterol • 696mg sodium • 6g fiber

1. Preheat the oven to 350°F. With a very sharp, small knife, carve a 3- to 4-inch zigzagged circle in the top of the squash or pumpkin and remove the top. (If the peel is too thick to cut easily, bake at 350°F. for 15 to 20 minutes to soften it.) Remove and discard the seeds (or reserve for toasting), and use a large spoon to scrape out the strings until the inside surface is clean.

2. In a large nonstick skillet, heat the olive oil over medium-high heat. Add the onions and cook, stirring, for 5 minutes. Add the mushrooms, zucchini, and turnip and cover the skillet; simmer for 5 minutes, until the mushrooms begin to exude their juices. Stir in the flour and simmer for 1 minute longer. Add 2 cups of the red wine and the remaining ingredients and simmer the *tagine* for about 15 minutes, stirring frequently.

3. Pour the stew into the squash, cover with the cut-out squash lid, and place in a large, shallow dish (such as a pie plate). Bake for about 1 hour, or until the squash is very soft. During baking, stir the *tagine* a couple of times, adding additional dry red wine if too much liquid has evaporated or been absorbed.

4. To serve, spoon out some stew and scrape out some of the squash flesh onto each plate.

greek okra and tomato stew

Rich and chunky, this warming stew combines okra and tomatoes with fragrant herbs and spices.
Serve it with rice or pita bread.

makes 6 servings

1 tablespoon olive oil

2 garlic cloves, minced

1 pound fresh young okra, cleaned, stemmed, and
sliced into ½-inch-thick pieces

1 pound (about 3 medium) ripe tomatoes, chopped

2 scallions, trimmed and minced

2 tablespoons white wine vinegar

1 tablespoon minced fresh mint (or ½ teaspoon
dried)

¼ teaspoon dried oregano

Pinch of allspice or nutmeg

Salt and freshly ground black pepper to taste

Per 1-cup serving: 69 calories • 2g protein
• 3g fat • 9g carbohydrates • 0 cholesterol
• 117mg sodium • 4g fiber

1. In a large skillet, heat the olive oil over medium heat. Add the garlic and cook, stirring frequently, until lightly golden, 1 to 2 minutes. Add the okra pieces and cook, stirring, for 5 minutes. Add all of the remaining ingredients and stir well.

2. Cover the skillet and simmer the stew for 15 to 20 minutes, stirring once or twice, until the tomatoes have been reduced to sauce. If the stew becomes too watery, simmer uncovered just until it thickens slightly.

italian tofu and spinach patties

Smoked mozzarella cheese gives these vegetarian patties a robust woodsy flavor.

makes 8 servings

1 pound soft tofu, crumbled

1 package (10 ounces) prewashed, ready-to-eat spinach

1 cup grated smoked mozzarella cheese

¼ cup freshly grated Parmesan cheese

2 garlic cloves, minced

1 teaspoon salt

¼ teaspoon freshly ground black pepper

¼ teaspoon ground nutmeg

2 cups dry bread crumbs

3 tablespoons olive oil

2 cups Mediterranean Tomato Sauce (page 298), warmed

Per patty with ¼ cup sauce: 282 calories

- 13g protein • 13g fat • 30g carbohydrates
- 10mg cholesterol • 1034mg sodium • 4g fiber

1. In a large bowl, mix the tofu, spinach, cheeses, garlic, salt, pepper, and nutmeg. Shape the mixture into 8 equal-size patties. Dip each patty in bread crumbs.
2. In a medium skillet, heat the olive oil over medium heat. Cook the patties until golden, 3 to 4 minutes per side. Serve in pool of tomato sauce.

eggplant manicotti

This eggplant manicotti recipe is rich with herbs and pine nuts. If you don't have any homemade tomato sauce on hand, use a good-quality prepared sauce. Extra ricotta filling from this easy recipe makes a great sandwich spread or pasta sauce.

makes 4 servings

For the filling

1½ cups ricotta cheese

1 cup loosely packed basil leaves

1 cup loosely packed parsley leaves

½ cup loosely packed spinach

1 tablespoon pine nuts, toasted
  (see Note, page 153)

1 tablespoon freshly grated Parmesan cheese

2 garlic cloves, minced

¼ teaspoon freshly ground black pepper

For the manicotti

1 eggplant, cut lengthwise into ¼-inch-thick slices

2 tablespoons olive oil

2 cups purchased or Mediterranean Tomato Sauce
  (page 298)

½ cup shredded fresh mozzarella

Per serving: 169 calories • 14g protein
• 7g fat • 14g carbohydrates • 16mg cholesterol
• 447mg sodium • 3g fiber

1. To prepare the filling, puree all the filling ingredients in a food processor. Refrigerate until ready to use.

2. If desired, salt the eggplant slices and let sit 30 minutes. Rinse, drain, and blot dry.

3. Preheat the broiler. Lightly oil a baking sheet; arrange the eggplant slices in a single layer on the sheet and brush them with more oil. Broil the eggplant 2 to 3 inches from the heat until softened, 3 to 5 minutes.

4. Preheat the oven to 375°F. Spread about ½ cup tomato sauce in a 9-by-12-inch baking dish. Place 1 to 2 tablespoons ricotta filling in the center of each eggplant slice; roll up. Arrange the rolls in the baking dish, seam side down. Top the rolls with the remaining sauce and sprinkle with the mozzarella. Bake for 45 minutes or until the eggplant is tender and heated through.

vegetable and bulgur kibbeh in yogurt sauce

Kibbeh, usually made with lamb or beef, are savory little meatballs served all over the Middle East. Crisp on the outside and meltingly tender within, our lentil- and bulgur-based version can make the centerpiece for a tantalizing meal. Parsley-imbued tabbouleh salad makes a fitting first course, while tart, icy pomegranate granita is a cooling finale.

makes 6 servings

For the *kibbeh*

3 cups water
1 cup lentils, picked over
1 teaspoon salt, or to taste
2 teaspoons tomato paste
¼ teaspoon cayenne pepper
½ cup fine bulgur
2 tablespoons olive oil
1 large onion, chopped
2 garlic cloves, minced
1 teaspoon ground cumin
½ teaspoon ground coriander
¼ cup chopped fresh parsley
2 tablespoons chopped fresh cilantro
½ tablespoon fresh lemon juice

For the sauce

2 cups plain yogurt
1 teaspoon extra-virgin olive oil
1 teaspoon fresh lemon juice
½ teaspoon ground cinnamon
½ teaspoon ground white pepper
Pinch of cayenne pepper
Salt to taste

Per serving with 2 tablespoons sauce: 221 calories
• 12g protein • 6g fat • 31g carbohydrates •
4mg cholesterol • 390mg sodium • 7g fiber

1. In a medium saucepan, bring the water to a boil. Add the lentils and salt and simmer over medium-low heat until tender, about 30 minutes. Stir in the tomato paste and cayenne until well combined, then stir in the bulgur. Remove the pan from the heat, cover, and let rest until the bulgur is tender and the liquid absorbed, about 30 minutes.

2. Preheat the oven to 450°F. Oil a baking pan with ½ tablespoon of the olive oil. In a large nonstick skillet, heat ½ tablespoon of the oil over medium heat. Add the onion and garlic and cook, stirring, until the vegetables are tender, about 5 minutes. Add the cumin and coriander and cook, stirring, for 1 minute longer.

3. Transfer the lentil mixture to a bowl and stir in the onion mixture. Add the parsley, cilantro, and lemon juice and knead well with your hands until the mixture begins to hold together.

4. Break off golf ball–size lumps of the *kibbeh* mixture and shape into ovals. Place on the prepared pan 1 inch apart and brush with the remaining tablespoon olive oil. Bake until the *kibbeh* are crisp on top, about 8 minutes.

5. Meanwhile, prepare the yogurt sauce. In a small bowl, whisk together all the ingredients. Serve alongside the warm *kibbeh*.

Side Dishes

■ Side dishes, like appetizers, can be so much more than mere accompaniments to a main course. Served several at a time, in company with breads, pasta, or grains, these side dishes can be the meal, no entree needed. Try making a meal of a few of the side dishes served in tandem with an array of appetizers. The diversity of tastes and textures can be astounding. ■ Across the Mediterranean, vegetables cooked into side dishes tend to be cooked or coated with olive oil and garlic, or tossed with zesty herbs, cheese, and sometimes grains. Of course, each country has a slight variation on the theme. Italians and Middle Easterners tend to like their vegetables slowly cooked and very soft, while the French seem to prefer their vegetables quickly sautéed or blanched until just tender yet crisp. ■ Stuffed vegetables are an incredibly popular side dish throughout the entire Mediterranean region and often include mushroom caps, tomatoes, peppers, squash, eggplant, cabbage leaves, and onions. Spinach, green beans, peas, potatoes, fennel, artichokes, and beet greens are some other vegetables that commonly appear as simple side dishes. For added texture and flavor, pine nuts, walnuts, or almonds (and sometimes raisins, too) may be sprinkled on top to make for a toothsome bite against soft, silky vegetables, especially vitamin-rich greens. ■ The temperate climate of the Mediterranean allows for a long growing season and almost every rural family has a vegetable garden. And if they don't, they can easily buy fresh regional produce every day at open-air city or village markets. In all Mediterranean countries, vegetables are served at every meal, as a side dish as well as part of the entree, and meals are traditionally vegetarian more often than not. In countries like Greece, side dishes really don't exist, except for roasted, fried, or baked potatoes. Rather, Greeks eat myriad vegetables together to form a meal. In Italy, vegetables can be served as a side dish, as part of an entree, or as an antipasto—the vivid Italian assortment of appetizers. One might be offered marinated zucchini, batter-fried beets, stuffed Swiss chard, or garlicky rapini. And in northern Africa, no matter what the vegetable served, you can be sure it will be made hot and spicy by a dab or two of *harissa*, that pungent chile-laden condiment so in favor there.

roasted mediterranean vegetables

As vegetables roast over high heat, their natural sugars caramelize and intensify the flavors. If you like, you can also roast green beans, yams, potatoes, zucchini, and eggplant.

makes 6 servings
2 yellow bell peppers
2 green bell peppers
1 pound carrots
Olive oil spray
Coarse or kosher salt (optional)

Per serving: 45 calories • 1g protein • 0 fat • 10g carbohydrates • 0 cholesterol • 289mg sodium • 3g fiber

Preheat the oven to 500°F. Remove the core and seeds from the bell peppers and cut each into 8 pieces. Cut the carrots on the diagonal into ¼-inch slices. Arrange the peppers and carrots in one layer on 2 baking sheets and mist lightly with olive oil spray. Roast the vegetables for 12 to 15 minutes, until well cooked but not burned. Sprinkle with salt to taste, if desired. Serve immediately.

mixed vegetable fritters

Italian-style fried vegetables are a favorite antipasti or side dish. Here, we've offered a simple batter into which any number of fresh vegetables can be dipped. Frying times, however, may vary according to the type of vegetable used, so if this makes you nervous, you might want to fry one piece of each type as a test to get the timing right.

makes 10 servings

For the batter

1½ cups all-purpose flour
½ teaspoon baking powder
½ teaspoon salt
¾ cup water
1 large egg, lightly beaten
1 tablespoon olive oil

For the vegetables

8 thin (about ½ inch in diameter) asparagus
   spears, trimmed
2 medium zucchini, cut into ½-inch slices
1 small eggplant, sliced in half lengthwise, then
   sliced into ½-inch pieces
1 small green bell pepper, cored, cut in half
   lengthwise, then cut into ¼-inch slices
½ small head broccoli or cauliflower, separated
   into 1-inch florets
Olive oil for frying
Salt to taste

Per serving: 132 calories • 5g protein • 4g fat
• 22g carbohydrates • 21mg cholesterol
• 124mg sodium • 4g fiber

1. In a large bowl, combine 1 cup of the flour, baking powder and salt and mix well. Stir in the water, egg, and olive oil and mix well. Let the mixture rest for 20 minutes at room temperature. Place the remaining ½ cup flour in a shallow dish.

2. When ready to fry, fill a large pot or wok one-third of the way with oil. Heat the oil until it reaches 365°F. on a deep-frying thermometer, or until a piece of bread turns golden brown in 60 seconds when immersed in the hot oil.

3. Working with one type of vegetable at a time, dip the vegetable pieces first into the flour, shaking off any excess, then into the batter, coating well. Carefully slide the coated vegetables into the oil (being careful not to crowd the pan; you will have to work in batches) and fry until crisp and golden brown on the outside and tender within. Cooking times will vary according to the type of vegetables used, but will fall somewhere between 1 and 4 minutes.

4. Using a slotted spoon, remove the fritters as they are cooked to a paper towel–lined plate to drain. Sprinkle with salt and serve hot.

artichokes stuffed with rice and yogurt

Native Mediterranean artichokes are used extensively throughout the region. In this elegant dish, artichokes are stuffed with herb-flecked rice mixed with yogurt. Serve it either as a side dish or as an appetizer.

makes 6 servings

4 cups water
1 cup rice
6 large artichokes
3 cups finely chopped onions
1 small leek, trimmed and finely chopped
3 tablespoons fresh dill, finely chopped
¼ cup olive oil
1 teaspoon salt
1½ cups low-fat yogurt
1 large egg, beaten
2 tablespoons white wine
Salt and freshly ground black pepper to taste

Per serving: 355 calories • 12g protein • 11g fat
• 54g carbohydrates • 39mg cholesterol
• 656mg sodium • 9g fiber

1. In a medium saucepan, bring 3 cups of the water and the rice to a boil. Lower the heat, cover the pot, and simmer until the rice is almost tender, about 10 minutes. Drain well.

2. Meanwhile, prepare the artichokes by cutting the stems evenly so that the artichokes can stand on their own. With a serrated knife, cut off the top portion of each artichoke. Remove the large outer leaves and snip off the tops of any pointed leaves. Spread the leaves open. Using a knife or a grapefruit spoon, remove the hairy chokes.

3. In a large bowl, combine the drained rice, 2 cups of the onions, the leek, and dill. Fill the prepared artichokes with the rice mixture and set aside.

4. In a large saucepan (large enough to fit artichokes), heat the oil over medium-high heat. Add the remaining 1 cup onion and cook, stirring, until softened, 2 to 3 minutes. Arrange the artichokes on top of the onion in the saucepan; add the remaining 1 cup water and salt to the bottom of the pan. Simmer, covered, for 20 to 25 minutes. Remove the artichokes carefully with tongs or a fork and place in a baking dish. Pour any sauce that has been formed in the saucepan over the artichokes.

5. Preheat the oven to 350°F. In a small bowl, combine the yogurt, egg, wine, and salt and pepper. Blend well. Pour the yogurt sauce over the artichokes. Bake for 20 minutes. Remove the artichokes to a platter and serve hot with the reserved sauce from the baking dish on the side.

garlicky beet greens with potatoes and olives

Take advantage of fresh beet greens in the spring, when they are tender and abundant. This healthy, iron-rich side dish will add substance to a light meal of cold soup and salad.

makes 6 servings

24 small new potatoes (about 2 pounds)
1 to 1½ pounds beet greens
2 tablespoons olive oil
1 small onion, minced
3 to 4 garlic cloves, smashed
¼ to ½ cup water
¼ cup coarsely chopped Kalamata olives
Freshly squeezed lemon juice to taste
Salt and freshly ground black pepper to taste

Per 1-cup serving: 231 calories • 8g protein
• 6g fat • 38g carbohydrates • 21mg cholesterol
• 366mg sodium • 6g fiber

1. Set a steamer insert into a large pot filled with 1 inch of water. Add the potatoes and steam until they are tender, about 20 minutes. When they are cool enough to handle, cut each potato in half.
2. Rinse the greens several times to make sure that all sand and grit are removed. Remove the stems from the beet greens and finely dice.
3. In a large pot or skillet, heat the olive oil over medium heat. Add the onion and garlic and cook, stirring frequently, for 2 to 3 minutes. Add the greens, cover, and steam until just tender, about 3 minutes.
4. In a serving bowl, combine the chopped greens, potatoes, olives, and lemon juice to taste and toss to mix. Season with salt and black pepper and serve.

marinated grilled eggplant

If you go shopping in an Italian deli you'll find prepared slices of grilled eggplant submerged in jars filled with golden olive oil. When they're lifted out with a fork, the oil runs off in a stream. If that seems like a little too much of a good thing, follow this delicious, easy-to-make recipe. You won't miss the fat.

To make thin chiffonade strips with the basil, stack the leaves on top of each other, roll into a cigar shape and cut crosswise into thin ribbons.

makes 4 servings

2 tablespoons extra-virgin olive oil, plus more as desired
1 large eggplant, sliced lengthwise into ¼- to ½-inch-thick slices
⅓ cup lightly packed fresh basil leaves, cut into a chiffonade (see headnote)
3 garlic cloves, minced
Pinch of crushed red pepper flakes
Salt to taste

Per serving: 99 calories • 1g protein • 7g fat • 9g carbohydrates • 0 cholesterol • 272mg sodium • 2g fiber

1. Lightly oil a stovetop grill or other grill and preheat to medium-high. Grill the eggplant slices until they are soft and cooked through, 5 minutes per side.
2. Transfer the slices to a shallow bowl. Brush the slices with olive oil and sprinkle them with the basil, garlic, red pepper flakes, and salt. Serve the eggplant immediately, with pasta, in sandwiches, or as part of an antipasto tray. You can also let it marinate for up to 1 week in the refrigerator.

fava beans with pesto sauce

In Genoa, the birthplace of pesto, the tangy basil sauce seems to find its way into many dishes, from pasta to soups to *bruschetta*. Pesto goes very well with fava beans and, believe it or not, this deliciously simple dish takes only ten minutes to prepare. If you can't find fava beans, use another type of white bean instead.

makes 6 servings

2 cups fresh basil

¼ cup walnuts

¼ cup freshly grated Parmesan cheese

3 tablespoons olive oil

2 garlic cloves, minced

Salt and freshly ground black pepper to taste

3 cans (15 ounces each) fava beans, rinsed and
  drained

6 lettuce leaves

2 to 4 scallions, trimmed and thinly sliced

Tomato wedges and/or red bell pepper rings, for
  garnish (optional)

Per serving: 343 calories • 19g protein
• 12g fat • 43g carbohydrates • 3mg cholesterol
• 565mg sodium • 12g fiber

1. In a blender or food processor, process the basil until finely chopped. Add the walnuts, Parmesan cheese, olive oil, and garlic and process until smooth. Season with salt and pepper.

2. In a small bowl, mix the pesto with the fava beans.

3. On a platter or individual salad plates, arrange the lettuce leaves. Mound the pesto-bean mixture on top of the lettuce leaves. Scatter the scallions over the tops. Garnish with tomato wedges and/or red bell pepper rings if desired. Serve at room temperature.

fennel à la grecque

Literally "in the Greek style," this French dish is bursting with the sweetness of fennel, cooked until just barely tender and offset by the unexpected tang of lemon.

makes 6 servings

4 cups water

3 medium fennel bulbs, trimmed and cut into ¼-inch sticks

⅓ cup chopped fresh parsley

Juice of 1 lemon

3 teaspoons red wine vinegar

2 teaspoons freshly grated lemon zest

Salt and freshly ground black pepper to taste

Per serving: 15 calories • 1g protein • 0 fat • 4g carbohydrates • 0 cholesterol • 30mg sodium • 0 fiber

1. In a large stockpot, bring the water to a boil and add the fennel sticks. Cover and cook for about 5 minutes, until the fennel is just barely tender.
2. While the fennel is cooking, in a small bowl, whisk together the parsley, lemon juice, vinegar, lemon zest, and salt and pepper.
3. Drain the fennel and transfer to a serving dish. Toss with the parsley-lemon mixture and serve.

navy beans with fennel

The distinct, delicate flavor of fennel is especially popular in French cuisine and in the French-influenced cuisine of the Maghreb, where the bulb is commonly baked, boiled, or sautéed with onions, wine, and a variety of complementary ingredients.

makes 6 servings

¼ cup olive oil

2 medium fennel bulbs, trimmed and diced into
   1-inch cubes

1 large onion, chopped

1 cup water

3 cups cooked navy beans, rinsed if canned

2 medium tomatoes, finely chopped

Salt and freshly ground black pepper to taste

Per 1-cup serving: 262 calories • 11g protein • 10g fat • 35g carbohydrates • 0 cholesterol • 126mg sodium • 8g fiber

In a large saucepan, heat the olive oil over medium heat. Add the fennel and onion and cook, stirring, until slightly softened, about 5 minutes. Add the water and simmer until tender, about 20 minutes. Add the beans, tomatoes, and salt and pepper, adding a little more water to prevent sticking if necessary. Simmer for 10 minutes more. Serve warm or cold.

garlicky greens sauté

Try this vibrant, healthful sauté with a rice or lentil pilaf and steamed carrots or squash. You can use whatever greens are in season.

makes 4 servings
2 tablespoons olive oil
1 large onion, minced
5 garlic cloves, minced
¼ cup sherry or white wine (optional)
¼ teaspoon dried oregano
¼ teaspoon dried basil
Salt and freshly ground black pepper to taste
8 cups dark leafy greens (spinach, chard, beet greens, etc.)
¼ to ½ cup freshly grated Parmesan cheese

Per serving: 97 calories • 4g protein • 5g fat • 9g carbohydrates • 4mg cholesterol • 200mg sodium • 4g fiber

1. In a large, deep skillet, heat the olive oil over medium-high heat. Add the onion and garlic and cook, stirring, until softened, about 5 minutes.
2. Add the sherry or white wine if desired, the oregano, basil, and salt and pepper; stir well.
3. Add the mixed greens to the skillet, pressing them down with the back of a spoon as they begin to wilt. Cook, stirring, until the greens are completely wilted, about 10 minutes. Transfer the greens to a serving dish, sprinkle with Parmesan cheese, and serve.

marinated mushrooms and hazelnuts

Crunchy, soft, sweet, and tart all at the same time, this marinated mushroom dish from Andalusia is anything but ordinary. Serve it with forks, wooden toothpicks, or bread for scooping. You can substitute blanched almonds for the hazelnuts.

makes 6 servings

1 cup hazelnuts

⅓ cup red wine

2 tablespoons olive oil

½ teaspoon salt

½ teaspoon dried thyme

½ teaspoon fennel seeds, slightly crushed

¼ teaspoon freshly ground black pepper

½ pound small button mushrooms, cut in half (about 3 cups)

Per serving: 207 calories • 5g protein • 18g fat • 6g carbohydrates • 0 cholesterol • 197mg sodium • 4g fiber

1. Preheat the oven to 350°F. Spread the hazelnuts on a baking sheet and toast them in the oven until fragrant, about 10 minutes. Let the nuts cool just slightly and rub them with a kitchen towel to remove their papery skins. Coarsely chop the nuts and set them aside.

2. In a medium skillet, combine the red wine, olive oil, salt, thyme, fennel seeds, and pepper. Warm the mixture over low heat until barely bubbling. Do not allow it to simmer. Add the fresh mushrooms and heat just until they exude a little moisture, about 5 minutes.

3. Transfer the mushroom mixture to a bowl and add the hazelnuts. Refrigerate, covered, for at least 2 hours, preferably overnight. Serve chilled or at room temperature.

mixed mushroom ragout

Traditional French ragouts are meat-based stews. In this recipe we have substituted a mélange of hearty, full-bodied mushrooms. Exotic mushrooms are less common and more expensive in the United States than in France, but this dish is worth the splurge. Serve it for special occasions or when entertaining good friends.

To make Mixed Mushroom Ramekins using this recipe, simply transfer the mushroom ragout to four small ovenproof ramekins or custard cups. Sprinkle each with 2 tablespoons shredded Gruyère cheese. Bake at 400°F. until the cheese begins to bubble and turn golden brown, 10 to 12 minutes. Serve hot with crusty French bread.

makes 4 servings

1 cup boiling water
½ ounce dried porcini mushrooms
1 tablespoon olive oil
1 large onion, chopped
3 garlic cloves, minced
8 ounces mixed fresh exotic mushrooms such as
    shiitake, oyster, chanterelles, or morels
1 tablespoon chopped fresh thyme leaves
    (or 1 teaspoon dried)
½ teaspoon salt
¼ teaspoon freshly ground black pepper
¼ cup heavy cream (optional)
4 slices sourdough bread, toasted
Chopped fresh thyme leaves (optional)

Per serving without cream: 141 calories • 4g protein • 5g fat • 22g carbohydrates • 0 cholesterol • 449mg sodium • 3g fiber

1. Pour the boiling water over the dried porcini mushrooms and let stand until the mushrooms are tender, about 25 minutes. Strain the mushrooms, reserving the liquid. Coarsely chop the rehydrated mushrooms; set aside.
2. In a large nonstick skillet, heat the olive oil over medium heat. Add the onion and garlic and cook, stirring, until the vegetables are tender and lightly golden, about 10 minutes. Set aside.
3. Remove and discard the stems of the shiitake mushrooms, and cut any large caps in half. Halve any large oyster mushrooms. Thinly slice the chanterelle mushrooms if they are large or very firm. Leave the morels whole. Add the mixed fresh mushrooms to the onion mixture in the skillet and cook, stirring, for 5 minutes. Pour the reserved mushroom liquid into the skillet, leaving any sediment in the bottom of the bowl. Add the reserved porcini mushrooms, thyme, salt, and pepper. Simmer until the mushrooms are tender, about 5 minutes. Add the cream, if using, and heat through. Serve the ragout over toast and sprinkle with fresh thyme if desired.

baked stuffed onions

Slightly sweetened with honey, these stuffed onions are delicious and warming. This hearty winter side dish stands up to reheating, so feel free to make it a day ahead.

makes 4 servings

4 medium onions, peeled
½ cup finely chopped walnuts
½ cup wheat germ or bread crumbs
2 tablespoons honey
1 tablespoon red wine vinegar
2 teaspoons Dijon-style mustard
½ teaspoon salt
¼ teaspoon freshly ground black pepper
¼ cup chopped fresh parsley, for garnish

Per serving: 245 calories • 9g protein • 11g fat • 33g carbohydrates • 0 cholesterol • 314mg sodium • 6g fiber

1. Preheat the oven to 350°F. Slice about ½ inch off the top of each onion. With a melon baller, hollow out a bowl-shaped space in each onion large enough to hold about ¼ cup filling. Slice off just enough of the bottom of each onion so that they stand upright.
2. In a medium bowl, combine the walnuts, wheat germ or bread crumbs, honey, vinegar, mustard, salt, and pepper; set aside.
3. Arrange the hollowed-out onions in a baking dish. Pour about ⅓ cup water around the onions and bake for 30 minutes. (Add water about ¼ cup at a time if it evaporates during baking.)
4. Remove the dish from the oven and spoon the filling into the onions and over their tops. Return them to the oven and bake until softened, about 30 minutes. Garnish stuffed onions with parsley. Serve warm.

honey-glazed onions

A filling of confetti-colored vegetables and a honey-mustard glaze elevates a simple onion to a lovely holiday dish. These stuffed onions can be made ahead and reheated just before serving time.

makes 20 servings
10 medium Vidalia onions

For the filling
1 cup seasoned bread crumbs
1 cup corn kernels, frozen or canned
1 cup diced zucchini
1 cup grated carrots
1 cup diced cooked beets
1 cup water

For the glaze
½ cup honey
3 tablespoons Dijon-style mustard
2 tablespoons balsamic or red wine vinegar
2 teaspoons paprika
1½ teaspoons salt
1 teaspoon freshly ground black pepper
½ teaspoon ground ginger

Per serving: 92 calories • 2g protein • 1g fat • 19g carbohydrates • 0 cholesterol • 303mg sodium • 2g fiber

1. Preheat the oven to 350°F. Peel the onions and slice them in half crosswise. Remove the centers, leaving a hollowed-out bowl in each onion half.
2. To prepare the filling, in a large bowl, stir together ½ cup of the bread crumbs, the corn, zucchini, carrots, and beets. Firmly pack the filling into the onion halves and arrange them in a shallow baking dish so that they fit snugly. Pour the water around the base of the onions; set aside.
3. To prepare the glaze, in a separate bowl, whisk together all of the glaze ingredients. Drizzle half of the glaze over the tops of the stuffed onions. Bake for 30 minutes. Drizzle the onions with the remaining glaze. Return the onions to the oven and bake for 30 minutes more.
4. Just before serving, sprinkle the onions with the remaining ½ cup bread crumbs and place them under the broiler until the crumbs are toasted and golden brown.

marinated pearl onions with tomato-saffron sauce

Saffron, made from the bright yellow stamens of the purple crocus flower, is a popular spice throughout the Mediterranean, and especially in the Maghreb, Spain, and Turkey. This colorful and sweet yet tangy side dish is especially good with grain-based dishes, such as pilafs. It will keep for up to ten days in the refrigerator.

makes 6 servings

30 pearl onions, peeled
¾ cup dry white wine
3 tablespoons olive oil
2 to 3 tablespoons red wine vinegar, or to taste
2 garlic cloves, sliced
½ teaspoon fresh thyme
½ teaspoon salt
1 bay leaf
⅓ cup raisins
2 tablespoons tomato paste
⅛ teaspoon saffron threads

Per serving: 123 calories • 1g protein • 7g fat • 11g carbohydrates • 0 cholesterol • 327mg sodium • 1g fiber

1. In a medium saucepan over medium-high heat, bring the onions, wine, olive oil, vinegar, garlic, thyme, salt, and bay leaf to a boil. Lower the heat to a simmer and cook, uncovered, for about 10 minutes. (Add water as needed to prevent sticking.)
2. Add the raisins, tomato paste, and saffron threads and simmer until the onions are tender, about 7 minutes. Remove from the heat and let cool.
3. Transfer to a serving dish, cover, and chill for at least 1 hour before serving;

pickled onions with honey sauce and black sesame seeds

Black sesame seeds add a slightly smoky flavor to this sweet sauce. They can be found in Middle Eastern or specialty food stores, or use regular sesame seeds instead. Because of their high oil content, sesame seeds tend to turn rancid relatively quickly and should be purchased in small quantities. They may be stored in a cool, dark place for no more than three months.

makes 8 servings

For the salad

2 cups cauliflower florets
1 cup broccoli florets
2 cups pickled onions or cocktail onions
1 cup finely chopped fresh cilantro
1 cup finely chopped onion

For the sauce

7 tablespoons olive oil
½ cup white wine vinegar
½ cup honey
1 teaspoon Dijon-style mustard
Pinch of salt
Black sesame seeds, for garnish

Per ½-cup serving: 105 calories • 1g protein • 6g fat • 13g carbohydrates • 0 cholesterol • 10mg sodium• 1g fiber

1. Bring a large pot of water to a boil. Add the cauliflower and broccoli and blanch for 1 minute. Drain well and coarsely chop.
2. Drain the pickled or cocktail onions and place them in a large bowl. Add the cauliflower and broccoli, cilantro, and onion. Set aside.
3. To make the sauce, in a blender, combine the olive oil, vinegar, honey, mustard, and salt and blend until fairly thick. Pour the sauce over the salad and sprinkle with the black sesame seeds.

canary islands potatoes with mojo sauce

In Spain's Canary Islands, off the northwest coast of Africa, the potatoes for this dish are cooked in seawater and liberally splashed with tart and fiery Mojo Sauce. You can also use this sauce as a dip. Cut the potatoes into quarters before boiling. Arrange the prepared potatoes on a serving platter, spear them with wooden toothpicks, and serve the Mojo sauce on the side.

makes 6 servings

12 medium red-skinned potatoes
½ cup red wine vinegar
2 tablespoons olive oil
2 garlic cloves, pressed
2 teaspoons minced fresh parsley
¾ teaspoon paprika
¾ teaspoon cumin seeds, toasted and slightly crushed
½ teaspoon salt, or to taste
⅛ teaspoon crushed red pepper flakes, or to taste

Per serving: 267 calories • 5g protein • 5g fat • 52g carbohydrates • 0 cholesterol • 1211mg sodium • 5g fiber

1. Cut the unpeeled potatoes in half. Bring a large pot of salted water to a boil and add the potatoes. Cook until tender but not mushy, about 15 minutes. Drain well.
2. Meanwhile, make the Mojo Sauce by whisking together the vinegar and olive oil in a small bowl. Add all of the remaining ingredients. Whisk again. Pour the sauce over the potatoes and serve hot or at room temperature.

potatoes in sweet-and-sour sauce

This potato dish is quick to prepare yet full of earthy, sophisticated flavors. Serve it warm with other antipasti, or chill it and serve it cold as a cooked salad side dish.

makes 6 servings

¼ cup olive oil

1 large onion, thinly sliced

12 small new potatoes, cut into quarters

12 black or green Italian olives, pitted and coarsely chopped

2 tablespoons water

2 tablespoons capers (optional)

3 tablespoons red wine vinegar

2 tablespoons sugar

Per serving: 223 calories • 2g protein • 11g fat • 33g carbohydrates • 0 cholesterol • 133mg sodium • 2g fiber

1. In a large skillet, heat the olive oil over high heat. Add the onion and cook, stirring, for 2 minutes. Add the potatoes, olives, water, and capers if using. Cover, lower the heat to medium, and cook, stirring occasionally, until the potatoes are barely soft, about 8 minutes.

2. Remove the cover and cook until all of the liquid evaporates. Mix the vinegar and the sugar and stir until the sugar is dissolved. Pour the mixture over the potatoes. Serve either warm or chilled. (The flavor is enhanced if the dish is refrigerated for a day or two.)

savory potato-fennel cake

This layered dish is a rustic, satisfying mixture of fennel, potatoes, and onions.

makes 6 servings

4 teaspoons olive oil

2 pounds red or white potatoes, thinly sliced (5 to 6 cups)

1 red onion, chopped

½ teaspoon dried thyme

Salt and freshly ground black pepper to taste

2 medium fennel bulbs, trimmed and thinly sliced

2 tablespoons freshly grated Parmesan cheese

Per serving: 189 calories • 4g protein • 4g fat • 36g carbohydrates • 1mg cholesterol • 55mg sodium • 3g fiber

1. Preheat the oven to 350°F. In a large cast-iron skillet, rub 2 teaspoons of the olive oil over the bottom and sides. As neatly as possible, place a layer of potato slices in a spiral fashion, using up half of the slices. Sprinkle with half of the chopped onion, half of the thyme, 1 teaspoon of the remaining oil, and the salt and pepper. Place a layer of fennel on top, using up half of the fennel. Repeat these 2 layers, ending with a layer of fennel slices.

2. Sprinkle the top fennel layer with Parmesan cheese, and press down hard on the layers with a plate. Remove the plate and bake until the fennel is tender and the potatoes are crispy and brown, 35 to 40 minutes. Allow to cool for 10 minutes before cutting into wedges and serving.

spinach with pine nuts and raisins

This is a typical Catalan dish that combines the sweet and buttery flavors of raisins and pine nuts. You can try substituting Swiss chard or beet greens for the spinach.

makes 4 servings

5 packages (10 ounces each) prewashed,
   ready-to-eat spinach
2 tablespoons olive oil
2 garlic cloves, minced
⅓ cup pine nuts, toasted (see Note, page 153)
⅓ cup raisins, coarsely chopped
½ teaspoon salt
¼ teaspoon freshly ground black pepper

Per serving: 219 calories • 12g protein
• 12g fat • 25g carbohydrates • 0 cholesterol
• 553mg sodium • 11g fiber

1. Bring a large pot of water to a boil. Blanch the spinach by dropping it in the boiling water for 45 seconds. Immediately drain the spinach, chop it, and set aside.

2. In a large, heavy skillet, heat the olive oil over medium heat. Cook the garlic, stirring, until just lightly browned, 2 to 3 minutes. Add the spinach and all of the remaining ingredients. Cook over medium heat for 10 minutes, stirring frequently, until the spinach has wilted. Serve hot or at room temperature.

sautéed spinach and fava beans

A *bouquet garni* is a classic French combination of herbs used to enhance the flavor of soups and stews. To make this herb bundle, simply wrap 3 sprigs parsley, 2 sprigs fresh rosemary, 1 sprig fresh thyme, and 2 bay leaves in a piece of cheesecloth, making sure to tie it securely with a small piece of string.

If you can't find dried fava beans (which are available in specialty and Middle Eastern markets), use lima beans instead.

makes 3 servings

1 cup dried fava beans
3 cups water
½ teaspoons salt
Bouquet garni (see headnote)
2 teaspoons olive oil
4 garlic cloves, minced
Pinch of cayenne
1 package (10 ounces) prewashed, ready-to-eat spinach
Salt to taste
Optional garnishes: wedge of lemon or lime, roasted red pepper, tomatoes, olives

Per serving: 224 calories • 16g protein • 2g fat • 34g carbohydrates • 0 cholesterol • 437mg sodium • 11g fiber

1. Soak the fava beans in water for at least 4 hours (or overnight). Pour off the soaking water and rinse the beans. Add the salt and fresh water to cover the beans by 1 inch. Bring the beans to a boil. Add the *bouquet garni* and cover the pot, leaving the lid slightly ajar. Lower the heat and simmer for 45 minutes or longer, until the beans are soft. Drain the beans and remove and discard the *bouquet garni*.
2. In a large skillet, heat the olive oil over medium heat. Add the garlic and cook, stirring, until it turns golden, about 5 minutes (do not let the garlic burn). Remove the garlic with a slotted spoon and set it aside. Add the cayenne to the pan. Stir in the spinach, cover, and let cook for 1 minute, until wilted. Season the spinach with salt.
3. Mound the spinach onto a large serving plate, top with beans, and sprinkle with the browned garlic. Add garnishes if desired.

string beans with walnuts and pomegranate

An impressive side dish, this recipe is easy and elegant. The addition of pomegranate gives a splash of color and an exotic Mediterranean flavor to a classic string bean preparation.

makes 4 servings

½ cup coarsely chopped walnuts
1 pound string beans
1 tablespoon fresh lemon juice
2 teaspoons extra-virgin olive oil
Salt to taste
2 tablespoons pomegranate seeds

Per serving: 158 calories • 4g protein • 11g fat • 13g carbohydrates • 0 cholesterol • 9mg sodium • 5g fiber

1. Preheat the oven to 350°F. Spread the nuts out on a baking sheet and toast them in the oven until golden and fragrant, about 5 minutes. Transfer the nuts to a plate to cool.
2. Bring a large pot of water to a boil. Add the string beans and blanch for 2 minutes. Drain well.
3. Mix the string beans with the walnuts, lemon juice, olive oil, and salt. Serve topped with the pomegranate seeds.

herbed tomatoes

At the height of the tomato season, or any time for that matter, you'll definitely want to try this cool summer dish. These tomatoes will spice up a simple cheese sandwich served on crusty slices of French bread.

8 ripe but firm tomatoes, preferably peeled
1 scallion, trimmed and thinly sliced
1 garlic clove, minced
2 tablespoons red wine vinegar
1 tablespoon minced fresh cilantro
1 tablespoon minced fresh parsley
Pinch of cayenne pepper (optional)

Per serving: 37 calories • 1g protein • 1g fat • 8g carbohydrates • 0 cholesterol • 16mg sodium • 2g fiber

1. Core 6 of the tomatoes and cut them horizontally into 1-inch-thick slices. Arrange in a large shallow dish and set aside.
2. Core the remaining 2 tomatoes and cut them into large chunks. Place the tomato chunks in a food processor and puree.
3. Strain the tomato puree into a small bowl to remove the seeds, add all of the remaining ingredients, and stir to blend.
4. Pour the tomato sauce over the tomato slices. Cover and let sit for 30 minutes before serving, if desired.

hot stuffed tomatoes

These Calabrese-style stuffed tomatoes are an exotic combination of sweet and savory flavors. Calabria's remote location in Italy's "toe" has allowed the unique, home-style cuisine of the region to persist. These tomatoes are perfect for entertaining guests; you can make them ahead, then bake them just before serving.

makes 6 servings

6 firm tomatoes
½ loaf stale Italian bread (about 4 ounces)
1 large garlic clove, cut in half
2 tablespoons extra-virgin olive oil
¼ cup black or green Italian olives, pitted and chopped
¼ cup pine nuts
¼ cup golden raisins, plumped in hot water and drained
2 tablespoons minced fresh parsley
1 teaspoon minced fresh basil
¼ teaspoon salt
¼ teaspoon freshly ground black pepper

Per serving: 171 calories • 4g protein • 8g fat • 22g carbohydrates • 0 cholesterol • 266mg sodium • 2g fiber

1. Preheat the oven to 350°F. Halve each tomato, scoop out the insides (leaving about a ¼-inch-thick wall), discard the seeds and pulp, and set the tomato shells aside.
2. Cut the bread into ½-inch-thick slices and rub each slice with the garlic until the clove is used up. Drizzle the bread with the olive oil. Shred or dice the bread and toss with the olives, pine nuts, raisins, parsley, basil, salt, and pepper. Stuff the tomato halves with the bread mixture. Place the tomatoes in a baking pan and bake until the stuffing is golden brown, about 20 minutes. Serve hot or warm.

mediterranean stuffed tomatoes with garlic

These delicious tomatoes are stuffed with feta, artichoke hearts, and plenty of sweet roasted garlic. Chile olive oil is available at specialty stores, or you can make your own by adding crushed red pepper flakes to extra-virgin olive oil.

makes 4 servings

4 large beefsteak tomatoes
Salt as needed
1 cup cubed French bread
1 tablespoon chile-infused olive oil
1 can (14 ounces) water-packed artichoke hearts,
   drained and coarsely chopped
¾ cup crumbled feta cheese
½ cup chopped fresh basil
½ cup coarsely chopped pitted black olives
2 heads Roasted Garlic (page 283), cloves
   squeezed from skins
1 tablespoon fresh oregano (or 1 teaspoon dried)
1 teaspoon freshly ground black pepper
½ cup freshly grated Parmesan cheese

Per serving: 329 calories • 16g protein •
19g fat • 26g carbohydrates • 50mg cholesterol
• 1104mg sodium • 2g fiber

1. Slice ½ inch off the tops of the tomatoes. Scoop out the pulp, leaving a ¼-inch-thick shell so that the tomatoes will hold their shape. Lightly sprinkle the inside of each tomato with salt. Invert the tomatoes onto paper towels and let them drain for 15 minutes.

2. Preheat the oven to 350°F. Toss the cubed bread with the chile olive oil. Spread the bread out onto a baking sheet. Bake until golden, 12 to 15 minutes. Place the bread in a large mixing bowl. Add the artichoke hearts, feta cheese, basil, olives, garlic, oregano, and pepper. Mix thoroughly.

3. Place the tomato shells on a baking sheet and stuff them with the artichoke-feta mixture. Top each tomato with some of the Parmesan cheese. Bake until golden, about 20 minutes.

white beans with fennel seeds

Although fresh fennel bulbs are more commonly used in Mediterranean cooking than dried fennel seeds, we've found that fennel seeds impart a distinctive and fragrant flavor to this dish without overwhelming the taste and texture of the white beans and spinach.

makes 6 servings

2 tablespoons extra-virgin olive oil

2 teaspoons fennel seeds

1 garlic clove, minced

1½ cups diced red bell pepper

1 cup diced celery

2 packages (10 ounces each) prewashed, ready-to-eat spinach

3½ cups cooked cannellini or other white beans, drained and rinsed if canned

Salt and freshly ground black pepper to taste

Per serving: 154 calories • 7g protein • 4g fat • 23g carbohydrates • 0 cholesterol • 260mg sodium • 7g fiber

1. In a large skillet, heat 1 tablespoon of the olive oil over medium-low heat. Add the fennel seeds and garlic and cook, stirring, until the seeds darken slightly. Stir in the bell pepper and celery and cook just until soft, 4 to 5 minutes.

2. Stack the spinach leaves one on top of another, roll them into a tight cigar shape, and cut crosswise into fine shreds. Add the shredded spinach and beans to the skillet and cook just until the beans are warmed through and the spinach is wilted. Season with salt and generous grindings of pepper, then drizzle with the remaining olive oil and serve.

zucchini sauté

Zucchini is a Mediterranean summertime favorite. If you can find them, the succulent deep yellow male flowers are edible and add color to any zucchini dish. To make quick work of slicing the zucchini, use the slicer side of a box grater.

makes 4 servings

1 tablespoon olive oil
4 medium zucchini, cut into ½-inch-thick slices
½ tablespoon chopped fresh basil
Salt and freshly ground black pepper to taste
Zucchini flowers for garnish (optional)

Per ½-cup serving: 48 calories • 1g protein • 4g fat • 4g carbohydrates • 0 cholesterol • 3mg sodium • 2g fiber

In a large skillet, heat the oil over medium heat. Add the zucchini and cook, stirring, until it becomes tender-crisp, 5 to 10 minutes. Sprinkle with basil and salt and pepper. Stir and cook for another minute. Serve immediately, garnished with fresh zucchini blossoms, if desired.

Pizza, Focaccia, Breads, and Sandwiches

As the foundation of the Mediterranean diet pyramid, bread is an essential mainstay. In fact, no Mediterranean meal would be complete without some form of bread to wipe one's plate or to serve as a base for cheeses and vegetables. Breads, made primarily from wheat flour, are baked every day in homes or communal ovens and served at breakfast, lunch, and dinner. They may be flat and crisp like traditional Israeli matzos, thick and crusty like our Bread for Crostini (page 259), or, like Middle Eastern pitas, may open to reveal steaming-hot pockets. ■ Traditional homemade Moroccan *kesra* dough is flavored with aniseed or sesame seeds, then traditionally sent to the village oven to be baked with other villagers' breads. These flat, round loaves are hearty, dense, and filled with healthful whole wheat. *Mouna* is an Algerian egg bread that is traditionally eaten by Sephardic Jews on the Sabbath. Light and fluffy, it is similar to the braided loaves of challah that are blessed and eaten by many Israeli Jews, and by Jews all over the globe. Indeed, bread—the fruit of the earth—is laden with sacred significance and revered by most world religions. ■ Thus, it is appropriate to find that even in wealthy households, stale bread is never simply thrown away. Italian *bruschetta*s and *crostini* are smeared with olive oil and garlic and toasted. Reconstituted with fruity olive oil and sharp vinegar, hard, stale bread can be eaten in salads such as Italian Panzanella (page 89) and Middle Eastern *fattoush*, which, not surprisingly, is made from pita breads. ■ Traditionally, the Italian flat bread called *focaccia* was covered with ashes and cooked in a skillet on the hearth. Now *focaccia* is usually oven baked, but it is still packed with herbs, onions, spices, and often an array of interesting vegetables. Pizza is another popular Italian creation that might possibly have been introduced as pita by Jewish immigrants from the eastern Mediterranean. Pizza in northern Italy is usually made with a very thin crust, while in the south it tends to be more doughy. Either way, it is topped with olive oil and often a rich, thick tomato sauce, cheese, and plenty of fresh vegetables, which can make a simple thin bread substantial enough to be a whole meal.

bread for crostini

This bread is slightly chewy with a crunchy crust and a texture that stands up to heaped-on toppings. Use it as a base for the *crostini* recipes in the appetizers and hors d'oeuvres chapter.

**makes 1 loaf
(16 slices)**

1 package active dry yeast

⅓ cup lukewarm water

2 ¾ cups all-purpose flour

½ cup whole wheat flour

1 teaspoon salt

¾ cup lukewarm water

Per slice without topping:

83 calories • 3g protein • 0 fat

• 17g carbohydrates

• 0 cholesterol • 145mg sodium

• 1g fiber

1. Dissolve the yeast in the ⅓ cup lukewarm water and set aside until foamy, about 10 minutes.

2. Place the flours and salt in a large bowl and stir in the yeast mixture. Slowly stir in ¾ cup lukewarm water until the dough is soft but not sticky. Turn the dough out onto a floured surface and knead it until uniform and springy, about 10 minutes. Alternatively, place the flours and salt in a food processor fitted with the dough blade. Pour the liquid ingredients through the feeder tube while the machine is running. Add water as necessary until the dough forms a ball and the sides of the bowl are clean. Turn the dough out onto a floured surface and knead for about 2 minutes.

3. Oil a large bowl. Place the dough in the bowl and turn to coat. Cover the dough with a damp kitchen towel and let rise in a warm, draft-free place until doubled in bulk, about 3 hours.

4. Punch the dough down. Turn the dough out onto a floured surface and knead until the dough can be handled easily. (If the dough is too sticky to handle, knead in some additional flour; if it is too dry, wet your hands and knead.)

5. Flatten the dough into a 7-by-11-inch rectangle. Roll up the short end to form a cylinder. Pinch the dough along the seam to seal and set the dough seam side down. Pull the top short ends of dough over to the bottom and pinch, closing the ends. Place the loaf on a floured peel or the back of a baking sheet and let rise until it doubles in bulk and a few air bubbles appear on the surface, 45 minutes to 1 hour.

6. Meanwhile, place baking tiles or a baking sheet in the oven and preheat to 400°F. Slash the top of the loaf with a knife. When fully risen, slide it onto the hot baking tiles or baking sheet. During the first 10 minutes of baking time, flick or spray a small amount of water in the oven 2 or 3 times. Bake until the top is golden brown and the loaf sounds hollow when tapped on the bottom, about 30 minutes. Cool before slicing and serving.

fennel sesame bread

Moroccans make this type of round flat bread, called *kesra*, fresh every day. Sometimes a little barley flour or cornmeal is added, as well as anise or sesame seeds. We have used fennel seeds, which give this bread a unique, delicate flavor. Slightly crunchy on the outside and chewy on the inside, it is the perfect vehicle for dipping in soup or sopping up the juices of a hearty *tagine*.

makes 2 loaves (12 slices each)

1 cup lukewarm water
1 teaspoon sugar or sugar substitute
1 packet active dry yeast
½ cup lukewarm milk, soy milk, or rice milk
3 ½ cups all-purpose flour
1 cup whole wheat flour
1 teaspoon salt
3 teaspoons crushed fennel seeds
3 teaspoons sesame seeds
Cornmeal as needed

Per Slice: 81 calories • 3g protein • 1g fat • 16g carbohydrates • 0 cholesterol • 90mg sodium • 1g fiber

1. In a large bowl, combine ¼ cup of the water and the sugar. Sprinkle in the yeast, stir, and set the bowl in a warm place until the yeast is foamy, about 10 minutes. Add the milk.

2. In a medium bowl, mix the flours with the salt. In 3 to 4 batches, stir the flour mixture into the yeast mixture. Add the remaining lukewarm water gradually, as you may need more or less than ¾ cup. Stir until the dough forms a stiff ball.

3. Turn the dough out onto a lightly floured surface and knead until smooth and elastic, 8 to 10 minutes. Sprinkle in the fennel seeds and sesame seeds during the last minute of kneading. Divide the dough in half. In a lightly oiled mixing bowl, form the dough into a ball by rolling it against the sides of the bowl. Repeat this procedure with the remaining dough half. Sprinkle a small amount of cornmeal on a baking sheet and flatten the balls slightly on the sheet. Cover the dough with oiled plastic wrap, oiled side down, and let rise for 2 hours in a warm place. (If you don't have a warm place, put the baking sheet on top of a large bowl filled part way with warm water.)

4. Preheat the oven to 400°F. Bake the dough for 12 minutes, then lower the heat to 350°F. and bake for 30 to 35 minutes more. The bread will be slightly browned and will sound hollow when you tap it on the bottom. Let it cool before slicing and serving.

big pizza dough

This homemade, half whole wheat dough is quick and easy to make, requires only one rising, and makes enough dough for two round or one big rectangular pizza. Use this dough for the pizza recipes that follow. Just one word of warning: Do not knead the dough after it has risen. This will make it tough and hard to roll out.

makes 2 thin 14-inch round crusts,
one 10-by-15-inch rectangular crust,
or the top and bottom crusts for a
12-inch stuffed pizza

1 ⅓ cup lukewarm water

1 packet active dry yeast

1 teaspoon salt

2 cups all-purpose flour, plus additional for kneading

1 ½ cups whole wheat or all-purpose flour

Per ⅛ recipe: 118 calories • 4g protein • 0 fat
• 25g carbohydrates • 0 cholesterol
• 179mg sodium • 2g fiber

1. Pour the water in a large bowl and sprinkle with the yeast. Whisk to dissolve. Add the salt and stir. Add the flours all at once. Stir to mix with a sturdy wooden or stainless steel spoon until the flour is incorporated and the dough forms a ball. Turn the dough out onto a lightly floured board and knead (adding flour as needed) for 5 to 8 minutes, until the dough is elastic and not sticky, but still soft.

2. Wash and dry the bowl, then coat it lightly with oil. Place the dough in the bowl, cover with a clean, damp kitchen towel, and let it rise in a warm place until doubled in bulk, about 1 hour.

3. Preheat the oven to 400°F. Turn the dough out onto a lightly floured board but do not knead. For 2 pizzas, divide the dough in half with a knife or dough cutter. Roll both pieces into 14-inch circles. Ease the circles into lightly oiled 14-inch round pizza pans. Or, roll out all of the dough to fit 1 cookie sheet that has been lightly oiled. Top the dough with sauce and desired toppings and bake as directed in the recipes that follow.

fast pizza dough

Make sure to use hot water (120° to 130°F.) when making this recipe, since that's what activates the rapid-rising yeast. Also, remember not to knead the dough for pizza after the first rising since it will be harder to roll out.

1¼ cups hot (120° to 130°F.) water

1 packet rapid-rising active dry yeast

3 tablespoons toasted wheat germ

1 teaspoon salt

3 cups all-purpose flour, plus additional for kneading

Per ⅛ recipe: 162 calories • 6g protein • 1g fat • 33g carbohydrates • 0 cholesterol • 267mg sodium • 2g fiber

1. Preheat the oven to 500° F. Pour the water into a medium bowl and sprinkle with the yeast. Stir with a wire whisk to dissolve. Add the wheat germ and salt and whisk again. Add the flour. With a sturdy wooden or stainless-steel spoon, stir until the dough forms a ball and leaves the sides of the bowl. Knead the dough briefly in the bowl, sprinkling in extra flour (if necessary) until the dough is smooth and not sticky but still soft, about 3 minutes. Set the bowl in a pie pan filled with 2 cups of hot water. Cover the bowl either with a sheet of lightly oiled waxed paper, oiled side down, or a damp kitchen towel. Let rise in a warm place for 15 minutes.
2. Turn the dough out with a spatula onto a floured board (do not knead). Shape and bake as directed in the recipes that follow.

salad pizza

Pizza's notoriety has grown by leaps and bounds since its humble beginnings as a simple Neapolitan snack. In keeping with the universal Mediterranean love for fresh vegetables, this dish is just what the name implies: pizza with tossed salad greens on top.

makes four 7-inch pizzas

½ cup milk plus ½ cup hot water, or 1 cup lukewarm water
1 package active dry yeast
2 tablespoons olive oil
2 ¼ cups all-purpose flour
1 tablespoon whole wheat flour
1 teaspoon salt
4 cups mixed salad greens
1 teaspoon balsamic vinegar

Per pizza: 318 calories • 9g protein • 7g fat • 53g carbohydrates • 1mg cholesterol • 599mg sodium • 3g fiber

1. In a large bowl, combine the milk and/or hot water (to make a lukewarm mixture). Stir in the yeast and let stand until foamy, about 10 minutes. Stir in 1 tablespoon of the olive oil.
2. Add the flours and salt and stir well to combine. If the dough seems dry, add water 1 teaspoon at a time until the dough forms a ball. If it seems wet, work in flour 1 teaspoon at a time. Turn the dough out onto a floured surface and knead until smooth and elastic but still slightly sticky, about 10 minutes.
3. Lightly oil a large bowl. Place the dough in the bowl and turn to coat both sides. Cover with a damp kitchen towel and let rise until doubled in bulk, about 1 hour.
4. Place baking tiles or a baking sheet in the oven and preheat to 500°F. Cut the dough into 4 equal pieces. On a floured surface, flatten out each ball of dough with the heel of your hand, then use a floured rolling pin to make each piece into a 7-inch circle. To make a slightly raised rim around each circle, place the heel of your hand in the center of the circle and push out while turning the dough about a quarter-turn, but do not push all the way out to the edge of the circle. Poke the dough circles a few times with a fork. Place the circles on a floured peel or the back of a second baking sheet. Slide onto baking tiles or hot baking sheet and bake until the top begins to brown, about 10 minutes.
5. Tear the greens into small pieces and toss with the remaining 1 tablespoon olive oil and the vinegar. When the crust is done, top with the salad and serve.

ciclista

This is the simplest of pizzas, but it becomes a meal when paired with vegetables or cheese. By itself, it makes a light appetizer.

makes 4 servings as main course,
8 as an appetizer

½ cup milk plus ½ cup hot water, or 1 cup
  lukewarm water
1 package active dry yeast
1 tablespoon olive oil
2 ¼ cups all-purpose white flour, plus additional
  for kneading
1 tablespoon whole wheat flour
1 teaspoon salt
¼ teaspoon kosher or coarse salt
1 tablespoon dried rosemary

Per main-course serving: 282 calories
• 8g protein • 4g fat • 52g carbohydrates
• 0 cholesterol • 738mg sodium • 2g fiber

1. In a large bowl, combine the milk and/or water (to make a lukewarm mixture) and yeast. Let stand until foamy, about 10 minutes. Stir in the olive oil.

2. Add the flours and regular salt and stir well to combine. If the dough seems dry, add water 1 teaspoon at a time until the dough forms a ball. If the dough seems wet, add flour 1 teaspoon at a time until the dough forms a ball. Turn the dough out onto a floured surface and knead until smooth and elastic but still slightly sticky, about 10 minutes. Alternatively, place the dry ingredients in a food processor fitted with the metal blade and pour the liquid ingredients through the feeder tube while the machine is running until the dough forms a ball and the sides come clean.

3. Oil a large bowl. Place the dough in the bowl and turn to coat both sides. Cover the bowl with a damp kitchen towel and let the dough rise until doubled in bulk, about 1 hour.

4. Place baking tiles or a baking sheet in the oven and preheat to 500°F. Turn the dough out onto a floured surface. Flatten the dough with the heel of your hand (do not knead), then use a floured rolling pin to roll the dough into a circle. With the heel of your hand, press the dough in the center and push out while turning about a quarter-turn until it forms a 14-inch circle. Place the dough on a floured peel or the back of a second baking sheet. Prick the dough with a fork a few times. Sprinkle the kosher or coarse salt and rosemary over the top and press gently into the dough. Slide onto the baking tiles or hot baking sheet and bake until the crust begins to brown, about 10 minutes.

onion pizza with niçoise olives

This lusty pizza, topped with Niçoise olives, goat cheese, basil, and red onions, has a true Provençal flair. If you use a prepared pizza crust, this meal can be made in no time at all. And if you can't imagine a pizza without tomatoes, sprinkle one large chopped tomato on the crust before adding the onion mixture. Proceed with the recipe as directed.

makes 8 slices

2 tablespoons olive oil

2 small red onions, thinly sliced

3 garlic cloves, minced

½ teaspoon salt

¼ teaspoon freshly ground black pepper

1 large prepared pizza crust, either purchased or homemade (see Big Pizza Dough recipe, page 261)

4 ounces goat cheese, crumbled, or soy cheese, grated (about ½ cup)

12 Niçoise olives, pitted and chopped

1 tablespoon chopped fresh basil

1 tablespoon chopped fresh rosemary

1 tablespoon chopped fresh thyme

Per slice: 301 calories • 9g protein • 8g fat • 47g carbohydrates • 14mg cholesterol • 630mg sodium • 5g fiber

1. Preheat the oven to 500°F. Heat the olive oil in a large skillet over high heat and add the onions. Lower the heat to medium and cook, stirring, for 3 minutes. Add the garlic, salt, and pepper and cook, stirring, for 3 minutes more.

2. Place the prepared pizza crust on a baking sheet. Spread the onion mixture evenly over the crust. Sprinkle the cheese and olives over the onions. Bake until the crust is browned around the edges, about 12 minutes. Sprinkle with the fresh basil, rosemary, and thyme and serve.

eggplant spinach pizza

Because the eggplant in this recipe is neither peeled nor salted, it's essential to choose a good one. Look for a firm texture, bright unblemished skin and no brown spots. The ideal weight is about ¾ pound for one recipe of Fast Pizza Dough. For an interesting variation, instead of pizza sauce, substitute ¼ cup Low-Fat Pesto (page 290).

makes 8 large slices

1 recipe Fast Pizza Dough (page 262), mixed and kneaded

1 medium eggplant

2 garlic cloves, minced

1 package (10 ounces) prewashed, ready-to-eat spinach

Salt and freshly ground black pepper to taste

1 cup Mediterranean Tomato Sauce (page 298) or prepared pizza sauce

8 ounces grated mozzarella or mozzarella-style soy cheese (about 2 cups grated)

Per slice: 339 calories • 16g protein • 13g fat • 43g carbohydrates • 16mg cholesterol • 591mg sodium • 6g fiber

1. Preheat the oven to 500°F. Lightly oil a 14-inch pizza pan. While the dough is rising, slice the top off the eggplant and discard. Cut the eggplant in half vertically. Halve each half again, vertically. Lay the eggplant quarters together to form halves flat on a cutting board. Slice quarters horizontally into ½-inch pieces. Toss the slices in a lightly oiled large nonstick skillet over medium-high heat. Cover and cook, stirring once or twice, until the eggplant pieces become slightly caramelized and tender, about 10 minutes. Add the garlic, cover, and cook for 2 more minutes. Add the spinach, cover, and steam for 5 minutes, stirring once or twice. Remove from the heat and uncover. Season with salt and pepper.

2. After the dough has risen for 15 minutes, turn it out onto a lightly floured surface. Roll out the dough to a 14-inch circle, dusting the top lightly with flour as needed to prevent sticking. Brush the excess flour from the dough and fit it into the prepared pan. Create a thin rim by pressing the dough down with your thumb about ¼ inch from the edge. Spread the dough with the prepared sauce and top with the eggplant-spinach mixture.

3. Bake for 12 minutes. Remove the pizza from the oven, top with the mozzarella cheese, and return to the oven immediately. Bake until the cheese is bubbly and the crust is golden brown and cooked through, 6 to 8 minutes.

rapini pizza

Rapini, also know as rape or broccoli rabe, is a favorite vegetable among Italians. It is a pungent bitter leafy green that has tiny broccoli-like buds clustered along its stems. It can be found in most markets and specialty stores from fall through spring.

makes 8 large slices

1 recipe Fast Pizza Dough (page 262), mixed and kneaded

2 tablespoons olive oil

2 garlic cloves, minced

1 bunch rapini, tough stems trimmed, cut into 1-inch pieces

½ cup water

Salt and freshly ground black pepper to taste

1 cup Mediterranean Tomato Sauce (page 298) or prepared pizza sauce

8 ounces grated mozzarella or mozzarella-style soy cheese (about 2 cups grated)

Per slice: 360 calories • 16g protein • 16g fat • 41g carbohydrates • 16mg cholesterol • 568mg sodium • 5g fiber

1. Preheat the oven to 500°F. Lightly oil a 14-inch pizza pan. While the pizza dough is rising, heat the olive oil over medium-high heat in a large nonstick skillet. Add the garlic and cook, stirring, until fragrant, about 1 minute. Add the rapini and water, cover, and cook, stirring once or twice, until the rapini is tender, 6 to 8 minutes. Uncover the pan and let any liquid evaporate if necessary. When the mixture is dry, remove from the heat and set aside. Season with salt and pepper.

2. When the dough has risen, turn it out onto a lightly floured surface. Dust the top with flour as needed to prevent sticking. Roll out into a 14-inch circle. Brush the excess flour from the dough and fit it into the prepared pan. Create a thin rim by pressing the dough down with your thumb about ¼ inch from the edge.

3. Spread the surface with the sauce. Sprinkle the sautéed rapini over the sauce. Bake for 12 minutes, remove from the oven, quickly sprinkle the cheese or soy cheese over the top, and immediately return to the oven. Bake until the cheese is melted and bubbling and the crust is golden and cooked through, 6 to 8 minutes.

pizza margherita

The world's most famous pizza—a combination of cheese, fresh basil, and tomatoes—is said to have been created in Italy in 1889 by *pizzaiolo* Raffaele Esposito, after the colors in the Italian flag and in honor of the reigning Queen Margherita, who loved pizza.

If fresh basil is out of season, combine ¼ cup chopped fresh Italian parsley and 1 rounded teaspoon dried basil and scatter evenly over the tomatoes before topping with cheese.

makes 8 large slices

1 can (14 ounces) diced peeled tomatoes with juice
1 recipe Fast Pizza Dough (page 262), mixed and kneaded
1 tablespoon balsamic vinegar
½ teaspoon freshly ground black pepper
18 fresh basil leaves, roughly chopped.
8 ounces grated mozzarella or mozzarella-style soy cheese (about 2 cups)

Per slice: 260 calories • 14g protein • 6g fat • 38g carbohydrates • 15mg cholesterol • 617mg sodium • 2g fiber

1. Preheat the oven to 500°F. Lightly oil a 14-inch pizza pan. While the dough is rising, empty the canned tomatoes into a sieve or small colander set over a deep bowl. Toss several times to speed draining. Pour about ⅔ cup of the collected tomato juice into a small saucepan. Add the vinegar and pepper and bring to a boil over high heat. Continue boiling over high heat to reduce the liquid. (You should end up with slightly more than ¼ cup sauce.) Remove the pan from the heat and stir to cool.

2. After the dough has risen for 15 minutes, turn it out onto a lightly floured board. Roll the dough into a 14-inch circle, dusting the top lightly with flour as needed to keep from sticking. Brush the excess flour from the dough and fit it into the prepared pan. Create a thin rim by pressing the dough down with your thumb about ¼ inch from the edge.

3. With a rubber spatula, scrape the reduced tomato liquid onto the crust, spreading to cover. Scatter the tomatoes over the sauce. Bake for 12 minutes then remove from the oven and quickly scatter the basil and cheese evenly over the pizza. Return the pizza to the oven and bake until the cheese is melted and bubbling and the crust is golden brown and baked through, 6 to 8 minutes.

four-vegetable, two-way pizza

The trick to being quick is to chop the vegetables roughly and scrape them directly from the cutting board into the skillet. Needless to say, the vegetables you use must be prime quality, especially the mushrooms, because even their stems are used.

For a vegan variation, instead of cheese, drizzle 1 to 1½ tablespoons extra-virgin olive oil over the cooked vegetables. Sprinkle with 1 teaspoon oregano and ½ teaspoon freshly ground black pepper. Toss to mix. Top the pizza and bake for 20 minutes.

makes 8 large slices

1 recipe Fast Pizza Dough (page 262), mixed and kneaded
1 tablespoon olive oil
1 large onion, chopped
1 green bell pepper, diced
1 red bell pepper, diced
2 garlic cloves, minced
1 pound white or brown mushrooms
1 cup Mediterranean Tomato Sauce (page 298) or prepared pizza sauce
8 ounces grated mozzarella or mozzarella-style soy cheese (about 2 cups)

Per slice: 278 calories • 15g protein • 6g fat • 42g carbohydrates • 15mg cholesterol • 604mg sodium • 4g fiber

1. Preheat the oven to 500°F. Lightly oil a 14-inch pizza pan. While the dough is rising, in a large skillet, heat the olive oil over medium-high heat. Add the onion and cook, stirring, until tender, about 5 minutes. Add the bell peppers to the skillet and cook, stirring occasionally, for about 5 minutes; add the garlic and cook, stirring, for 1 minute longer.

2. While the onion-pepper mixture cooks, put the fresh mushrooms into a colander. Toss them under rapidly running water to clean. Turn the mushrooms out onto paper toweling and quickly pat to dry. Dice the mushrooms (stems included), into ½-inch pieces. Add them to the skillet and cook, stirring, over high heat until they are cooked through and any pan liquid has evaporated, about 5 minutes. Remove the skillet from the heat and let cool.

3. After the dough has risen for 15 minutes, turn it out onto a lightly floured surface. Roll the dough into a 14-inch circle, dusting the top lightly with flour as needed to prevent sticking. Brush any excess flour from the dough and fit the dough into the prepared pan. Create a thin rim by pressing the dough down with your thumb about ¼ inch from the edge.

4. Spread the dough with the prepared tomato sauce. Distribute the reserved vegetables evenly over the top. Bake for 12 minutes. Remove the pizza from the oven, quickly sprinkle the cheese over the top and immediately return the pizza to the oven. Bake until the cheese is bubbly and the crust is golden brown and baked through, 6 to 8 minutes.

tofu "ricotta" calzone

This savory stuffed pastry from Naples translates literally as "trouser leg." Add any number of filling ingredients to a calzone, such as our Tofu "Ricotta" Filling (or several types of cheese), grilled vegetables, marinated artichokes, or roasted peppers. If you have a bread machine, set the timer to have the dough all ready when you get home from work. If you use frozen bread dough, be sure it is thawed in time before you start to make the calzones.

makes 4 calzones

1 pound bread dough or 1 recipe Fast Pizza
 Dough (page 262), mixed and kneaded
1 recipe Tofu "Ricotta" Filling (page 295)
1 tablespoon olive oil
1 green bell pepper, diced
1 medium onion, diced
Salt and freshly ground black pepper to taste
2 cups Mediterranean Tomato Sauce (page 298),
 or prepared marinara sauce, divided
½ cup sliced black olives
Cornmeal for dusting

Per calzone: 544 calories • 23g protein • 18g fat
• 76g carbohydrates • 8mg cholesterol
• 146mg sodium • 10g fiber

1. Preheat the oven to 400°F. Divide the dough into 4 equal pieces and roll out on a floured surface to make 6-inch circles. Cover the circles with a damp kitchen towel and let them rise.
2. Meanwhile, prepare the Tofu "Ricotta" Filling.
3. In a large skillet, heat the olive oil over medium-high heat. Add the bell pepper and onion and cook, stirring, until softened, about 5 minutes. Remove from the heat and season with salt and pepper. Place 1 tablespoon tomato sauce in the center of each dough circle and spread to make a 4-inch circle over the dough. Spoon the filling evenly over the sauce. Spoon the bell pepper and onion mixture over the filling, and sprinkle with sliced olives. Brush a little water around the edges of the dough. Fold the dough in half and crimp the edges well.
4. Place the calzones on a cookie sheet or a pizza stone lightly sprinkled with cornmeal. Make 2 small slashes in the top of each calzone to let steam escape. Bake the calzones until the crusts are crisp and brown, about 20 to 25 minutes. Serve with the remaining warmed marinara sauce on the side.

focaccia

Focaccia breads are thicker than pizzas and are made with a wide variety of ingredients from sweet raisins and walnuts to savory tomatoes, onions, garlic, and oregano. The predecessor of today's pizza, *focaccia* is meant to be eaten as a bread or a snack, and for that reason it is not heavily garnished. With any leftover *focaccia,* you can make traditional bread salad, or Panzanella (page 89).

Focaccia has endless variations; here are four for you to try:

- For added flavor, sprinkle rosemary and red pepper flakes over tomato sauce.
- Instead of tomato sauce, sprinkle *focaccia* lightly with kosher or coarse salt and freshly ground pepper.
- Top plain dough with 2 diced onions and 1 to 2 cloves minced garlic that have been sautéed in a lightly oiled pan until soft but not browned.
- Add 1 tablespoon minced fresh herbs (such as basil, thyme, rosemary, or sage) to Fast Pizza Dough when mixing. Brush rolled out dough with 1 tablespoon extra-virgin olive oil. Sprinkle with kosher salt and freshly ground pepper.

makes 12 squares

1 recipe Fast Pizza Dough (page 262), mixed and kneaded but not risen
½ to ¾ cup Mediterranean Tomato Sauce (page 298)

Per square: 111 calories • 4g protein • 1g fat • 23g carbohydrates • 0 cholesterol • 239mg sodium • 1g fiber

1. Preheat the oven to 450°F. On a lightly floured surface, roll out the dough into a rectangle measuring roughly 11 by 17 inches. Lightly dust the top with flour during rolling to prevent sticking.
2. Ease the dough into a lightly oiled 11½-by-17-inch baking pan, stretching to fit. Cover the dough with a sheet of lightly oiled waxed paper, oiled side down. Let rise in a warm place for 25 minutes.
3. Top the dough with the tomato sauce, spreading to cover ¼ inch from the edges. Press down with your index finger to make little dimples over the entire surface.
4. Bake until the dough is cooked through and lightly browned on the bottom, 20 to 25 minutes. Remove the *focaccia* from the oven and let cool on a wire rack for 10 minutes. Slice into 12 large squares with a serrated knife and serve.

grape focaccia

During the autumn grape harvest in Tuscany bakers make this sweet *focaccia* bread, called *schiacciata all'uva*, bursting with Sangiovese wine grapes. This bread, which began as a rustic country tradition, has now found its way into even the most refined city bakeries. With such an exquisite flavor, it's no surprise.

makes 8 servings

For the dough

1 small apple, cored and
   quartered
2 cups all-purpose flour, plus
   additional for kneading
1 tablespoon sugar or 2
   teaspoons honey
1 scant teaspoon rapid-rising
   yeast
½ teaspoon salt (optional)
1 tablespoon olive oil
⅓ to ½ cup hot tap water
⅓ cup raisins

For the filling

3 cups red seedless grapes
½ cup walnuts
Pinch of ground cloves
¼ cup sugar or honey
¼ cup brown sugar (optional)
1 teaspoon cornstarch
   (2 teaspoons if using honey
   instead of sugar)

Per serving: 258 calories
• 6g protein • 7g fat • 46g
carbohydrates • 0 cholesterol
• 3mg sodium • 2g fiber

1. Process the quartered apple in a food processor for about 20 seconds, then transfer to a separate bowl.
2. Add 2 cups of the flour, the sugar or honey, yeast, and salt to the food processor and process for 5 seconds. Add the processed apple and oil and process for an additional 5 seconds. With the processor running, gradually add ⅓ cup hot water through the feeder tube. Stop the machine and let the dough rest for about 20 seconds. Continue processing and adding water (if necessary) gradually through the feeder tube until the dough forms a soft ball and the sides of the bowl are clean. Pulse 2 or 3 more times.
3. Sprinkle a work surface with flour. Add the raisins and roll them in the flour to coat. Turn the dough out onto the surface and knead for about 1 minute to incorporate the raisins, adding flour if the dough is very sticky. Lightly flour the inside of a plastic bag. Place the dough in the bag, seal, and let it rest for 15 to 20 minutes in a warm, dark place.
4. Roll the dough into a circle 12 to 14 inches in diameter. Place it in an oiled skillet or baking dish. Cover the dough with a kitchen towel and set aside in a warm place while you prepare the filling.
5. Preheat the oven to 400°F. To prepare the filling, place all the ingredients in a bowl and mix well.
6. Spoon the filling onto the dough. Bake for 20 minutes, then rotate the pan 180 degrees. Reduce the oven temperature to 375°F. and bake for an additional 10 minutes, or until the grapes are tender and the crust is browned. Cool in the pan for 5 minutes. Remove the *focaccia* from the pan and cool thoroughly on wire rack.

farro and sun-dried tomato focaccia

Farro, an ancient grain, has a nutty taste and lightly chewy texture. Here, it lends its delicate flavor to an otherwise robust *focaccia*, topped with intense nuggets of sun-dried tomato. Start this recipe the day before you plan to serve it.

makes 6 to 8 servings

½ cup farro
1 cup warm water
1 package active dry yeast
3 tablespoons olive oil
¼ cup firmly packed, minced, oil-packed sun-dried tomatoes
1 teaspoon light brown sugar
2 cups all-purpose flour, plus additional for kneading
½ cup whole wheat flour
½ teaspoon salt
Kosher or coarse salt, for the top
Dried oregano, for the top

Per serving: 312 calories • 9g protein • 10g fat • 45g carbohydrates • 0 cholesterol • 390mg sodium • 4g fiber

1. Place the farro in a medium bowl with water to cover. Let the farro soak overnight.
2. Drain the farro and place it in a small saucepan covered by 2 inches of water. Bring the mixture to a boil over high heat, then reduce the heat to medium and simmer the farro until tender, about 45 minutes. Drain and reserve.
3. Combine the warm water and yeast in a small bowl and let stand until foamy, 5 to 10 minutes. Stir in 1 tablespoon of the olive oil, the tomatoes, and brown sugar.
4. In a large mixing bowl, combine the flours and salt. Add the yeast mixture and drained farro and mix until well combined. Turn the dough out onto a well-floured surface. Knead for 5 minutes, adding additional flour if the dough is too sticky. Shape the dough into a ball, then roll out into a circle about 12 inches in diameter. Place the dough on a lightly oiled baking sheet. Cover with a cloth and let rise in a warm place for 40 minutes.
5. Preheat the oven to 400°F. With your fingertips, gently make equal-spaced dimples all over the surface of the dough. Drizzle the remaining olive oil evenly over the top, then sprinkle with kosher salt and oregano, to taste. Bake for 20 to 25 minutes, or until the top is golden. Cut the *focaccia* into wedges and serve warm.

focaccia with stracchino and arugula

Stracchino, also known as *crescenza* or gorgonzola, is a northern Italian creation made with fresh cow's milk plus any leftover milk from the day before. It is a mild, spreadable cheese with a tangy aftertaste. If you can't find *stracchino*, substitute *taleggio*, the unripened version. You can also use mozzarella. Baked *focaccia* topped with greens is a classic Italian dish; this one calls for spicy-tasting arugula.

makes 6 servings

1 package active dry yeast
2¼ cups warm water
2 tablespoons olive oil
2 teaspoons salt
5 cups all-purpose flour
½ pound *stracchino* or other soft cheese, or silken tofu
1 bunch arugula leaves (not the stems)

Per serving: 481 calories • 14g protein • 4g fat • 74g carbohydrates • 30mg cholesterol • 925mg sodium • 3g fiber

1. In a large bowl, sprinkle the yeast over ¼ cup of the water. Let it stand until foamy, about 10 minutes.
2. Stir in the remaining 2 cups water, olive oil, and salt. Add the flour 1 cup at a time, stirring well after each addition. When the dough is too stiff to stir, turn it out onto a floured surface and knead in enough of the remaining flour to make a stiff but pliable dough.
3. Oil a large bowl. Place the dough in the bowl and turn over to coat both sides. Cover with a damp kitchen towel and let the dough rise in a warm spot until doubled in bulk, about 2 hours.
4. Place baking tiles or a baking sheet in the oven and pre-heat to 500°F. On a floured surface, roll out the dough into a 12-inch square. Place the dough on a floured peel or the back of a second baking sheet. Poke the dough all over with a fork and let it rise, uncovered, for about 30 minutes.
5. Slide the dough onto the baking tiles or a hot baking sheet and bake for 20 to 25 minutes, until golden brown on top. Remove from the oven and immediately spread the cheese or tofu on top. Lay the arugula leaves on top of the cheese or tofu, cut into wedges, and serve.

pita-wrapped salads with honey dressing

These hand-held, fresh salads are easy to assemble and are great for outdoor, spur-of-the-moment gatherings.

makes 4 pockets

For the honey dressing

¼ cup balsamic vinegar

¼ cup olive oil

2 tablespoons red wine vinegar

2 tablespoons honey

½ teaspoon paprika

Salt and freshly ground black pepper to taste

For the pocket salads

4 large pita breads

4 cups spinach leaves, stemmed and torn into
  pieces

1 cup bell pepper strips

½ cup crumbled feta cheese (optional)

½ small red onion, sliced thinly

1 tablespoon pine nuts, toasted
  (see Note, page 153)

Per pocket with 1 tablespoon dressing without feta: 265 calories • 8g protein • 5g fat • 47g carbohydrates • 0 cholesterol • 424mg sodium • 3g fiber

1. To make the dressing, place all of the ingredients in a microwave-safe container and microwave on high for 2 minutes. Remove from the microwave and stir until the honey is completely dissolved. Alternatively, combine ingredients in the top of a double-boiler set over simmering (not boiling) water and stir until the honey is completely dissolved. Cool to room temperature and refrigerate until thoroughly chilled.

2. Cut the pita breads in half crosswise. Divide the spinach, bell pepper, cheese, onion, and toasted pine nuts among the pita pockets. Drizzle each with some dressing. Serve the remaining dressing on the side.

the ultimate grilled eggplant sandwich

This Grecian-inspired sandwich, slathered in tomato pesto and goat cheese, is bursting with flavor and makes an elegant party dish when thinly sliced. It is easy to assemble and makes good use of other recipes in this collection.

makes 4 servings
1 sourdough *baguette*
½ cup Tangy Sun-Dried Tomato Pesto (page 289)
½ recipe Marinated Goat Cheese (page 53) or
   8 slices smoked mozzarella cheese
8 leaves romaine or green leaf lettuce
1 recipe Marinated Grilled Eggplant (page 235)

Per serving: 349 calories • 10g protein • 19g fat • 33g carbohydrates • 31mg cholesterol • 780mg sodium • 4g fiber

Slice the *baquette* lengthwise, cutting it almost, but not quite, all the way through. Spread both sides of the cut bread with the pesto. Spread the goat cheese on one side and place lettuce leaves on the other side. Top the lettuce with the grilled eggplant. Close the sandwich and cut into 4 pieces; serve.

pepper and provolone sandwich

This is fabulous summer fare. Succulent roasted peppers and grilled red onions on crusty bread topped with tangy melted provolone cheese make these sandwiches perfect for picnics or, cut into smaller portions, as appetizers for a summer dinner party.

makes 4 sandwiches

2 tablespoons minced fresh oregano
   (or 1 tablespoon dried)
1 tablespoon olive oil
1 tablespoon balsamic vinegar
1 small garlic clove, minced
1 small red onion, blanched and sliced into 4 thick
   rounds
4 Italian-style hard rolls, split (or 8 thick slices
   Italian bread)
2 green bell peppers, roasted (see Note,
   page 63)
2 red bell peppers, roasted (see Note, page 63)
⅔ cup shredded provolone cheese

Per sandwich: 295 calories • 12g protein
• 8g fat • 40g carbohydrates • 13mg cholesterol
• 516mg sodium • 2g fiber

1. Preheat the broiler or grill. In a small bowl, stir together the oregano, olive oil, vinegar, and garlic. Brush the mixture onto the red onion slices. Grill the onion until it is light brown on both sides, turning once, about 6 minutes.

2. Place the bottoms of the rolls, or 4 slices of bread, on a large piece of foil. Distribute equal amounts of peppers, onion, and cheese onto each roll or slice. Top with the remaining bread and fold the foil over the sandwiches. Grill for 5 to 7 minutes or until heated through.

sesame flat bread

People all over the world make some version of simple flat breads. This one is flavored with sesame seeds for a taste of the Middle East. Flat breads are made without yeast and cook quickly.

makes 6 flat breads

1 cup all-purpose flour
1 cup whole wheat flour
½ teaspoon salt
½ to ¾ cup water
2 to 3 tablespoons sesame seeds
1 tablespoon olive oil

Per bread: 178 calories • 5g protein • 4g fat • 29g carbohydrates • 0 cholesterol • 181mg sodium • 3g fiber

1. Mix the flours and ¼ teaspoon of the salt in a medium bowl. Add enough water to bind the dough, starting with ½ cup. Knead the dough until it becomes smooth and silky, 4 to 5 minutes. Wrap the dough in plastic wrap and let it rest for 15 minutes.

2. Meanwhile, in a dry skillet over medium-high heat, toast the sesame seeds until golden brown and fragrant, about 2 minutes. Remove the toasted seeds from the heat and mix with the remaining ¼ teaspoon salt. Crush the salted seeds slightly with a mortar and pestle or in a spice grinder; set aside.

3. Divide the dough into 6 balls. Flatten the first ball with floured hands. On a surface lightly dusted with flour, roll out the flattened ball to a circle about 6 inches in diameter. Repeat this procedure with the remaining balls. Brush the circles lightly with olive oil, then sprinkle with the sesame mixture.

4. Preheat a heavy skillet over medium-high heat. Cook the breads, one at a time, until small brownish spots appear, 3 to 4 minutes on each side. Wrap the breads in a clean kitchen towel to keep warm and serve immediately.

rosemary breadsticks

There's no such thing as an imperfect breadstick. If one stick is too long for the pan, simply bend one end over to fit, like a shepherd's crook. Breadsticks are always a welcome snack, appetizer, or accompaniment to soups, salads, and pasta dishes.

makes thirty-two 10-inch breadsticks

1 recipe Fast Pizza Dough (page 262), mixed, kneaded, and risen
1 tablespoon olive oil
1 teaspoon dried rosemary, crumbled
½ teaspoon kosher or coarse salt
¼ teaspoon freshly ground black pepper

Per breadstick: 40 calories • 1g protein • 0 fat • 8g carbohydrates • 0 cholesterol • 67mg sodium • 0 fiber

1. Preheat the oven to 500°F. Turn out the risen dough onto a lightly floured surface. Roll it out into a rectangle measuring roughly 12 by 16 inches, dusting the top with flour lightly as needed to prevent sticking.
2. With a knife or pizza dough cutter, cut the dough in sixteen 1-inch-wide strips.
3. Lift each strip individually and cut in half crosswise. Quickly twist and pull the half strips to form a twisted rope about 10 inches long. Repeat this procedure until all of the strips are cut and twisted.
4. Lay the strips side by side vertically in three 11½-by-17-inch lightly oiled baking pans. Brush the oil over the breadsticks, then sprinkle evenly with the rosemary, salt and pepper. Bake until the breadsticks are golden brown, about 15 minutes. Cool on rack.

Note: Electric ovens tend to cook faster; this recipe was tested in a gas oven. You may need to lower the heat of an electric oven to 450°F.

sesame sticks

The story goes that breadsticks were invented by Antonio Brunero, a baker for the royal family of Turin, who touted them as a healthy form of bread that was to be eaten during Italy's plague years, 1679–1698. In any case, we know you will enjoy these crunchy sesame-coated breadsticks as a light snack, or as an accompaniment to a pasta dish or salad.

makes 8 breadsticks

2 cups all-purpose flour, plus additional for kneading

1 tablespoon sugar or 2 teaspoons honey

1 scant teaspoon rapid-rising yeast

½ teaspoon salt

⅓ to ⅔ cup hot tap water

1 tablespoon baking soda

1 cup cold water

¼ to ½ cup sesame seeds

¼ teaspoon kosher or coarse salt (optional)

Per serving: 87 calories • 3g protein • 2g fat • 14g carbohydrates • 0 cholesterol • 383mg sodium • 1g fiber

1. Place the flour, sugar or honey, yeast, and salt in a food processor and process for 10 seconds. With the processor running, add ⅓ cup hot water gradually through the feeder tube. Stop the machine and let the mixture rest for 20 seconds so that the flour can absorb the water. Continue processing and adding water (if necessary) until the dough forms a ball and the sides of the work bowl are clean. Pulse 2 or 3 more times, then turn the dough out onto a floured surface.

2. Knead the dough for about 1 minute, adding 1 to 2 tablespoons flour as necessary if the dough is sticky. Lightly flour the inside of a plastic bag. Place the dough in the bag, seal, and let rest for 15 to 30 minutes in a warm, dark place.

3. Preheat the oven to 400°F. Grease a baking sheet. In a large shallow bowl, dissolve the baking soda in cold water. Place the sesame seeds in a separate, shallow bowl. Divide the dough into 8 equal pieces. Keep the pieces covered with a kitchen towel so that they won't dry out. Roll 1 piece of dough into a rope about 8 inches long, dip it into the baking soda solution, then drain the rope briefly on a kitchen towel. Roll the rope in the sesame seeds. Place the rope on the prepared baking sheet. Repeat this procedure with the remaining dough. Sprinkle with kosher salt if desired. Cover the sesame sticks with a kitchen towel and let rest for 15 minutes. Bake for 10 minutes, until the sticks are golden brown and the sesame seeds are toasted. Cool briefly on a wire rack before serving.

Sauces, Marinades, and Fillings

Sauces are the spice of Mediterranean cuisine. Whether made to top nubby grains of couscous, firm strands of pasta, or a variety of crisp, fresh vegetables, sauces add color, flavor, and depth to Mediterranean cooking. ■ Mediterranean sauces come in myriad incarnations. *Aïoli*, called the "butter of Provence," is a classic French garlicky mayonnaise made with olive oil and as many as two cloves of garlic per person. Indeed, garlic is used widely in sauces, marinades, and fillings throughout the Mediterranean. The Lebanese make a similar sauce, only without the eggs. *Aïoli* may also contain finely chopped fresh parsley and often appears dolloped over green beans, carrots, potatoes, or whatever vegetable happens to be in season. *Aïoli* is also served with egg and seafood dishes. France has also popularized *pistou*, like Italian pesto, a concoction made with basil, garlic, olive oil, and pine nuts. A healthy spoonful of *pistou* is enjoyed in *soupe au pistou* (see our Provençal Soup with Pistou on page 107), which is similar to Italian minestrone. ■ Other types of pesto also abound. In addition to the classic Genovese basil and pine nut sauce, we include creative recipes calling for parsley and other herbs (page 291), and even sun-dried tomatoes (page 289). They can all be used in a manner similar to classic pesto—that is, as a sauce for pasta or vegetables, as a spread for bread, or as a tangy dip for crudités and breadsticks. ■ In northern Africa, cooks generally make good use of incendiary chile peppers in their sauces, especially in Tunisia, a country famous for its *harissa*, which is used in most Tunisian dishes. *Harissa* is also often eaten plain, simply smeared on a piece of bread. Tahini, a savory sauce made from sesame paste (from which it takes its name), garlic, and lemon juice, is a common Middle Eastern condiment used on falafel and as a dip for crudités. Mild yogurt sauces are also common throughout Greece, Turkey, the Middle East, and northern Africa. ■ Finally, there's the widely loved sauce that's rich with tomatoes and fresh herbs—the classic Mediterranean Tomato Sauce (page 298). It's served over pasta, polenta, and even steamed vegetables. The Italians, who are most famous for their tomato sauce, make it an imperative not to smother their food with sauces; rather, they pour them on lightly, allowing the food to speak for itself, which is what all good sauces really should do.

roasted garlic

When roasted, garlic takes on a sweet and nutty flavor while the flesh becomes soft and creamy.
Roasted garlic makes an excellent spread for crusty Italian bread.

makes 6 servings as a spread for
bread
3 whole garlic bulbs
3 teaspoons extra-virgin olive oil (optional)
1½ teaspoons salt (optional)

Per serving without bread: 38 calories • 1g protein
• 2g fat • 4g carbohydrates • 0 cholesterol • 2mg
sodium • 0 fiber

1. Preheat the oven to 300°F. Place each bulb of garlic on a
   5-inch square piece of aluminum foil. If desired, top each
   bulb with a teaspoon of olive oil and ½ teaspoon salt.
   Wrap each bulb in foil, twisting the top closed. Bake for
   45 minutes, until the garlic reaches the desired creaminess.
2. To serve, place the whole bulbs of roasted garlic on a serving platter surrounded by thick slices of fresh Italian
   bread. Let your guests squeeze the garlic onto their bread.

aïoli à la estella

This classic mayonnaise-like sauce is commonly used to garnish soups and entrees. It is a pungent and heady invention that is an essential component of French Mediterranean cooking. You can store *aïoli*, covered, in the refrigerator for up to three days.

makes approximately 1½ cups or 22 tablespoons

1 cup fresh bread crumbs
¼ cup fresh lemon juice
2 to 4 garlic cloves, minced
Pinch of salt
⅓ cup extra-virgin olive oil
2 teaspoons prepared mustard (optional)

Per tablespoon: 36 calories • 0 protein • 3g fat • 2g carbohydrates • 0 cholesterol • 25mg sodium • 0 fiber

1. Place the bread crumbs in a small bowl. Sprinkle them with the lemon juice and let sit for 2 minutes. In a food processor or mortar (with pestle), combine the minced garlic and salt and process or pound to a paste.
2. If using a mortar and pestle, transfer the mixture to a small bowl. Add the lemon-soaked crumbs and puree, adding the olive oil a few teaspoons at a time (while the food processor is running), and blend or pound to a thick paste. Add mustard, if desired.
3. To serve, place a teaspoon of *aïoli* on top of hot soups or over cooked or raw vegetables. If the *aïoli* separates, simply mix it with a fork or spoon before serving.

romesco sauce

One of the five fabled Catalan sauces, *romesco* takes its name from a variety of small, hot red chiles grown in Spain. Though *romesco* chiles are not available in the United States, you'll get good results with any kind of small, dried hot pepper. Full of intriguing and unexpected flavors, this sauce is excellent served over steamed new potatoes or as a dipping sauce for steamed or raw vegetables.

makes 1 to 1½ cups or 16 to 22 tablespoons

1 small dried hot chile pepper
½ cup hot water
3 medium ripe tomatoes
½ cup blanched slivered almonds
2 garlic cloves, minced
1 teaspoon paprika
½ teaspoon salt
¼ to ⅓ cup extra-virgin olive oil
2 to 3 tablespoons red wine vinegar

Per tablespoon: 60 calories • 1g protein • 6g fat • 2g carbohydrates • 0 cholesterol • 80mg sodium • 1g fiber

1. Preheat the broiler. Soak the dried pepper in the hot water until soft, about 10 minutes.
2. Meanwhile, broil the tomatoes until they become soft, about 6 minutes. Peel, seed, and mash the tomatoes and set them aside.
3. In a small, dry skillet over low heat, toast the almonds until they turn golden brown, about 3 minutes. Chop the almonds in a blender or food processor until finely ground and set them aside.
4. Drain the rehydrated hot pepper, remove the seeds, and chop coarsely. In a blender or food processor, grind the pepper, tomatoes, garlic, paprika, and salt until smooth. Drizzle in the olive oil a little at a time, blending until the sauce reaches a creamy consistency. Add the vinegar 1 tablespoon at a time, to taste. Stir in the ground toasted almonds by hand and serve.

red wine, tomato, and rosemary sauce

This is a rich, heady sauce that can be used on pasta, grains, or vegetables. By thickening the sauce with arrowroot or cornstarch instead of the traditional butter-and-flour roux, you can drop the fat count to virtually nil. For a richer-flavored sauce, substitute another cup of red wine for one of the cups of water and add 1 cup of sautéed sliced mushrooms to the sauce just before thickening with the arrowroot powder or cornstarch.

makes 8 servings

1 teaspoon olive oil
1 cup finely chopped onion
1 cup peeled and diced carrots
½ cup diced celery
3 garlic cloves, minced
2¼ cups water
2 cups dry red wine
2 tablespoons red wine vinegar
1 tablespoon tomato paste
1 tablespoon chopped fresh rosemary
   (or 1 teaspoon dried)
1 teaspoon dried basil
½ teaspoon dried thyme
½ teaspoon white pepper
Salt to taste
2 tablespoons arrowroot powder or cornstarch

Per serving: 75 calories • 1g protein • 1g fat • 8g carbohydrates • 0 cholesterol • 19mg sodium • 1g fiber

1. In a large nonstick skillet, heat the olive oil over medium heat. Add the onion, carrots, celery, and garlic and cook, stirring, until softened, about 5 minutes. Transfer the cooked vegetables to a heavy 3-quart pot and add 2 cups of the water, the red wine, vinegar, tomato paste, rosemary, basil, thyme, pepper, and salt. Bring the mixture to a boil, then reduce the heat, partially cover the pot, and simmer for 15 to 20 minutes, until the vegetables are tender.

2. Whisk together the remaining water and arrowroot or cornstarch until smooth and fully dissolved. Slowly pour into the simmering sauce, stirring constantly. Lower the heat and continue to stir as the sauce thickens and becomes shiny, about 5 minutes. If necessary, add more dissolved arrowroot or cornstarch, 1 teaspoon at a time, until the sauce reaches desired consistency.

mediterranean marinade

This sauce is recommended for basting or marinating a variety of Mediterranean vegetables including artichoke hearts, asparagus, broccoli, cherry tomatoes, eggplant, leeks, mushrooms, onions, and zucchini, as well as cubed tofu. It will keep for up to one week in the refrigerator, if you have any leftovers or need to make it in advance.

makes about ¾ cup marinade or 12 tablespoons; enough for 2 pounds of vegetables

½ cup extra-virgin olive oil
¼ cup white wine or balsamic vinegar
¼ cup minced onion
1 garlic clove, crushed
1 tablespoon crumbled dried oregano
Salt and freshly ground black pepper to taste

Per tablespoon: 85 calories • 1g protein
• 9g fat • 1g carbohydrates • 0 cholesterol
• 45mg sodium • 0 fiber

In a large glass bowl, whisk together all of the ingredients. Add the vegetables or tofu and let sit for 30 minutes. For basting, brush the marinade directly onto the vegetables before and during grilling.

basil-garlic marinade

Fresh basil adds a taste of the Mediterranean summer to this basic marinade for steamed, grilled, or raw vegetables, or cubed tofu. It will keep for up to one week in the refrigerator.

**makes about ⅓ cup or about
5 tablespoons**

2 to 4 tablespoons extra-virgin olive oil

Juice of 1 lemon

10 leaves fresh basil (or 2 teaspoons dried)

2 garlic cloves

Salt and freshly ground black pepper to taste

Per tablespoon: 50 calories • 1g protein
• 5g fat • 1g carbohydrates • 0 cholesterol
• 100mg sodium • 0 fiber

In a blender or food processor, add all of the ingredients and puree. Place the marinade in a large glass bowl, add ingredients to marinate, and let sit for 30 minutes. For basting, brush the marinade directly onto the ingredients (vegetables, tofu, etc.) before and during grilling.

tangy sun-dried tomato pesto

Sun-dried tomatoes lend a strong, earthy flavor to this pesto. For a dip or spread, blend in 8 ounces of softened cream cheese. The pesto will keep, covered and refrigerated, for up to two weeks.

makes ½ cup or 8 tablespoons

4 ounces sun-dried tomatoes (not oil-packed)
2 garlic cloves
Juice of 1 lemon
Salt and freshly ground black pepper to taste
Water as needed

Per tablespoon: 19 calories • 1g protein • 0 fat • 4g carbohydrates • 0 cholesterol • 73mg sodium • 1g fiber

1. Place the dried tomatoes in a shallow bowl. Cover with boiling water and let soak until they become soft and pliable, about 8 minutes. Drain.
2. Place the rehydrated tomatoes, garlic, lemon juice, and salt and pepper in a food processor or blender and process until smooth, adding water as needed 1 tablespoon at a time until the pesto reaches desired consistency. (If using a blender, you might have to add a little more water to aid the processing.)

low-fat pesto

Pesto is great tossed with pasta or dabbed on homemade pizzas. You can store any unused portions covered in the refrigerator for up to one week, or freeze for up to one month.

2 cups chopped fresh basil leaves

1 cup chopped fresh Italian parsley

¼ to ⅓ cup bread crumbs, toasted
(see Note, page 174)

2 tablespoons freshly grated Parmesan or
Parmesan-style soy cheese

2 or 3 garlic cloves

3 tablespoons white miso

¼ to ⅓ cup water

Per tablespoon: 19 calories • 1g protein • 1g fat • 3g carbohydrates • 1mg cholesterol • 146mg sodium • 1g fiber

Put all of the ingredients except for the water in a blender or food processor and pulse until minced. With the machine running, add the water a bit at a time until the desired consistency is reached.

herb pesto

This is a twist on the classic Genovese basil pesto and can be tossed with pasta, dolloped on bread and in soup, or served as a condiment with steamed vegetables. For a vegan alternative you may omit the Parmesan cheese.

makes about ¾ cup or 12 tablespoons

2 cups packed fresh herbs, such as Genovese basil, cilantro, Italian parsley, mint or spinach, or any combination of 2 or 3 herbs

1 to 2 tablespoons fresh thyme, marjoram, or oregano (optional)

¼ cup extra-virgin olive oil

¼ cup pine nuts or walnuts, toasted (see Note, page 153)

¼ cup freshly grated Parmesan cheese (optional)

3 garlic cloves

Salt and freshly ground black pepper to taste

Water as needed

Per tablespoon: 60 calories • 1g protein • 6g fat • 1g carbohydrates • 0 cholesterol • 92mg sodium • 1g fiber

Add all of the ingredients, except for the water, to a food processor and puree until well blended. For a smooth, creamy pesto, add water, 1 tablespoon at a time, until the pesto reaches desired consistency. For a thicker, chunkier pesto, do not add any water.

pesto alla trapanese

This sauce resembles the famous basil pesto sauce that originated in Genoa, Italy, but is made with the beguiling additions of tomato and almonds.

makes about 1 cup or 16 tablespoons

4 plum tomatoes, peeled (see headnote,
   page 223), seeded and chopped
½ cup roughly chopped blanched almonds
½ cup fresh basil leaves
2 garlic cloves, minced
1 tablespoon extra-virgin olive oil
Salt and freshly ground black pepper to taste

Per tablespoon: 41 calories • 1g protein • 3g fat
• 2g carbohydrates • 0 cholesterol • 3mg sodium
• 1g fiber

Place the tomatoes, almonds, basil, and garlic in a blender, food processor, or mortar. Drizzle in the olive oil and blend, process, or grind with a pestle until pureed to the desired consistency (the almonds should still provide a little crunch). Add salt and pepper. Serve over cooked pasta if desired.

spinach and sun-dried tomato pasta sauce

This hearty, Greek-inspired sauce is easy to prepare and will impress your guests when served over the pasta of your choice, with a light sprinkling of feta cheese.

makes 4 servings

¼ cup sun-dried tomatoes (not packed in oil)

2 teaspoons olive oil

1 small onion, chopped

4 or 5 garlic cloves, minced

8 ounces fresh mushrooms, sliced

2 tablespoons tamari soy sauce

1 can (16 ounces) artichoke hearts, drained and chopped

¼ cup chopped Kalamata olives

¼ cup pine nuts

1 package (10 ounces) prewashed, ready-to-eat spinach

Per serving: 200 calories • 13g protein • 9g fat • 27g carbohydrates • 0 cholesterol • 809mg sodium • 11g fiber

1. Soak the sun-dried tomatoes in hot water for 30 minutes.
2. Meanwhile, in a medium skillet, heat the olive oil over medium-high heat. Add the onion and garlic and cook, stirring, until softened, about 3 minutes. Add the mushrooms and tamari and cook, stirring, for another 3 minutes, until the vegetables become tender. Drain the rehydrated tomatoes and slice them into thin strips. Add the tomatoes, artichoke hearts, olives, and pine nuts to the saucepan and toss to mix. Add the spinach, toss, and heat until the spinach wilts.

red pepper harissa sauce

"A little dab'll do ya" with this fiery condiment. This version is less of a traditional Tunisian paste and more of a chunky sauce. We've also added cooked red bell peppers and shallots to the mandatory red chile peppers and garlic for a milder flavor. The Tunisians serve *harissa* with almost all of their savory dishes. Try it over couscous, add a spoonful to soup, and, if you dare, spread it on bread. The sauce can be stored in the refrigerator for up to two weeks.

**makes about 2 cups or
32 tablespoons**
6 to 8 small dried red chile peppers
1 cup hot water
3 tablespoons extra-virgin olive oil
2 red bell peppers, seeded and quartered
3 shallots, quartered
3 or 4 garlic cloves, minced
2 tablespoons fresh lemon juice
Salt to taste

Per tablespoon: 14 calories • 0 protein • 1g fat
• 1g carbohydrates • 0 cholesterol • 0 sodium
• 0 fiber

1. Soak the dried chile peppers in the hot water until they soften.
2. Meanwhile, in a medium skillet, heat 1 tablespoon of the olive oil over medium-high heat. Add the bell peppers, shallots, and garlic and cook, stirring, until soft, about 10 minutes. Set aside.
3. Add the chile peppers and their soaking liquid to a blender or food processor and process for 30 seconds. Strain through a fine-meshed sieve, reserving the liquid and discarding the chile debris.
4. Add the red bell pepper mixture and the chile pepper liquid to the blender or food processor and process to a slightly chunky consistency. Strain the mixture once more, discarding the liquid. Spoon the sauce into a serving bowl or covered jar and stir in the remaining olive oil, the lemon juice, and salt. Serve immediately. If reserving for later use, layer the top of the jar with a little additional olive oil, cover tightly, and refrigerate.

tofu "ricotta" filling

Use this easy-to-prepare vegan filling to stuff pasta shells, manicotti, rigatoni, cannelloni, or in our recipe for Calzones (page 270), or just toss with cooked penne pasta and marinara sauce and bake in a casserole. For a slightly different flavor, mix in some chopped spinach and soy Parmesan cheese.

makes about 3 cups filling

1 pound hard or extra-firm silken tofu, drained, squeezed, and crumbled

⅓ cup olive oil

1 teaspoon salt

1 teaspoon garlic powder

1 teaspoon onion powder

1 teaspoon dried basil

1 teaspoon dried oregano

Per ¼-cup filling: 77 calories • 3g protein • 7g fat • 1g carbohydrates • 0 cholesterol • 13mg sodium • 1g fiber

In a large bowl, mix all of the ingredients and toss well. Adjust the seasonings to taste.

sautéed garlic crumbs

These crisp crumbs are an excellent substitute for grated cheese. Always use soft, fresh (not dried) bread crumbs. Purchase soft crumbs from a bakery or make them yourself by cubing slices of bread. You can store unused crumbs in an airtight container at room temperature for up to four days, or freeze in airtight plastic bags for up to six months.

makes 1½ cups or 22 tablespoons

2 tablespoons olive oil

2 garlic cloves, minced

1¾ cups soft whole wheat or white bread crumbs, cubed

Per tablespoon: 32 calories • 1g protein • 1g fat • 4g carbohydrates • 0 cholesterol • 153mg sodium • 0 fiber

1. In a large nonstick skillet, heat the olive oil over medium-high heat. Add the garlic and cook, stirring constantly, until opaque but not brown. Add the bread crumbs and cook, stirring often, until the crumbs turn golden, 5 to 8 minutes. Be careful not to let them burn.
2. Scrape the crumbs onto paper towels and let cool before using or storing.

roasted red sauce

Essential to many Italian pasta dishes, this is an especially hearty and flavorful red sauce. Don't let the amount of garlic frighten you away from this recipe. When roasted, the garlic becomes sweet and mild and adds great flavor to the sauce. Use this recipe for Quick Layered Polenta and Red Sauce (page 185) or as a topping for pasta, grains, or steamed vegetables.

makes 8 cups

1 can (28 ounces) whole Italian plum tomatoes in juice
1 large onion
1 large garlic head
1 large carrot
3 teaspoons olive oil
1 large celery stalk, finely chopped
1 jalapeño pepper, seeded and finely chopped
2 teaspoons dried oregano
1 teaspoon dried thyme
1 teaspoon dried rosemary
½ teaspoon sugar
1 can (28 ounces) crushed Italian plum tomatoes
Salt and freshly ground black pepper to taste

Per ½-cup serving: 39 calories • 1g protein • 1g fat • 7g carbohydrates • 0 cholesterol • 131mg sodium • 1g fiber

1. Preheat the oven to 325°F. Drain the whole plum tomatoes and reserve the juice. Peel and quarter the onion. Remove some of the papery outer peel from the garlic head but do not separate the cloves. Cut the carrot into 3 or 4 large pieces.

2. In a large, shallow baking pan, combine the tomatoes, onion, garlic, and carrot. Add 2 teaspoons of the olive oil and toss the vegetables to coat. Roast the vegetables until the head of garlic is soft, the onion looks wilted, and the tomatoes are just slightly charred, about 1 hour.

3. When the vegetables are cool enough to handle, finely chop (or coarsely puree in a food processor) the roasted tomatoes, onion, and carrot pieces.

4. In a large pot, heat the remaining teaspoon of olive oil over medium heat. Add the chopped celery and jalapeño and cook, stirring often, until softened, about 5 minutes. Separate the garlic cloves and squeeze the roasted garlic into the pot. Add the roasted vegetables, oregano, thyme, rosemary, and sugar and cook, stirring occasionally, for 5 minutes. Add the crushed tomatoes and simmer for about 1 hour. If the sauce becomes too thick, add the reserved liquid from the can of whole plum tomatoes. Season with salt and pepper to taste.

mediterranean tomato sauce

Use this basic recipe anytime you need a zesty, flavorful tomato sauce. It keeps for up to one week in the refrigerator or for up to six months frozen.

makes 6 servings
¼ cup olive oil
1 small onion, minced
2 garlic cloves, minced
1 can (28 ounces) Italian plum tomatoes
Salt and freshly ground black pepper to taste
Pinch of crushed red pepper flakes (optional)
12 whole basil leaves, shredded, or 1 tablespoon
  minced fresh parsley

Per serving: 118 calories • 2g protein • 9g fat • 8g carbohydrates • 0 cholesterol • 217mg sodium • 2g fiber

1. In a large skillet, heat the olive oil over medium-high heat. Add the onion and cook, stirring, for 2 minutes, until softened slightly. Add the garlic and cook, stirring, for 1 minute longer.
2. Add the remaining ingredients and simmer the sauce, crushing the tomatoes against the sides of the pan with a wooden spoon to break them up, until thickened, about 40 minutes.

Desserts

Most Mediterranean meals end simply, with a colorful platter of fresh fruits. Peaches, plums, strawberries, apricots, figs, grapes, cherries, pomegranates, melons, apples, pears, blood oranges, and tangerines each have their season in the Mediterranean, and only at that time (or in their dried form) do they grace tables for dessert. Lightly cooked compotes, such as our Compote of Peaches, Pistachios, and Marsala (page 303), glossy fresh fruit tarts, decorative Moroccan fruit salads sprinkled with rose or orange blossom water, and subtly sweetened granitas are delicious and simple ways of using fresh seasonal fruit, which most people of the region will tell you is the dessert of choice. But this in no way means that Mediterranean peoples are not fond of more sugary sweets. Rather, they have a huge collective sweet tooth, and satisfy it daily, enjoying pastries and confections with coffee or tea as midmorning or afternoon snacks, or even late at night, well after the dinner table has been cleared. These sweets are often made from nuts and flaky phyllo dough, which is a favorite throughout the area. Honeyed pastries like baklava are adored in Greece, Turkey, and the Middle East, and can use almonds, pistachios, hazelnuts, walnuts, or a combination. Our version (page 315) is a bit less sweet than usual, but is otherwise a perfect example. Nuts also show up in cakes, tarts, and tortes, which are often scented with orange blossom or rose water, or equally fragrant fruit liqueurs. Almond paste, an Italian and Middle Eastern favorite, lends its intensely sweet, nutty flavor to pastries, dried fruits, candies, and creamy, puddinglike tortes, such as Chocolate-Glazed Almond Ricotta Torte (page 310). Although chocolate is not as beloved in the Middle East and northern Africa as it is in other parts of the world, the French and the Italians do not follow their Mediterranean cousins in this sentiment. Cakes, cookies, candies, and tarts can all be flavored and enriched by both cocoa powder and chocolate, and are particularly sought out during the winter holidays, when the feasting is as important to some people as the holidays themselves. Sweet custards and olive oil–enriched cakes, candied or stuffed dried fruit, and sweet couscous or milk-based rice puddings are also luscious examples of the vast array of Mediterranean desserts.

minted fig and orange salad

Typical Mediterranean meals end with huge platters of fresh seasonal fruit rather than sweet dessert pastries and puddings. This Moroccan-inspired mélange is colorful and refreshing. When the days are long and hot, this vibrant dish really hits the spot.

makes 4 servings

2 navel oranges
8 fresh figs, sliced
1 cup raspberries
1 cup plain yogurt
2 to 3 tablespoons chopped fresh mint leaves,
   plus sprigs for garnish
1 tablespoon honey
½ teaspoon ground cinnamon

Per 1-cup serving: 175 calories • 4g protein • 3g fat • 38g carbohydrates • 2mg cholesterol • 30mg sodium • 6g fiber

1. Peel the oranges, taking care to remove as much of the white pith as possible. Separate the oranges into sections and then cut each section into 1-inch pieces. Place the oranges and any juice that accumulated on the cutting board into a large bowl.
2. Add all of the remaining ingredients to the bowl and toss to mix. Chill until ready to serve. Garnish the salad with sprigs of mint.

fragrant orange salad with dates

Heaping platters of fruit are enjoyed by all the people of the Mediterranean after lunch and dinner. Make this traditional southern Moroccan dessert the crowning touch to your northern African feast. Orange blossom water is available in Middle Eastern and gourmet specialty shops.

makes 6 servings

5 large navel oranges
2 teaspoons orange blossom water
2 teaspoons granulated sugar
½ cup chopped dates
¼ cup toasted chopped almonds
½ teaspoon ground cinnamon
Fresh mint leaves, for garnish

Per serving: 139 calories • 2g protein • 3g fat
• 28g carbohydrates • 0 cholesterol
• 2mg sodium • 5g fiber

1. With a knife, peel the skin and the white pith from the oranges. Place a strainer over a bowl and section the oranges between membranes so that there is nothing left but orange flesh. Excess juice should collect in the bowl; use it for something else.
2. In another bowl, combine the orange blossom water and sugar and mix until the sugar dissolves. Add the orange sections, dates, almonds, and cinnamon and toss lightly to mix. Garnish the salad with mint and serve.

compote of peaches, pistachios, and marsala

Compotes make delicious, light desserts that are the perfect endings to hearty lunches and dinners. This one is scented with the delicate flavors of vanilla bean, cinnamon, and Marsala, Sicily's sweet golden wine. Although Marsala has since become a favorite all over Italy, originally this libation was created by an English wine shipper in 1773 specifically for the English market. He discovered that fortifying the wine with grape spirits eliminated possible spoilage during transport.

makes 6 servings

5 ounces pistachios in the shell (about 1 cup)
6 cups water
¾ cup granulated sugar or sugar substitute
½ cup Marsala wine
1 cinnamon stick
½ vanilla bean, split in half lengthwise
6 ripe peaches, cut in half lengthwise and pitted

Per serving: 292 calories • 4g protein • 12g fat • 42g carbohydrates • 0 cholesterol • 3mg sodium • 4g fiber

1. Remove the pistachios from their shells. Blanch them in boiling water for 1 minute. Drain and remove any loose skins.

2. In a large pot, combine the water, sugar, Marsala, cinnamon stick, and vanilla bean and bring the mixture to a boil. Add the peaches and simmer until tender, about 5 minutes. Transfer the peach halves to a serving dish.

3. Continue simmering until the liquid has been reduced to about 1½ cups syrup, about 30 minutes. Remove and discard the vanilla bean and cinnamon stick. Stir in the blanched pistachios, spoon the syrup over the peaches, and serve.

baked quince with red wine and almonds

Originally from Crete, quince are fragrant yellow-skinned autumn fruits that look like a cross between an apple and a pear. Because they have a hard texture and slightly bitter flavor when eaten raw, quince are usually cooked. Then, they mellow into a delightfully fragrant fruit with a distinct, almost floral flavor.

In Greece and Italy, beloved quince are often used to make candies and jams. Sweet, flaky pastries are made with quince and almonds in Spain, and the fruits are baked with cinnamon and sugar in Israel. In northern Africa and countries in the eastern Mediterranean, it is not uncommon to find quince used in main dishes and *tagines*. If you can't find quince at your supermarket, try a local farmer's market. Or, substitute firm Granny Smith apples.

makes 6 servings

6 ripe quince (or apples)
1 cup sweet red wine
3 tablespoons chopped almonds
3 tablespoons brown sugar
4 or 5 whole cloves
Ground cinnamon, for dusting

Per serving: 134 calories • 1g protein • 2g fat • 23g carbohydrates • 0 cholesterol • 9mg sodium • 3g fiber

1. Preheat the oven to 350°F. Core the quince, keeping the fruit as intact as possible for stuffing. If using apples, core them.
2. In a medium bowl, stir together the wine, almonds, brown sugar, and cloves.
3. Place the quince or apples in a buttered baking dish. Stuff the quince or apples with the filling and dust the tops with cinnamon.
4. Bake until the quince or apples are tender, about 50 minutes. Let them cool before serving topped with the syrup from the baking dish.

lemon sorbet

Some say that the Italians adopted sorbet (called *sorbettos*) from the traditional Middle Eastern iced fruit drinks called *sharbats*, though legend has it that sorbet was invented by an experimental Sicilian who mixed snow from Mt. Etna with fruit juice. However the story goes, ice creams and sorbets persist as cooling refreshments in the warm Italian climate. To speed freezing, pour the sorbet mixture into several glass bowls. If stirred about every hour, sorbet made in our test kitchen was ready to eat in only four hours. Or, if you have an ice cream maker, you can use it here.

makes 8 servings

4 cups water
2 cups granulated sugar, or to taste
Zest of 2 lemons
12 lemons

Per serving: 203 calories • 1g protein • 0 fat • 54g carbohydrates • 0 cholesterol • 1mg sodium • 0 fiber

1. In a medium pot over high heat, stir together the water, sugar, and lemon zest. Bring the mixture to a boil, then reduce the heat to medium and simmer briskly for 10 minutes. (The mixture should become slightly syrupy.)

2. Meanwhile, halve the lemons horizontally and squeeze out the juice. (If you wish to use the lemon halves as serving cups, reserve them.) Strain the sugar syrup through a sieve into a large glass bowl and let it cool to room temperature.

3. Once the syrup has cooled, line a strainer with cheesecloth or a coffee filter and strain the fresh lemon juice into the syrup. Discard the lemon pulp. Add additional sugar if desired.

4. Place the bowl in the freezer. After 1 hour, break up the ice that has formed and stir until the sorbet becomes liquid. Continue freezing, breaking up the ice and stirring at regular intervals until the sorbet is frozen to desired consistency, 4 to 8 hours.

two-three sugar syrup

This simple syrup is used as an ingredient in the two granita recipes that follow. You can start with less sugar and sweeten to taste. It will keep, covered and refrigerated, for two months.

makes 1 quart or 4 cups

3 cups granulated sugar
2 cups water

Per ½-cup serving: 290 calories • 0 protein
• 0 fat • 75g carbohydrates • 0 cholesterol
• 0 sodium • 0 fiber

In a medium saucepan, combine the sugar and water. Bring the mixture to a boil over medium heat, stirring to dissolve the sugar. Reduce the heat and simmer for 5 minutes. Remove the syrup from the heat and allow it to cool. Pour the syrup into a container, cover and refrigerate until ready to use.

coffee granita

On a hot summer night, serve this refreshing granita as dessert and coffee in one. For a real caffeine kick, make double-strength coffee by using 2 tablespoons of freshly ground coffee for every 6 ounces of boiling water. Of course, you can also make this with decaffeinated coffee.

makes about 6 cups

1 quart freshly brewed double-strength coffee, chilled
¾ cup Two-Three Sugar Syrup (above)
½ teaspoon vanilla extract

Per ½-cup serving: 98 calories • 0 protein
• 0 fat • 25g carbohydrates • 0 cholesterol
• 1mg sodium • 0 fiber

1. Chill a 13-by-9-inch baking dish, preferably metal.
2. Meanwhile, in a medium bowl, mix the coffee, syrup, and vanilla until blended. Pour the mixture into the chilled dish. Freeze until ice crystals form around the edges of the dish, about 30 minutes. With a fork, stir well to incorporate ice crystals. Continue freezing and stirring every 30 to 40 minutes, until the mixture is thick and slushy, about 3 hours.
3. To serve, scrape the surface with a strong fork to create crystals. Pile the granita into individual glass dishes and serve right away.

pomegranate granita

Granitas gets their name from "*granum,*" Latin for "grain," and these refreshing desserts do indeed have an icy granular texture to them. This vibrant ruby granita gets a flavor kick from a secret ingredient—balsamic vinegar. Serve garnished with fresh raspberries and don't identify that mysterious ingredient.

makes about 8 cups

1 quart pomegranate juice (available in natural food stores)

½ cup Two-Three Sugar Syrup (page 306)

2 tablespoons fresh lemon juice

1 tablespoon balsamic vinegar

Per ½-cup serving: 86 calories • 0 protein • 0 fat • 22g carbohydrates • 0 cholesterol • 9mg sodium • 0 fiber

1. Chill a 13-by-9-inch baking dish, preferably metal.
2. Meanwhile, in a medium bowl, mix all of the ingredients until blended. Pour the mixture into the chilled dish. Freeze until ice crystals form around the edges of the dish, about 30 minutes. With a fork, stir well to incorporate the ice crystals. Continue freezing and stirring every 30 to 40 minutes, until the mixture is thick and slushy, about 3 hours.
3. To serve, scrape the surface with a strong fork to create crystals. Pile the granita into individual glass dishes and serve right away.

blood orange custard

This custard is a typical homemade Italian dessert that uses the tart ruby juice from Sicilian-derived blood oranges (*arancia rossa*). Here, we serve it over ladyfingers, but it is also wonderful over pound cake slices or as a filling for an angel food layer cake.

makes 6 servings

12 ladyfingers

1 cup blood orange juice (or mixture of blood orange juice and regular orange juice)

3 large egg yolks

½ cup sugar

1½ cups milk

⅓ cup all-purpose flour

Zest of ½ orange

1 blood orange, peeled and sliced into ¼-inch-thick half-circles

Per serving: 251 calories • 7g protein • 7g fat • 41g carbohydrates • 197 cholesterol • 66mg sodium • 0 fiber

1. Line the sides and bottom of a 9-by-9-inch pan with the ladyfingers. Sprinkle the ladyfingers with ½ cup blood orange juice and set aside.

2. Meanwhile, in a small saucepan, whisk together the egg yolks. Add the sugar and whisk until thoroughly combined. In a small bowl, whisk together ½ cup of the milk with the flour, breaking up any lumps. In small batches, mix the flour paste into the egg mixture, whisking after each addition. Whisk in the remaining 1 cup milk. Strain the remaining ½ cup of blood orange juice and add it to the custard. Add the orange zest. Cook over very low heat, stirring constantly, until the custard becomes thick, 15 to 20 minutes. (Make sure that you do not allow the mixture to boil.)

3. Pour the custard over the ladyfingers, spreading it evenly with a spatula. Cover the pan with plastic wrap, letting the wrap rest directly on top of custard to prevent a skin from forming. Refrigerate until completely cool, about 1 hour. Top with fresh blood orange slices and serve.

sweet couscous dessert

Couscous, the pillar of Maghrebi cuisine, even shows up in desserts. Here it is mixed with dates and nuts and flavored with cinnamon and *ras el hanout*, a Moroccan blend of sweet spices including nutmeg, mace, cloves, ginger, pepper, and allspice. If you can't find it, use a combination of nutmeg and allspice instead.

makes 10 servings

1 cup slivered almonds
½ cup coarsely chopped walnuts
½ cup shelled pistachio nuts
6½ cups water
¾ cup granulated sugar
1 tablespoon freshly squeezed lemon juice
3 cups couscous
2 tablespoons orange blossom water (optional)
1 cup chopped dates
5 tablespoons unsalted butter (optional)
1 teaspoon cinnamon, plus additional for garnish
½ teaspoon *ras el hanout* (see headnote)
2 tablespoons confectioners' sugar

Per serving: 367 calories • 9g protein • 14g fat • 65g carbohydrates • 0 cholesterol • 8mg sodium • 5g fiber

1. Preheat the oven to 350°F. Lay all the nuts out on a baking sheet and toast them in the oven, stirring once or twice, until golden and fragrant, about 5 minutes. Transfer the nuts to a plate to cool.

2. In a medium saucepan, bring 5½ cups of the water, the sugar, and lemon juice to a boil. Stir the mixture as it boils until the sugar is dissolved. Remove from the heat and stir in the couscous and orange blossom water, if using. Cover the pan and let sit until the couscous has absorbed all the water and is tender, about 30 minutes.

3. Meanwhile, in a small saucepan, bring the remaining 1 cup water and the dates to a simmer over medium heat. Let the mixture simmer until the dates are quite tender. Add the butter, cinnamon, and *ras el hanout* to the pan and stir well. Add the mixture to the couscous and stir it well, using your fingers to break up any lumps and to incorporate the dates.

4. When ready to serve, mound the couscous on a serving platter and sift the confectioners' sugar over the top. Decorate with the nuts and a sprinkle of additional cinnamon and serve immediately.

chocolate-glazed almond ricotta torte

This creamy torte falls somewhere between a cheesecake and a silky pudding. Soft almond paste, sold either in bulk or in cans in the supermarket, is best for this smooth torte, since it easily combines with the sugar. If you can't find it, you can use the solid type sold in tubes, but you may have to process it longer with the sugar.

makes 8 servings

For the cake

½ cup sugar

¼ cup almond paste

3 ½ cups ricotta cheese

3 large eggs

¼ cup all-purpose flour

2 tablespoons Amaretto liqueur

For the glaze

8 ounces bittersweet chocolate, chopped

½ cup heavy cream

2 tablespoons light corn syrup

Per serving: 589 calories • 20g protein • 35g fat • 55g carbohydrates • 154mg cholesterol • 127mg sodium • 2g fiber

1. Preheat the oven to 325°F. Grease an 8-inch springform pan. In a food processor fitted with a steel blade, process the sugar and almond paste until well combined and smooth, about 1 minute. Add the ricotta cheese and process until the mixture is smooth, about 1 minute longer. Add the eggs one at a time, processing for a few seconds between additions. Add the flour and Amaretto and pulse to combine.

2. Scrape the mixture into the prepared pan and bake until the center jiggles only very slightly and feels firm to a gentle touch, about 45 minutes. Transfer the pan to a wire rack to cool. Cover the torte and refrigerate it (still in the pan) until cold, at least 2 hours.

3. To make the glaze, in a medium saucepan, combine the chocolate, cream, and corn syrup. Bring the mixture to a simmer, stirring constantly, and stir until the chocolate is melted. Remove the pan from the heat and let cool for a few minutes.

4. Unmold the cake and set it on a wire rack with a sheet of waxed paper underneath it. Pour the glaze over the cake, using a spatula to spread the glaze over any white spots. If necessary, scrape the glaze drips off the waxed paper, reheat, and use to patch any imperfections on the torte. Let the glaze set for at least 30 minutes before serving.

chocolate-mascarpone torte

Mascarpone, a buttery, fresh cow's milk cheese, is a favorite throughout Italy. It is made into both sweet and savory dishes, one of the most popular being tiramisù, made from espresso-soaked ladyfingers and mascarpone. The creamy cheese is also often mixed with liqueur and served as a substitute for whipped cream.

In this festive tart, we've marbled rich mascarpone cheese with a chocolate, brownielike filling. You can make this tart well ahead of time (or save any leftovers) and freeze it. Simply cover the baked tart with plastic wrap, place in large plastic freezer bag, and freeze for up to six weeks. Allow the tart to thaw completely to room temperature before serving.

makes 12 servings

8 ounces bittersweet chocolate, broken into 1-inch chunks

5 tablespoons unsalted butter or margarine

2 large eggs, at room temperature

1 teaspoon vanilla extract

⅓ cup sugar

¾ cup all-purpose flour

¼ teaspoon salt

4 ounces mascarpone cheese, at room temperature

Per serving: 233 calories • 4g protein • 16g fat • 23g carbohydrates • 44mg cholesterol • 155mg sodium • 12g fiber

1. Preheat the oven to 350°F. Grease a 9-inch round tart pan with a removable bottom and set aside.

2. In a small, heavy saucepan, melt the chocolate and butter or margarine over low heat, stirring frequently. Remove from the heat.

3. In a medium bowl, beat the eggs and vanilla with an electric mixer at medium speed for 30 seconds. Gradually add the sugar and beat for 1 minute. Beat in the chocolate and butter mixture, making sure to scrape down the sides of the bowl. Beat in the flour and salt at low speed until just blended. Spread the batter evenly in the prepared pan.

4. Put the cheese into a small bowl and stir well with a fork. Drop the cheese by teaspoonfuls randomly over the surface of the chocolate batter. Using a sharp knife, swirl the cheese mixture into the chocolate mixture to create a marbled effect.

5. Bake the tart until the center is just set, 20 to 25 minutes. Remove the pan to a wire rack and cool completely. Remove from the tart pan, cut into 12 wedges and serve.

chocolate-espresso cake with espresso sauce

How better to end an Italian dinner than with this rich and delicious cake? Our vegan version uses tofu, honey, and whole wheat flour so you know that you can safely indulge in this decadent dessert without feeling guilty!

makes 8 servings

For the cake

7 ounces soft tofu

½ cup mild honey

1 teaspoon vanilla extract

½ cup brewed espresso or very strong coffee

½ cup unsweetened cocoa

1½ cups all-purpose flour or whole wheat pastry flour

1 tablespoon baking powder

1 teaspoon baking soda

For the sauce

10 ounces soft tofu

¾ cup brewed espresso or very strong coffee

½ cup mild honey

1 to 2 tablespoons brandy or cognac

1 teaspoon vanilla extract

For the garnish (optional)

Fresh or frozen berries of choice

Mint sprigs

Confectioners' sugar

Per serving with sauce: 196 calories • 6g protein • 2g fat • 17g carbohydrates • 0 cholesterol • 268mg sodium • 3g fiber

1. Preheat the oven to 350°F. Lightly oil an 8½-inch Bundt pan. To make the cake, in a blender or food processor, puree the tofu with the honey and vanilla. Add the espresso or coffee and cocoa. In a medium bowl, sift the flour with baking powder and baking soda. If using a food processor, add the flour mixture to the tofu mixture and process until smooth. If using a blender, transfer the tofu mixture to a bowl, add the flour mixture, and beat well until smooth. Pour the batter into the prepared pan and bake until firm to the touch, about 25 minutes. Transfer the cake to a wire rack and allow it to cool.

2. Combine all of the sauce ingredients in a blender or food processor and blend until smooth and creamy. Chill the sauce for at least 1 hour. (The sauce will thicken as it cools; dilute with more espresso if necessary.)

3. Remove the cooled cake from the pan, place on a serving platter, and cut into 8 to 10 slices. Spoon ¼ cup of the sauce onto each of 8 to 10 dessert plates and top each plate with a slice of cake. If desired, garnish with berries, sprigs of mint and a light dusting of confectioners' sugar.

yogurt cheesecake with black pepper and honey

The success of this luscious cheesecake depends upon the quality of the yogurt used. A creamy, whole-milk yogurt without any stabilizers will give the most satiny texture. To drain the yogurt, place it in a very fine sieve or in a strainer or colander lined with a double layer of cheesecloth, suspend it over a bowl, and let drain for three hours. You can drain the yogurt several days in advance and store it in the refrigerator.

makes 10 servings

For the crust

1½ cups all-purpose flour
3 tablespoons sugar
Freshly grated zest of ½ lemon
Pinch of salt
½ cup (1 stick) cold unsalted butter, cut into ½-inch slices
1 large egg yolk

For the filling

1 quart whole-milk yogurt, drained for 3 hours (see headnote)
⅔ cup sugar
2 large eggs
1 tablespoon cornstarch
½ teaspoon coarsely ground black pepper
⅛ teaspoon salt
1 tablespoon honey
Freshly grated zest of ½ lemon

Per serving: 306 calories • 7g protein • 14g fat • 39g carbohydrates • 101mg cholesterol • 87mg sodium • 1g fiber

1. To make the crust, combine the flour, sugar, lemon zest, and salt in a large bowl. Cut in the butter with a pastry blender or 2 knives until mixture resembles coarse crumbs. Alternatively, pulse the mixture together in a food processor. Add the egg yolk and pulse or stir until the mixture forms a ball and holds together. Flatten the dough into a disk, wrap in plastic wrap, and refrigerate for 30 minutes.

2. Roll the dough out between 2 pieces of waxed paper to a 12-inch circle. Fit the circle into a 10-inch springform pan. Cover and chill the crust for at least 30 minutes.

3. Preheat the oven to 375°F. Uncover the crust and line it with foil or waxed paper. Fill the crust with pie weights, raw rice, or dried beans. Bake for 15 minutes, then remove the foil and weights. Bake the crust until golden, about 15 minutes longer. Transfer to a wire rack to cool. Lower the oven temperature to 350°F.

4. To prepare the filling, in a food processor or bowl, combine the yogurt, sugar, and eggs and process until creamy and smooth, about 1 minute. Add the cornstarch, pepper, and salt and pulse to combine. Pour the filling into the crust and bake the tart until the center is set and firm to a gentle touch, about 35 minutes. Transfer to a wire rack to cool completely. When the tart is cool, cover and refrigerate until cold, at least 3 hours.

5. To serve, unmold the cake and place on a serving platter. Place the honey and lemon zest in a small microwave-safe dish and heat it on high power for 20 seconds, until thin and liquid. (Alternatively, heat in a small saucepan on the stove.) Drizzle the honey mixture over the top of the cake, then cut into slices and serve.

olive oil cake

This light, simple-to-make cake has a predominantly citrus flavor with a faint, fruity hint of olive oil. Make sure to use extra-virgin olive oil or the cake will taste bland. Using olive oil instead of butter also makes this cake kosher, without your resorting to margarine.

makes 8 servings

4 large eggs, at room temperature
1 cup granulated sugar
½ cup extra-virgin olive oil
½ teaspoon baking powder
⅛ teaspoon salt
1 cup all-purpose flour
Grated zest of 1 orange
Grated zest of 1 lemon
Confectioners' sugar, for sprinkling

Per serving: 310 calories • 5g protein • 16g fat • 37g carbohydrates • 107mg cholesterol • 65mg sodium • 1g fiber

1. Preheat the oven to 350°F. Grease and flour an 8-inch cake pan. Using an electric beater set on high speed, beat the eggs and sugar until very light and thick, about 5 minutes. Add the oil, baking powder, and salt and mix on low speed to incorporate. Using a rubber spatula, fold in the flour and citrus zests.
2. Pour the mixture into the prepared pan and bake until the top is golden brown and the cake springs back when lightly pressed with a finger, about 55 minutes. If the cake gets too brown before the center is done, cover the top of the pan with foil. Transfer the cake to a wire rack to cool.
3. When ready to serve, unmold the cake and sprinkle the top with confectioners' sugar.

baklava

One of the best-known Turkish desserts, baklava is traditionally composed of crisp sheets of phyllo dough layered with a cinnamon-flavored nut filling and then soaked in a sweet syrup fragrant with rose or orange blossom water. You are likely to find some form of baklava in virtually every region that was occupied by the Turks during the Ottoman Empire.

Baklava can be assembled the day before serving and refrigerated. Once baked, however, it should not be refrigerated, as this may cause the pastry to become soggy. Stored at room temperature, sweet baklava can keep for over a week.

makes 24 pieces

For the baklava

3¾ cups chopped, unsalted mixed nuts, such as almonds, walnuts, hazelnuts, or pistachios

¼ cup sugar

1 teaspoon ground cinnamon

1¼ sticks unsalted butter, melted

14 sheets phyllo dough

For the sugar syrup

1 cup sugar

1 cup water

2 cinnamon sticks or ½ teaspoon ground cinnamon

2 teaspoons rose water or orange blossom water, or 1 teaspoon vanilla extract

1 teaspoon fresh lemon juice

Per piece: 255 calories • 5g protein • 18g fat • 20g carbohydrates • 17mg cholesterol • 164mg sodium • 2g fiber

1. Preheat the oven to 325°F. In a small bowl, combine the nuts, sugar, and cinnamon.

2. Lightly brush a 12-by-17-inch baking pan (or the nearest size pan you have) with melted butter. Lay a sheet of phyllo dough in the bottom of the pan and brush it lightly with butter. Repeat this procedure with 3 more sheets of phyllo dough, buttering each one after it has been laid over the others.

3. Evenly spread the top sheet with a third of the nut mixture. Cover the filling with 3 more sheets of phyllo dough, brushing each sheet with butter as before. Repeat these layers twice more, covering the last nut layer with the remaining 4 sheets of phyllo dough, brushing each sheet with butter as before (fold in any excess dough before placing the top sheet on top and brushing with butter). Using a sharp knife, carefully score the top layers of pastry into 24 diamond or square shapes.

4. Bake the pastry for 30 minutes. Increase the heat to 350°F. and bake until the pastry is golden brown and puffed, about 10 minutes.

5. Meanwhile, prepare the sugar syrup. In a medium saucepan, combine the sugar, water, and cinnamon sticks. Bring the mixture to a boil over medium heat. Reduce the heat and simmer for 10 minutes, until the syrup thickens. Remove the saucepan from the heat, stir in the rose water and lemon juice (and ground cinnamon if using) and set aside.

6. Pour the syrup over the hot, baked pastry and allow to cool. Cut the pastry along the score lines before serving.

pistachio butter rings

Delicate, crumbly butternut cookies of this sort are popular all over the Middle East. These use pistachio nuts, which give them a nubby, green- and purple-flecked surface peeking out from a dusting of confectioners' sugar.

makes about 2 dozen cookies

1 cup (2 sticks) unsalted butter, at room temperature

¾ cup confectioners' sugar, plus additional for sprinkling

½ teaspoon orange blossom water or vanilla extract

2 cups all-purpose flour, plus additional for rolling

½ teaspoon baking powder

¼ teaspoon salt

¼ cup finely chopped pistachio nuts

Per cookie: 126 calories • 1g protein • 8g fat • 11g carbohydrates • 21mg cholesterol • 24mg sodium • 0 fiber

1. Preheat the oven to 325°F. In a large bowl, using an electric beater set on medium speed, beat the butter and sugar until light and fluffy, about 2 minutes. Beat in the orange blossom water or vanilla. Add the flour, baking powder, and salt and beat to combine. Stir in the nuts.

2. On a lightly floured surface, using lightly floured hands, divide the dough into walnut-size balls. Roll the balls into 2½-inch-long snakes and form into rings, pinching the seam to seal. Place the rings 1 inch apart on baking sheets. Bake the cookies until they are pale gold and set, about 20 minutes. Transfer the baking sheets to wire racks to cool.

3. Before serving, dust the cookies with additional confectioners' sugar.

lacy honey cups

These thin wafers can be shaped into decorative little cups, then filled with whipped cream or ice cream and fresh fruit. Be sure to bake the wafers until they are medium brown in color—not a light or pale brown—or they will not hold their shape. You can also be creative and form the wafers into a variety of other shapes. To make cylinders, roll each wafer around the handle of a wooden spoon. If the wafers cool before you've had a chance to shape them, pop them back into the oven for a minute or two; they should once again become pliable.

makes 8 wafers

½ cup honey
2½ tablespoons unsalted butter or soy margarine
½ cup all-purpose flour or whole wheat pastry flour
1 teaspoon vanilla extract
½ teaspoon freshly grated lemon zest
Pinch of salt

Per wafer: 126 calories • 1g protein • 4g fat • 23g carbohydrates • 10mg cholesterol • 2mg sodium • 0 fiber

1. Preheat the oven to 350°F. Lightly grease a cookie sheet. In a small pot over high heat, combine the honey and butter; bring the mixture to a rapid boil. Continue boiling for 1 minute. Remove the pan from the heat, then stir in the flour, vanilla, lemon zest, and salt. The mixture will be runny.

2. Drop the wafer mixture, 2 tablespoons at a time, several inches apart, on the prepared cookie sheet. (The wafers will double or triple in size, so you may be able to bake only 2 to 4 at a time.) Immediately place the cookie sheet into the oven and bake for 8 to 9 minutes, until the wafers are lacy and medium brown in color.

3. Remove the wafers from the oven and allow them to cool for a mere 20 to 30 seconds. Remove the wafers from the baking sheet with a spatula and quickly place them, while still warm and pliable, in small bowls or cups with steep sides and mold each into a cup shape. Allow the wafers to cool and set before removing them from the molds. Repeat the process with the remaining batter, using the same cookie sheet, lightly greasing it in between batches.

fig and almond crescents

Figs are especially popular in the eastern Mediterranean and Middle Eastern countries where they are eaten fresh or dried and are made into sweets, jams, and desserts, such as these delightful filled pastries.

makes 10 crescents

For the dough

2 cups unbleached all-purpose flour, plus about 2 tablespoons for kneading

1 tablespoon sugar or 2 teaspoons honey

1 tablespoon olive oil (optional)

1 scant teaspoon rapid-rising yeast

½ teaspoon salt

⅓ to ⅔ cup hot water

For the fig filling

⅓ cup plus 1 tablespoon finely chopped almonds

2 cups (about 10 ounces) coarsely chopped dried figs

1 cup orange juice

2 tablespoons honey

1 teaspoon freshly grated orange zest

2 teaspoons olive oil

Per crescent: 213 calories • 5g protein • 4g fat • 42g carbohydrates • 0 cholesterol • 111mg sodium • 4g fiber

1. Preheat the oven to 400°F. Grease a baking sheet. In a food processor, combine 2 cups of the flour, the sugar or honey, olive oil if desired, yeast, and salt and process for 10 seconds. With the processor running, gradually add about ⅓ cup of the hot water through the feeder tube. Stop the machine and let the dough rest for about 20 seconds. Continue adding hot water if necessary and process until the dough forms a ball and the sides of the bowl are clean. Pulse for an additional 2 or 3 times, then turn the dough out onto a floured surface.

2. Knead the dough for about 1 minute, adding flour as necessary if the dough becomes sticky. Lightly flour the inside of a plastic bag. Place the dough in the bag, seal, and let it rest for 15 to 20 minutes in a warm place.

3. Meanwhile, make the filling. Add the almonds, figs, orange juice, honey, and orange zest to a 1-quart saucepan and bring the mixture to a boil. Reduce the heat and continue cooking, stirring occasionally, until the figs soften and all the juice is absorbed, about 10 minutes. Let the mixture cool, then return the filling to the food processor, process for 5 seconds, and set aside.

4. Turn the dough out onto a floured surface. Cut it into 10 equal pieces. Keep the pieces covered with a damp kitchen towel until you are ready to use them so that they won't dry out. Roll each piece into a thin circle about 4 inches in diameter. Spread 1 tablespoon of filling over the bottom two-thirds of each circle. Fold the remaining third over the filling to form a crescent. (The dough won't cover the filling completely.) Place the crescents on the prepared baking sheet.

5. Brush the crescents with the olive oil. Bake for 10 minutes. Rotate the pan 180° and bake for an additional 15 to 20 minutes, until the crescents are golden brown. Cool briefly on a wire rack before serving.

hazelnut biscotti

Biscotto, Italian for "twice baked," means that these delicious hazelnut-studded cookies turn out crunchy and hard. *Biscotti* come in many flavors and shapes, from the traditional crescent-shaped almond *biscotti* of Tuscany to the anise-flavored diamonds found in Sicily. Oddly enough, in Rome, delicious orange and almond *biscotti* are reserved for the penitential days of Lent. These dessert biscuits will soften up immediately when dunked into a steaming cup of espresso or a glass of sweet dessert wine.

Biscotti will freeze for up to two months. To serve, simply transfer as many cookies as desired to a plate, cover with plastic wrap, and let them thaw at room temperature.

makes 30 biscotti

1 cup hazelnuts
2 cups all-purpose flour
1 teaspoon baking powder
¼ teaspoon salt
¾ cup sugar
⅓ cup unsalted butter or margarine, softened
2 large eggs, at room temperature
3 tablespoons hazelnut or almond flavored liqueur

Per biscotto: 108 calories • 2g protein • 6g fat • 13g carbohydrates • 14mg cholesterol • 101mg sodium • 1g fiber

1. Preheat the oven to 350°F. Spread the hazelnuts on a baking sheet and toast in the oven until they turn golden brown and their skins crack and loosen, about 15 minutes. Wrap the hot hazelnuts in a kitchen towel and firmly rub them together to loosen most of the skins. Discard the skins. Let the nuts cool, then coarsely chop and set aside. Turn off the oven for now.

2. In a medium bowl, combine the flour, baking powder, and salt and set aside.

3. In a large bowl, beat the sugar and butter with an electric mixer until light and fluffy. Beat in the eggs, one at a time, beating well after each addition. Scrape down the sides of the bowl as necessary. Beat in the liqueur. With the mixer on low speed, beat in the flour mixture until just blended. Stir in the chopped hazelnuts.

4. Divide the dough in half. Spread each half evenly down the center of a sheet of waxed paper and roll into two 13-inch logs. Wrap the logs in plastic wrap and refrigerate until firm, about 2 hours or for up to 24 hours.

5. About 15 minutes before you're ready to continue, preheat the oven to 375°F. Unwrap the logs and place them 2 inches apart on a lightly greased baking sheet. With floured hands, shape each log to measure 2 inches wide and ½ inch thick.

6. Bake until set and golden brown, about 20 minutes. Remove the logs from the oven and, using a serrated knife, cut each log into 1-inch-thick diagonal slices. Place the slices, cut side up, on a baking sheet and bake until the cut surfaces are golden brown, about 7 minutes per side, flip the slices, and bake for about 7 minutes more. Remove the biscotti to a wire rack and cool completely before serving or freezing.

turkish apricot candies

Often served at the end of a meal with tiny cups of dark Turkish coffee, these rich, sweet candies are regularly made to have on hand for unexpected visitors. Traditional Mediterranean hospitality persists in Turkey, where it is customary to give a warm welcome to the casual caller at all times. These treats will store at room temperature in an airtight container for up to two weeks.

makes 24 candies

1 cup (packed) dried apricots, minced
½ cup sugar
4 tablespoons unsalted butter
2 tablespoons water
1 tablespoon orange blossom water
1 cup chopped, shelled pistachios (unsalted)

Per candy: 156 calories • 3g protein • 9g fat • 18g carbohydrates • 11mg cholesterol • 43mg sodium • 1g fiber

1. In a medium saucepan, combine the apricots, sugar, butter, water, and orange blossom water. Cook over low heat, stirring occasionally with a wooden spoon, until the mixture becomes a thick puree, 15 to 20 minutes. Remove the pan from the heat and beat until smooth. Transfer the mixture to a plate and spread it out into an even circle. Allow to cool.

2. Divide the mixture into 24 equal pieces and roll each into a ball. Coat each ball with chopped pistachios and place in small petit four papers if desired.

minted yogurt drink

Cooling iced yogurt beverages, called *ayran*, are enjoyed everywhere in Turkey, whether on street corners, in bars, or at home. The eastern Mediterranean's answer to the smoothie, this refreshingly simple recipe for *ayran* goes well with many regional dishes. Or, serve it as a snack in between meals.

makes 4 servings

3 cups plain yogurt
3 cups water, or to taste
3 to 4 tablespoons chopped fresh mint
Salt to taste

Per serving: 104 calories • 6g protein • 6g fat • 9g carbohydrates • 22mg cholesterol • 79mg sodium • 0 fiber

In a blender, combine all of the ingredients and process until smooth. Pour the drink into a large pitcher and chill for at least 1 hour. Serve in tall glasses with ice.

moroccan tea

Served after every meal and sometimes before, tea is a very important part of Moroccan dining, although it was introduced by the British only during the Crimean War in 1854. The Moroccans have adapted European tea by infusing it with fresh sprigs of mint and adding plenty of sugar. Mint tea is ritually served in glasses by the master of the house to guests who, traditionally, drink three cups of tea. In this recipe, we've added cinnamon for a twist.

makes 4 cups tea

¼ cup sugar
2 bags or 2 tablespoons green tea
1 small bunch fresh mint, including stems
1 cinnamon stick
4 cups boiling water
Mint leaves, for garnish

Per serving: 49 calories • 0 protein • 0 fat • 13g carbohydrates • 0 cholesterol • 7mg sodium • 0 fiber

1. Rinse a medium tea pot with boiling water. Place the sugar, tea bags or loose tea, mint, and cinnamon stick in the teapot. Fill with boiling water.
2. Cover the pot and let the tea steep for at least 5 minutes. Pour a small amount of tea into a cup, then pour the tea from the cup back into the teapot. Repeat this procedure 3 times in order to fully blend the ingredients. Pour the tea into teacups, garnish each cup with a mint leaf, and serve.

Menu Suggestions

Maghrebi Feast

Mouhammara (page 64) ▪ Sesame Flat Bread (page 278) ▪ Moroccan Carrot Soup (page 100) ▪

Warm Couscous Tabbouleh (page 194) ▪ Moroccan Stew (page 220) ▪ Fragrant Orange Salad with Dates

(page 302) ▪ Moroccan Tea (page 322)

Buffet of Hot and Cold *Mezze*

Marinated Roasted Red Peppers (page 63) ▪ Marinated Olives (page 51) ▪ Spinach Phyllo Kisses

(page 48) ▪ Herb-Stuffed Grape Leaves (page 55) ▪ Mixed Plate of Lentil and Olive Crostini (pages 58

and 59) ▪ Herbed White Bean Pâté (page 43) ▪ Focaccia (page 271) ▪ Turkish Apricot Candies

(page 320) ▪ Fig and Almond Crescents (page 318)

Italian Dinner Party

Stuffed Garlicky Mushroom Caps (page 47) ▪ Roasted Tomato Bruschetta (page 62) ▪ Raw Artichoke Salad with Parmesan (page 79) ▪ Goat Cheese and Radicchio Agnolotti (page 145) ▪ Sautéed Spinach and Fava Beans (page 250) ▪ Chocolate-Mascarpone Torte (page 311)

Summer Brunch (Vegan)

Cool Cantaloupe Soup (page 105) ▪ Riviera Salad (page 77) ▪ Artichoke and Fennel Tart (page 132) ▪ Lentil Bulgur Pilaf (page 196) ▪ Compote of Peaches, Pistachios, and Marsala (page 303)

Mediterranean Picnic

Triple Bean and Artichoke Salad (page 95) ▪ Provençal Mushroom Tart (page 140) ▪ Pepper and Provolone Sandwich (page 277) ▪ The Ultimate Grilled Eggplant Sandwich (page 276) ▪ Hazelnut Biscotti (page 319)

Autumn in Provence

Arugula with Roasted Garlic Viniagrette (page 83) ▪ Provençal Soup with Pistou (page 107) ▪ Rosemary Breadsticks (page 279) ▪ Baked Quince with Red Wine and Almonds (page 304)

Spanish Sunday Brunch

Garden Gazpacho (page 101) ▪ Spanish Tortilla (page 122) ▪ Garlicky Greens Sauté (page 239) ▪ Pomegranate Granita (page 307)

Birthday Party Menu

Caprese Salad (page 80) ■ Sesame Sticks (page 280) ■ Four-Vegetable, Two-Way Pizza (page 269) ■

Lemon Sorbet (page 305) ■ Olive Oil Cake (page 314)

Greek Harvest Dinner

Spanakopita (page 118) ■ Tomato and Fennel Soup (page 110) ■ Herb and Rice Stuffed Peppers

(page 180) ■ String Beans with Walnuts and Pomegranate (page 251) ■ Baklava (page 315)

Light Springtime Luncheon Buffet

Herbed White Bean Pâté (page 43) ■ Sesame Flat Bread (page 278) ■ Spring Salad with Goat Cheese

Medallions (page 87) ■ Roasted Asparagus Salad with Orange (page 75) ■ Yogurt Cheesecake with Black

Pepper and Honey (page 313)

Warming Winter Dinner

Winter Fig Salad (page 86) ■ Hearty Root Vegetable and Bean Stew (page 203) ■ Farro and Sun-Dried

Tomato Focaccia (page 273) ■ Chocolate-Glazed Almond Ricotta Torte (page 310)

A Turkish Delight

Grape Leaves Stuffed with Bulgur, Apricots, and Mint (page 54) ■ Turkish Fennel Salad (page 84) ■

Stuffed Baby Eggplants (page 210) ■ Pistachio Butter Rings (page 316)

Glossary

Arborio Rice   An Italian short-grain rice that is considered the best for making risotto because of its ability to absorb liquids while retaining its shape. Arborio rice is Italy's biggest rice export and is therefore easy to find in this country.

Arrowroot Powder   A plant-derived white powder used as a thickening and binding agent and as a substitute for eggs, cornstarch, and flour roux.

Arugula   A sharp mustard green that originated in Asia and is used most commonly in salads and soups.

Asiago Cheese   A sharp cow's milk cheese from the area of Asiago in Italy. It can be purchased *d'allevo* (fresh), *fresco* (two months' aging), *mezzano* (three to five months') and *vecchio* (nine months' or longer).

Blood Oranges   Sweet oranges with deep red flesh, brought to America in the 1930s by Italian and Spanish immigrants. They are expensive and somewhat difficult to find, but their stunning color can't be beat.

Bulgur   Also called *burghul*. Wheat kernels that have been steamed, dried, and crushed. (It is not the same as cracked wheat.) It has a tender, chewy texture and comes in coarse, medium, and fine grinds.

Cannellini Beans   In Italian, *cannellini* means "tiny rods." These white kidney beans are used in Italian soups or stews, and mixed with herbs as a filling side dish.

Capers   The unopened flower buds of the scrubby caper bush, which grows in poor dry soil and between the stones of thousand-year-old Mediterranean buildings. Capers are preserved in vinegar brine and eaten with salads or used to add flavor to main dishes.

Chanterelle Mushrooms   Trumpet-shaped mushrooms that vary in taste from mild and meaty to flowery, nutty and even subtly cinnamony. Fresh chanterelles are generally available from summer through winter.

Compote   Stewed fresh or dried fruits, often with a sweet liqueur added to the mixture.

Cremini Mushrooms   These mushrooms look like common cultivated mushrooms but are brown, not white, and are much more flavorful. They are the standard cultivated mushroom in European Mediterranean countries. When cremini mushrooms grow large and their caps unfurl, they are called portobello mushrooms.

Curly Endive   A dark leafy green that is usually blanched or sautéed before eating to reduce the vegetable's bitter taste. Curly endive is also added to soups and stews.

Emmentaler Cheese   Also called Emmental, this part-skim cow's milk cheese comes in huge wheels and is filled with large holes. French Emmentaler has a somewhat fruity nutty taste and a semifirm texture. It melts well and is used extensively in French cooking.

Enoki Mushrooms   A well-loved mushroom in Japan, these tiny mushrooms have a slightly acid and fruity taste. They are available year-round in most Oriental specialty stores.

Farro   A distinctive grain that has a complex nutty taste with undertones of oats and barley. It is not quite as heavy as most whole grains and looks and tastes somewhat like a light-brown rice.

Fava Beans   These pale green beans can be found canned or dried in most Middle Eastern specialty stores. *Ful mudammas* are smaller, brown-skinned fava beans, used most commonly in northern Africa.

Fennel   A French favorite, these pale green rounded fennel bulbs and stalks are used in savory dishes, soups, and stews. Fennel has a crisp texture and a mild, fresh anise flavor. Dried fennel seeds come from the flowers of this vegetable.

Gruyère Cheese   Originally from Switzerland, Gruyère is a versatile cow's milk cheese with a slightly sweet nutty flavor. Gruyère is often used in fondue and grated fresh over vegetable and pasta dishes.

Julienne   Foods that have been cut into thin, matchstick-like strips.

Kabocha Squash   A Japanese winter squash with a mottled dark-green rind and soft, fine-grained yellow-orange flesh. Cooked kabocha squash is tender, floury, and sweet.

Kalamata Olives   Greek olives that are a defining feature of the classic Greek salad. These uniquely flavored dark purple gems have practically infinite uses in Mediterranean cookery.

Manchego Cheese   A popular Spanish sheep's milk cheese with a rich, semifirm texture and a full, mellow flavor. It is a great snack cheese and is also melted over baked vegetable dishes.

Mascarpone Cheese   A soft, mild fresh cow's milk cheese that originated in Lodi, Italy. It is versatile enough to be blended with other flavors and is sometimes sweetened and eaten with fruit.

Mesclun   A mixture of tender young leafy greens, such as baby lettuces, various mustard greens, and radicchio.

Morel Mushrooms   A tasty wild mushroom that has a rounded treelike shape and fruits only in the springtime. This honeycomb-textured mushroom refuses to be cultivated and comes highly prized as a rare wild treat.

Niçoise Olives   These little black or dark purple olives can usually be found in specialty or gourmet shops. You can substitute any other oil-cured black olives for Niçoise olives.

Orzo   Tiny rice-shaped pasta. In Italian, orzo also refers to barley; don't be confused!

Oyster Mushrooms   The cultivated variety of this delicate and tender mushroom is more common in stores than its wild, darker and more flavorful cousin.

Porcini Mushrooms   The name *porcini* means "little pigs" in Italian. Italy's most popular mushrooms are in season from August through October and are available both fresh and dried.

Portobello Mushrooms   See *Cremini Mushrooms*.

Provolone Cheese   A sharp and spicy cow's milk cheese from southern Italy. It comes in a globe-shaped ball (*prova*, from which the name derives) with a hard wax rind.

Radicchio   A purplish red-leaf chicory with a slightly sharp taste. Radicchio is usually used in salads or as a garnish.

Rapini/Broccoli Rabe   A sharp-tasting green closely related to broccoli. Rapini is used in soups or stews and as a side vegetable. The stem, leaves, buds, and even the yellow flowers may be eaten.

Riccota Salata Cheese   A type of soft cow's milk ricotta that is firmer and saltier than regular riccota cheese. Regular ricotta is not a good substitute—try a mild feta cheese (preferably French) if it's not available.

Saffron   This expensive spice, which gets its name from *zafaran,* Arabic for "yellow" is native to Asia and comes from the pistils of purple crocuses, which must be painstakingly separated from the rest of the flower. Saffron threads are the whole pistils, not the powdered form. Saffron will keep for several years when sealed in an airtight container and stored in a dry, dark place. Spanish saffron is reputed to be the best.

Semolina   Roughly ground durum wheat used to make pasta and bread. Technically, semolina is not a grain; rather, it is the milled endosperm, or nutritive tissue of durum wheat, the hardest of all wheat varieties.

Serrano Peppers   Small (about 2 inches long), smooth-skinned, medium-green chiles. Beware, these are among the hottest peppers around!

Seville Oranges   Popular bitter Mediterranean oranges. They are high in acid and used most commonly in marmalade, sauces, and relishes. The peel is often candied or dried and used as a seasoning.

Spelt   A species related to wheat with grains that do not thresh free of the chaff. This nutty, chewy grain, as well as its flour, can be found in most natural food stores. Many people who are allergic to normal wheat find that they do not have an adverse reaction to moderate amounts of spelt.

Stracchino Cheese   A cow's milk cheese from northern Italy. Stracchino's distinction is that it is made with fresh cow's milk mixed with the milk from the night before. It is a soft cheese with a unique tart flavor. The more aged the cheese, the more fruity and pronounced the flavor. It is often served with fresh fruits.

Tagine   A hearty northern African stew. *Tagines* may be made of chickpeas, onions, garlic, dried fruits, and fresh cilantro, and seasoned with spices such as cinnamon, cumin, and turmeric. The name *tagine* also refers to the earthenware pot in which the stew slowly simmers all day long.

Tahini   A thick sesame seed paste, used most commonly in the eastern Mediterranean and Middle Eastern parts of the region. It is commonly mixed with lemon juice to make sauces and dips.

Tamari   A dark Japanese soy sauce that is thicker and has a mellower flavor than other types of soy sauce.

Valencia Oranges   Sweet, thin-skinned oranges with sweet juicy flesh. Valencia oranges are often used as juice fruits.

Valencia Rice   A short, stubby rice from Valencia, Spain. This rice is considered to be the best for making paella.

Watercress   A tangy salad green in the mustard family. Watercress is used in salads and on sandwiches.

Mail-Order Sources

Balducci's
P.O. Box 10373, Newark, NJ 07193-0373; tel. (800) BALDUCCI; Web site, www.Balducci.com

Dean & DeLuca,
560 Broadway, New York, NY 10012; tel. (212) 431-1691 or (800) 221-7714

Fillo Factor, Inc. (Fresh phyllo),
56 Cortland Avenue, Dumont, NJ 07628; tel. (800) OK-FILLO

Kalustyan Orient Export Co.,
123 Lexington Avenue, New York, NY 10016; tel. (212) 685-3888, fax (212) 683-8458

Mozzarella Company (Fresh mozzarella and ricotta),
2944 Elm Street, Dallas, TX 75226; tel. (800) 798-2954, fax (214) 741-4076; E-mail, mozzCo@aol.com

Oasis Brands (Tunisian products),
P.O. Box 12871, La Jolla, CA 92039; tel. (619) 276-1440

Spice House (Spices from around the world),
103 N. Old World Third Street, Milwaukee, WI 53203; tel. (414) 272-0977

Sultan's Delight,

59-88th Street, Brooklyn, NY 11209; tel. (718) 745-2121, fax (718) 745-2563

Sur la Table,

84 Pine Street, Pike Place Farmers' Market, Seattle, WA 98101; tel. (800) 243-0852

Vanilla Saffron Imports,

949 Valencia Street, San Francisco, CA 94110; tel. (415) 648-8990, fax (415) 648-2240

Vivande,

2125 Fillmore Street, San Francisco, CA 94115; tel. (415) 346-4430

Williams-Sonoma,

P.O. Box 7456, San Francisco, CA 94120-7456; tel. (800) 541-2233

Zabar's,

2245 Broadway, New York, NY 10024; tel. (212) 787-2000

Zingerman's,

422 Detroit Street, Ann Arbor, MI 48104; tel. (734) 663-3354

INDEX